ROUTLEDGE LIBRARY EDITIONS: MANAGEMENT

Volume 16

MANAGEMENT CONTROL IN A VOLUNTARY ORGANIZATION

MANAGEMENT CONTROL IN A VOLUNTARY ORGANIZATION

Accounting and Accountants in Organizational Context

PETER BOOTH

LONDON AND NEW YORK

First published in 1995 by Garland Publishing, Inc.

This edition first published in 2018
by Routledge
2 Park Square, Milton Park, Abingdon, Oxon OX14 4RN

and by Routledge
711 Third Avenue, New York, NY 10017

Routledge is an imprint of the Taylor & Francis Group, an informa business

© 1995 Peter Booth

All rights reserved. No part of this book may be reprinted or reproduced or utilised in any form or by any electronic, mechanical, or other means, now known or hereafter invented, including photocopying and recording, or in any information storage or retrieval system, without permission in writing from the publishers.

Trademark notice: Product or corporate names may be trademarks or registered trademarks, and are used only for identification and explanation without intent to infringe.

British Library Cataloguing in Publication Data
A catalogue record for this book is available from the British Library

ISBN: 978-1-138-55938-7 (Set)
ISBN: 978-1-351-05538-3 (Set) (ebk)
ISBN: 978-0-8153-6698-0 (Volume 16) (hbk)
ISBN: 978-1-351-25824-1 (Volume 16) (ebk)

Publisher's Note
The publisher has gone to great lengths to ensure the quality of this reprint but points out that some imperfections in the original copies may be apparent.

Disclaimer
The publisher has made every effort to trace copyright holders and would welcome correspondence from those they have been unable to trace.

MANAGEMENT CONTROL IN A VOLUNTARY ORGANIZATION

Accounting and Accountants in Organizational Context

Peter Booth

Garland Publishing, Inc.
New York and London 1995

Copyright © 1995 by Peter Booth

Library of Congress Cataloging-in-Publication Data

Booth, Peter.
   Management control in a voluntary organization : accounting and
accountants in organizational context / Peter Booth.
   p. cm.—(New works in accounting history)
Includes bibliographical references and index.
   ISBN 0-8153-2239-9
   1. Associations, institutions, etc.—Accounting. 2. Associations,
institutions, etc.—Management. I. Title. II. Series.
HF5686.A76B66   1995   95–22958
657—dc20   CIP

All volumes printed on acid-free, 250-year-life paper.
Manufactured in the United States of America.

Design by Marisel Tavarez

DEDICATION

I wish to dedicate this book to Suzanne, Katherine, James and Ross, who make life bearable in more ways than they can ever know.

CONTENTS

LIST OF TABLES xi

LIST OF FIGURES xiii

PREFACE xv

ACKNOWLEDGMENTS xvii

CHAPTER 1: BACKGROUND AND RATIONALE

I.   INTRODUCTION 3

II. FOCUSING THE PROBLEMATIC 4

   A SKELETAL MODEL OF THE PURPOSEFULNESS OF ACCOUNTING .. 6

   APPLYING THE MODEL TO VOLUNTARY ORGANIZATIONS 11

III. A TYPOLOGY OF VOLUNTARY ORGANIZATIONS 16

IV. OVERVIEW OF FINDINGS 21

V.   CHAPTER SUMMARY 22

CHAPTER 2: A CRITICAL STRUCTURALIST FRAMEWORK

I.   INTRODUCTION 27

II. A CRITICAL STRUCTURALIST ANALYSIS OF
     MANAGEMENT 28

   THE MANAGEMENT PROCESS AND INTER-PROFESSIONAL
   COMPETITION 29

   ACCOUNTING AND MANAGEMENT CONTROL 36

   SUMMARY OF MAJOR POINTS 43

III. MANAGEMENT CONTROL IN VOLUNTARY
     ORGANIZATIONS 45

   WHAT IS THE VOLUNTARY SECTOR? 46

   THE DYNAMICS OF DIFFUSION TO THE VOLUNTARY SECTOR 49

viii

MANAGING VOLUNTARY ORGANIZATIONS 53

SUMMARY OF MAJOR POINTS 58

IV. A CRITICAL STRUCTURALIST FRAMEWORK FOR CHURCHES 60

V. CHAPTER SUMMARY 69

CHAPTER 3: RESEARCH METHOD

I. INTRODUCTION 73

II. THE SUBJECT ORGANIZATION 76

THE NORTHERN DIVISION OF MAINSTREAM CHURCH 76

SELECTION JUSTIFICATION 82

Access 82

The Significance of Mainstream Church 83

Theoretical Appropriateness 83

III. CASE STUDY DESIGN 85

BASIC DESIGN TYPE 85

BOUNDARIES OF THE CASE 86

SOURCES OF DATA 89

Observation 90

Interviews..92

Documents...95

IV. CHAPTER SUMMARY 96

CHAPTER 4: ACCOUNTING SYSTEMS I: FORMAL FEATURES AND FINANCIAL DYNAMICS

I. INTRODUCTION 101

II. FORMAL ACCOUNTING SYSTEMS 102

THE MANAGEMENT ACCOUNTING CONTROL SYSTEM 104

THE BUDGETING SYSTEM 108

ACCOUNTING SYSTEMS ACROSS THE DEPARTMENTS 112

Coverage of the Accounting Systems 114

Independent Department Accounting Systems 116

Accounting Expertise 118

Implications of the Comparative Analysis 120

SUMMARY OF FORMAL ACCOUNTING SYSTEMS 121

III. FINANCIAL DYNAMICS AND ACCOUNTING 123

FINANCIAL CRISES AND BUDGET FORMULATION 124

FINANCIAL TRENDS AND IMPACTS 128

SUMMARY AND IMPLICATIONS 134

IV. CHAPTER SUMMARY 136

**CHAPTER 5: ACCOUNTING SYSTEMS II: HOW IS
ACCOUNTING USED IN PRACTICE?**

I. INTRODUCTION 141

II. USES OF ACCOUNTING BY SACRED OCCUPATIONAL
GROUPS 143

VARIATIONS IN THE EXTENT OF USE OF ACCOUNTING BY SACRED
OCCUPATIONAL GROUPS...143

DEPARTMENT OF EDUCATIONAL ACTIVITIES 149

Board 149

Directorate 152

DEPARTMENT OF MISSION OUTREACH 157

DIVISIONAL COUNCIL 164

III. USES OF ACCOUNTING BY ACCOUNTANTS 167

IV. TENSIONS BETWEEN OCCUPATIONAL GROUPS 174

x

V. CHAPTER SUMMARY 179

CHAPTER 6: ACCOUNTING SYSTEMS III: THE DYNAMICS OF THE BUDGETING PROCESS

I. INTRODUCTION 187

II. HISTORICAL TRENDS IN THE BUDGETING PROCESS ... 188

III. A CASE STUDY OF THE BUDGETING PROCESS UNDER FINANCIAL STRESS 197

      STAGE ONE—CONSTRUCTING CLEAR OPTIONS 199

      STAGE TWO—MARSHALLING RESISTANCE 206

      STAGE THREE—ENFORCEMENT OF BUDGET DISCIPLINE 208

IV. CHAPTER SUMMARY 215

CHAPTER 7: CONCLUSIONS

I. INTRODUCTION 221

II. MAJOR FINDINGS 224

III. A COMPARISON WITH TRENDS IN VOLUNTARY ORGANIZATIONS 239

IV. CONCLUDING COMMENTS 248

APPENDIX 251

BIBLIOGRAPHY 255

      GENERAL REFERENCES 255

      MAINSTREAM CHURCH REFERENCES 270

INDEX 273

xi

LIST OF TABLES

Table 1.1 Major Characteristics of Voluntary Organizations 16

Table 2.1 A Summary of Armstrong's Analysis of the Rise of Accounting Controls in British Capitalist Enterprises ... 39

Table 3.1 Functions of the Northern Division Departments 80

Table 3.2 Overall Pattern of Multiple Data Sources Used 89

Table 3.3 Observation Pattern of Division Head Office From February to December 1987 91

Table 3.4 Interview Schedule of Senior Division Staff 94

Table 4.1 Distinctive Descriptive Features of an Accounting System 103

Table 4.2 Distinctive Features of the Management Accounting Control System 105

Table 4.3 Distinctive Features of the Budgeting System 109

Table 4.4 Typical Budget Formulation Timetable 110

Table 4.5 A Chronology of Major Budget Formulation Issues 125

Table 4.6 Percentage of Total Parish Income Derived from Offerings 131

Table 4.7 Budget Allocations to Departments: 1983 to 1986 133

Table 5.1 Coding System Used to Classify Interactions During Meetings 145

Table 5.2 Significance of Accounting in Forums Dominated by Sacred Occupational Groups 147

Table 5.3 Significance of Accounting in a Forum Dominated by Accountants 168

Table 5.4 Significance of Accounting in the Senior Management Group 174

Table 5.5 Frequency of References to Accounting in Documents of Various Forums 181

xii

Table 6.1	Major Features of the Budgeting Process in the Northern Division	189
Table 6.2	A Chronology of Stage One of the 1988 Budget Process	200
Table 6.3	A Chronology of Stage Two of the 1988 Budget Process	206
Table 6.4	A Chronology of Stage Three of the 1988 Budget Process	209

xiii

LIST OF FIGURES

Figure 1.1 Summary of General Boundary Conditions on the Purposefulness of Accounting 7

Figure 1.2 A Form of Membership Involvement Based Spectrum of Voluntary Organizations 18

Figure 1.3 A Funding Source Based Spectrum of Voluntary Organizations 19

Figure 2.1 The Sacred and Secular Divide and the Process of Rationalization in Churches 66

Figure 3.1 Organizational Structure of the Northern Division 78

Figure 3.2 Time Periods of Involvement with the Subject Organization 87

Figure 4.1 Total Income and Expenditure Patterns (1978 $) 129

Figure 4.2 Trends in Parish and Agency Contributions (1978 $)...130

Figure 6.1 A Consultative Budgeting Process 191

PREFACE

This book is concerned with the study of accounting within its organizational and social context. A major problematic under such an approach is; how does accounting obtain and maintain a position of organizational significance? This problematic is approached theoretically in this book by analysing accounting as having potential effects at both an ideological level and at an occupational level. Empirically, it is explored within the context of voluntary organizations as theoretically interesting extreme cases, where the conditions for accounting to be significant should be most open to question.

The theoretical framework of the book draws upon the work of Richard Laughlin on the Church of England and the writings of Peter Armstrong on the variations in management control strategies in business organizations to develop a critical structuralist framework for the analysis of management control and the use of accounting within voluntary organizations in general, and churches more specifically. This framework emphasizes; the interaction of different forms of organizational control problems within voluntary organizations; the actions of differing occupational groups, in particular the confrontations between accountants and occupational groups more concerned with the core ends of voluntary organizations; and the impacts of various organizational crises.

This framework is applied to a case study of the significance of accounting within a major Protestant Australian church, where accounting is found to be of generally low, but variable, significance. The critical structuralist framework developed in the first section is found to have considerable utility in explaining these findings. Tensions between the clergy and accountants over the use of accounting, and the prioritization of secular financial control problems by the financial crisis being experienced by the church, were especially relevant to understanding the observed variable significance of accounting. The findings are then compared to research on churches and voluntary organizations more generally.

ACKNOWLEDGMENTS

This book is based upon my doctoral thesis. In the preparation of that thesis, and this book, I owe a great many debts of gratitude to a wide range of people. First, I owe a great personal and academic debt to my supervisor, Craig Littler, whose critical insight and guidance, and pragmatic advice, has immeasurably improved both this study and my own thinking on this area of research. Also, many thanks to his wife, Liz, and daughter, Nyree, for their forbearance of the many intrusions into their home life that my thesis resulted in, and their own support and encouragement.

Second, I wish to thank my academic colleagues at Griffith University and the University of New South Wales, where I worked when completing my doctoral work, and now at the University of Technology, Sydney, who have provided critical comment on various aspects of this project over the years, and moral support and encouragement when I needed it. In particular, thanks are due to David Limerick, Lee Parker, Bill Birkett and Wai Fong Chua for their helpful comments and to Ken Moores for his continued support over the years, and for pushing me into this type of research in the first place.

Third, I owe a huge debt to the members of the subject church, who allowed the study to be undertaken and this book to be published. Without their openness, honesty, and willingness to allow another demand on their very busy lives, this study would never have been possible, let alone have allowed me the depth of understanding of their life that I felt that I achieved during our time together. In particular, I would like to thank the three Johns, Glenn, Duncan, Bill, Peter, Sid, Col and Stan for their personal efforts towards ensuring that the project was completed, and for their friendship and warm encouragement.

Finally, my thanks to Stephanie for painstakingly proofing the manuscript and making useful suggestions on standardizing my style.

MANAGEMENT CONTROL IN A VOLUNTARY ORGANIZATION

Chapter 1
Background and Rationale

I.   INTRODUCTION

This book is about accounting as a situated practice (Chua 1988). It analyses the uses of accounting in a voluntary organization, a division of a major Protestant Australian church. Instead of seeing accounting practices as functionally or dysfunctionally fitted to the organization, they are viewed as reflexive constructions of the context of the everyday activities of the members of the organization at a specific time in its history. As such this study seeks to add to the increasing body of research on accounting in its social and organizational context (for example, Berry et al 1985; Burchell et al 1980; Hopwood 1978, 1983; Nahapiet 1988; Preston 1986).

The traditional, dominant perspective on the usefulness of accounting in organizations sees it as possessing inherent functional imperatives, in particular the satisfaction of financial information needs that are fundamental to the operation of rational economic decision-making in any form of organization (Burchell et al 1980). Within this perspective three main problematics are raised: How can accounting techniques be improved to better serve decision-makers? How can accounting systems be designed to overcome the cognitive limits of decision-makers? How can accounting systems and/or decision-makers be 'changed' to avoid dysfunctional responses to such systems? Many worthwhile research findings have resulted from the addressing of these questions, but their particular focus has also limited the consideration of why and how accounting is used in organizations.

Burchell et al (1980) argued that accounting does not have any inherent usefulness, its prominence in modern organizational affairs is

4   *Managment Control in a Voluntary Organization*

the result of specific organizational and social historical patterns; that is, the various uses of accounting accepted as basic premises under the traditional approach have been, and continue to be, socially constructed. This means that the 'purposefulness' of accounting itself should be the problematic of study. How did accounting come to be what it is? How has 'what it is' changed? How do new uses emerge? For, as Hopwood (1983) argued, accounting is always becoming what it was not.

In essence then, the problematic addressed in this study is "...how... does accounting achieve and maintain a position of organizational significance" (Hopwood 1983, p.291)? It identifies some of the uses of accounting in the Northern Division of the Mainstream Church at a specific time in its history (the name of the division and church have been disguised). These are analysed using a critical structuralist approach that emphasizes the importance of particular organizational control problems, the activities of occupational groups and specific social conditions in facilitating such uses (Armstrong 1984, 1985, 1986, 1987a). A church is chosen as the focus of interest as a compelling extreme case where the claimed 'inherent purposes' of accounting should be highly in doubt (Thompson 1975).

In this chapter two main tasks are addressed. First, the problematic identified above is developed and justified in more depth. This involves a general questioning of the basic nature of accounting practices and how they may become purposeful in organizations. Second, a typology of voluntary organizations is developed to justify the selection of a church as a potentially fruitful site for the study of the problematic. This identifies key characteristics and dimensions of voluntary organizations that may be linked to the use of accounting. The chapter concludes with an overview of the findings, a summary of the discussion and the structure of the book.

II.   FOCUSING THE PROBLEMATIC

This book is based upon the premise that it is a generally irrefutable fact that accounting has obtained and continues to maintain a position of organizational significance (see, for example, the arguments in Anthony and Young 1984; Chandler and Deams 1979; Hopwood and Tomkins 1984; Horngren and Foster 1987; Johnson

Background and Rationale 5

1978, 1983; Lavoie 1987). In addressing this question, the view that accounting has certain inherent functional uses for action in organizations is rejected. As Burchell et al state "...we have uncritically adopted a rather particular set of views of human, organizational and social rationality and the relationships between accounting, decision making and organizational action" (1980, p.13). To counter such tendencies, the view that the purposefulness of accounting is socially constructed is adopted (see Burchell et al 1980; Hopwood 1983). This view proposes that there is no obvious, self-evident answer to the prominence of accounting in organizations in modern industrial societies. The general problematic therefore, is how accounting practices have been made purposeful in organizations; to enquire into how accounting came to have, and has maintained, a position of organizational significance.

In arguing for the rejection of the inherent functional imperatives view of accounting practices, Burchell et al state that "...accounting can no longer be regarded as a mere collection of techniques for the assessment of economic magnitudes" (1980, p.6). They argue that the uses to which various accounting practices are put and the names in which they are used have much wider effects than just the calculation of sets of economic numbers. However, while such arguments are important in drawing our attention to the dynamic, multiple uses of accounting, they should not divert it from the essential point that a system of financial measurement is the core of accounting practices. In this regard the operational definition of an accounting system suggested by Laughlin (1984) is adopted for this study. An organizational accounting system is a

> "...formal system which expresses in fundamentally numerical terms
> past, present and future financial actions of such an enterprise"
> (Laughlin, 1984, p.8).

The identification, interpretation, coding, and aggregation of these actions is accomplished by the application of various sets of rules of a general, industry or organizational specific nature.

Laughlin (1984) makes two important general points about this definition. First, no distinction is made between various sorts of accounting systems. Both financial and management accounting distinctions can be accommodated within the definition. At the organizational level of analysis such distinctions may be either difficult or arbitrary in practice anyway (Swanson, 1978). Second, the definition makes no direct claims about the purposefulness of

6 *Managment Control in a Voluntary Organization*

accounting. However, this is already implicit to some extent in the notion of what is measured, and in the conception of an accounting system as a measurement and communication system.

The essential point is that, as an initial working hypothesis, the financial magnitudes produced by accounting systems as abstractions of some of the actions of an organization should be seen as the core of the dynamic, myriad practices labelled accounting at various points in time. An understanding of how these practices can become purposeful should start from an understanding of how these types of measurements may be purposeful. Always allowing for the case, of course, that some uses may only be loosely connected to the attributes of these numbers.

When proposing the problematic in these broad terms, it is proposed that three major points should be noted. First, accounting is not a coherent entity. It both changes over time, and at any particular point in time and space the purposes, if any, that accounting serves may vary (Hopwood 1983; Loft 1986; Miller and O'Leary 1987). Therefore, any analysis needs to recognise that accounting is a generic term for a myriad of different practices that can be used in many different ways. Second, human rationality cannot be tightly defined as the traditional notion of logical decision making, rather multiple forms of rationality exist (for example, Berry et al 1985; Dermer and Lucas 1986). Rationality should be more broadly viewed as socially constructed meaning systems which provide sets of rules for meaningful action (Brunsson 1982; Schutz 1967). Third, given the two preceding points, any understanding of the relationship between accounting and human action must be contextualized. It must consider the various uses of particular accounting practices, the forms of rationality to which they are linked and the nature of the settings in which this takes place. These points focus attention on the social nature of the production and reproduction of the purposefulness of accounting and thereby the indeterminate nature of the significance of accounting in organizations.

A Skeletal Model of the Purposefulness of Accounting

However, a danger of such a focus is that it can lead to the adoption of an extremely relativist position on the nature of the significance of accounting. In an attempt to avoid this, Figure 1.1

Background and Rationale

suggests some tentative and incomplete answers to some general boundary conditions on the potential for accounting to be purposeful in organizations.

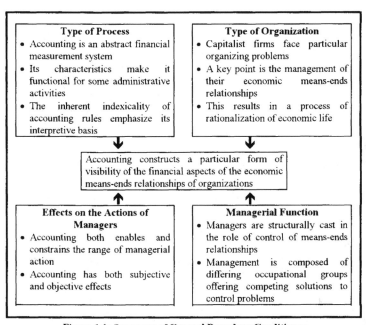

Figure 1.1: Summary of General Boundary Conditions on the Purposefulness of Accounting

The basic premise of the potential purposefulness of accounting expressed in Figure 1.1 is that accounting can be 'functional' for the administration of organizations because it provides a particular form of visibility into and of economic means-ends relationships. This potential flows from the basic nature of accounting as an abstract financial measurement system. As such it possesses a range of characteristics common to written communication systems which are functional for certain administrative processes. Stinchcombe (1974) has argued that written communication is an important basis for the functioning of industrial administration. This is because it possesses four distinctive features that oral communication does not:

1. Writing abstracts from the complexities of the subject of communication.

8   *Managment Control in a Voluntary Organization*

2. Writing provides a relatively immutable record of its subject.
3. Writing enables the use of algorithms, sequential methods of calculation of complex problems, or systematic organization of the elements of thought.
4. Writing provides a portable product with minimal chance of change in the elements upon transfer.

These features enable a more systematic, analytic and potentially remote (that is, longer chains of command) form of management than would otherwise be possible. Accounting possesses all of these features, thereby creating a potential for its 'usefulness' for industrial administration; a potential that was explicitly recognised by Stinchcombe (1974). In addition, as an interpretive process, the indexical nature of accounting rules[1] increases the potential range of uses that accounting numbers may fulfil.

However, the potential purposefulness of accounting is also dependent on an appropriate organizational context for the above characteristics to be useful. In a very general sense, this requires a capitalist firm. In such firms a central problem is the management of their economic means-ends relationships. These propositions are taken from the writings of Max Weber (1927, 1947), who emphasized the achievement of narrowly specified economic goals in rational-legal bureaucracies through the use of a rational calculative basis of management (see also, Albrow 1970; Salaman 1979). Further, Weber proposed a general tendency towards such rationalization of all forms of capitalist organizations. While there are many complexities of modern organizational existence and a variety of points of resistance that restrict the extent of this rationalization of economic life, it is still seen as the dominant theme of capitalist organization (see Morgan 1990).

Accounting is directly relevant to this process of rationalization. As Stinchcombe argued:

> "The rationalization of economic life involves setting up systematic dictates or norms for efficient productive activity, and then governing factories or commerce by them. Weber emphasized, especially, the analysis of activities in terms of money and the control of such activities in terms of financial accounts" (1974, p.45).

Thus, a central role in the rationalization process is the movement from qualitative to quantitative, especially monetary, modes of thinking and acting.

Background and Rationale

> "In particular, organizations had to be able to measure and think in terms of costs, revenues, etc.; the relationship between means (the utilization of capital and labour) and ends (the goal of profit - indeed, in more general terms, what profit was) had to be clarified" (Morgan, 1990, p.95).

Accounting, therefore, was 'functional' for the rationalization of economic life in capitalist organizations[2] because it provided a means of thinking about and acting upon the basic economic means-ends relationships central to these organizations [The form of the above argument and other ways in which Weber's work may impact upon an understanding of accounting in action are explored more fully in Colignon and Covaleski (1991)]. The basic characteristics of accounting and this particular capitalist firm context for its use, therefore, are both actively implicated in creating the potential for accounting to be purposeful[3].

However, this does not imply that accounting is purposeful for all organizational participants. The control problem of the management of their economic means-ends relationships is essentially a managers' problem as they are structurally cast in roles where they have to give effect to actions aimed at developing and achieving the ends of the organization (Clegg 1989; Storey 1985). To do so they have to intervene in and influence both technical processes and the actions of other managers and workers; and hold the actions of these other to account (see, also, Batstone 1979; Gowler and Legge 1983; Roberts and Scapens 1985). Therefore, the characteristics of accounting are most potentially relevant for managers. But in modern capitalist firms, managers are composed of a range of occupational groups with differing expertise. These groups may possess alternative solutions to the control problems of the firm (Armstrong 1984, 1985, 1986, 1987a). These different solutions can form an 'occupational ideology' which a group uses to promote its own importance within the management function and which other occupational groups resist. Such ideologies may be expected to be particularly strong for occupational groups who are linked to a profession.

Accounting is not the sole, or even obviously the 'best', way in which the economic means-ends relationships may be managed. Accountants within the firm, as a management group, will be more likely to see accounting as purposeful and can be expected to be actively involved in the construction of the relevance of accounting to the control problems of the capitalist firm, both by promoting their own occupational solutions and in constructing how the problems are

10   *Managment Control in a Voluntary Organization*

perceived in the first place. The ability to do so is enhanced by the role the accounting profession plays in the general development of accounting within capitalist societies. Accountants, therefore, may play a significant role in constructing accounting as a 'better' solution than those of other occupational groups.

Finally, the potential purposefulness of accounting is also affected by the types of effects that it can have on managers' actions. The above discussion of its creation of the visibility of means-ends relationships emphasizes the enabling by accounting of a wider range of managerial action which generally draw upon its objective effects. For example, it has been proposed above that accounting allowed managers to get a practical grasp on their costs, revenues and profits, and even to construct a clearer view of what the goal of profit meant and how costs and revenues could be controlled to achieve it (Morgan 1990; Stinchcombe 1974).

However, this visibility can also be constraining to the extent that it penetrates and dominates other alternative ways of thinking and acting. For example, Hopwood (1983) has argued that the visibility made possible by accounting makes more prominent and significant an economic conception of organizational life and has also propagated a view of a disinterested, neutral and rational way of administrative action (see, also, Burchell et al 1985; Hopwood 1984, 1987; Loft 1986; Miller and O'Leary 1987). Accounting thereby tends to allow only the articulation of a particular set of interests and to restrict action to that to which a calculative form of logic can be applied. It particular, this can be linked to the subjective effects[4] of accounting, whereby it constructs restricted views of rationality and moral orders in the firm; that is, what it means to be a 'good' and a 'bad' manager (Batstone 1979; Bariff and Galbraith 1978; Booth 1988; Gowler and Legge 1983; Markus and Pfeffer 1983; Roberts and Scapens 1985). Paradoxically, this constraining aspect of accounting may also increase the potential for its significance by allowing for its penetration into areas where the relevance of its 'functional' characteristics are less clear.

The potential for the purposefulness of accounting, therefore, is a complex construction of its particular characteristics, the organizational type within which these characteristics are 'relevant', the occupational groups which may use and/or promote and/or resist this relevance, and the dual positive and negative effects that

Background and Rationale *11*

accounting may have. It is not proposed that the very general argument developed above fully explains the purposefulness of accounting, or that it even necessarily captures all the major factors involved. Rather, it is proposed as a 'skeletal' model (Laughlin 1990a). Laughlin (1990a) states that skeletal model are incomplete theorizations which may be applicable across a wide range of situations, but which require specific empirics to flesh them out. They allow both variety and generality in thinking. In this sense, the simple model in Figure 1.1 is a basic schematic that allows more specific questions to be formulated both about whether the various factors identified are important (for example, what is the role of the accounting profession) and if, and under what circumstances, the boundary conditions hold (for example, for type of organization). Used in this way, the model can sensitize the researcher to potentially interesting dimensions of the complex question of the purposefulness of accounting.

Applying the Model to Voluntary Organizations

A central dimension of the skeletal model was the rationalization of economic life. It was argued to be a prime basis for the characteristics of accounting to be seen as functional. Also, these very characteristics themselves could play a part in enabling the forms of thinking and acting necessary for rationalization to develop. Weber (1947) argued that rationalization was an increasing feature of modern capitalist societies. This type of argument has been a feature of much of the labour process literature (see Thompson 1989 for a detailed review). It has also been argued that this process of increasing rationalization has gone beyond capitalist firms and has also penetrated state and other non-capitalist organizational types (for example, DiMaggio and Powell 1983; Hopwood and Tomkins 1984; Meyer and Rowan 1977). If this is so, then using the skeletal model, it would be expected that the purposefulness of accounting has also spread beyond the specific setting of the capitalist firm.

Morgan (1990), in a useful summary of some of this literature, argued that this process has indeed occurred. He states that the use of accounting and control systems which focus managerial strategies on measurable characteristics of work performance and measure success or failure in terms of financial criteria have become a powerful image in modern organizations, particularly where work relations are money-

12 *Managment Control in a Voluntary Organization*

based (see also, Hopwood 1983; Hopper et al 1987; Miller and O'Leary 1987). Also, the dominance of calculability and rationalization in capitalist firms has developed into a powerful, legitimate model of management in industrial societies which it is increasingly difficult for other firms to avoid. Therefore, Morgan argued, the "...structure of rationalized relations in capitalist organizations are imposed on other money-based forms of organization" (1990, p.125).

However, these processes of rationalization are not complete or without resistance for at least two reasons (Morgan 1990). First, rationalization is based on the imposition of particular forms of knowledge, and, as Foucault (1979, 1980) argued, such power-knowledge relations continually give rise to forms of resistance and non-compliance; for example, the gap between the myth and actuality of rational control in educational organizations argued by Meyer and Rowan (1977). Second, there are also other bases of organizational legitimization, particularly in non-capitalist organizations. "Within the organization, ...[therefore]..., the techniques of rationalization, etc., continually run up against problems, particularly the recalcitrance of human beings and technology. which within the state and civil society is magnified by competing non-calculable ideals such as citizenship and formal equality" (Morgan 1990, p.126).

This argument suggests that there may be specific limits to the purposefulness of accounting. Organizations in the 'state and civil society' may be sites where there is significant resistance to the processes of rationalization and thus, to the significance of accounting. In particular, Morgan (1990) proposes that the most extreme general sites of such resistance may be voluntary organizations, as they are based on strong non-calculable ideals.

A further basis for such an assessment can be seen if we consider another of the boundary conditions specified in the proposed skeletal model; the role of managers in the control function. It was argued that managers are structurally cast in roles where they have to address the control problems of organizations and that they often have to achieve this through other managers. The accounting literature has long recognised that an important attribute of relations between managers is their agency nature (Baiman 1982, 1990; Scapens 1984). However, the purely economic conception of the agency relationship

Background and Rationale 13

used has been widely criticised (Chua 1986b; Tinker 1980, 1985). Recently, Simon stated that:

> "The problem I have with the agency literature ... is that this theory seems to look almost entirely at economic inducements. This theory also seems to assume that leisure is such a desirable good that people are intrinsically shirkers and that they will only do what can be enforced. There is a tremendous amount of psychological evidence that contradicts this: human beings are not only capable of acquiring strong loyalties to organizations ..., they are also incapable of not acquiring them. We must look at loyalty structures to learn what ties people to organizations" (1990, pp.660-661).

Similarly, Armstrong (1989a) has argued that trust and loyalty are generic features of the relationships between managers and a key to understanding the nature of agency in management. He proposed that trust and management control systems are alternative modes of solving the agency problem - how to ensure that managers with delegated responsibility act in the interests of their superiors. As Fox (1974) points out, trust and management control systems are conflicting mechanisms. The whole underlying assumption of management control systems, particularly their monitoring functions, is distrust of managers. Armstrong (1989a) extends this further by arguing that it may be more expensive to maintain trust than alternative control systems for some situations. Therefore, a contradiction exists in that trust is the basis of manager relationships but managers may have economic incentives to use cheaper management control systems based on distrust. Management, therefore, has to make choices about the trade-off between their reliance on trust and on management control systems.

It can be argued that the importance attached to trust by managers and the relevance of economic incentives varies between capitalist and voluntary organizations. In the capitalist firm the strong conception of control problems in terms of economic means-ends relations emphasizes the relevance of economic incentives over reliance on trust. Also, as Armstrong (1989a) points out, some managers may increase their trust relation with their superiors by sacrificing such relations with their subordinates through the implementation of more cost effective controls. The relevance of a broad range of accounting practices may be increased in such circumstances as their design is based on a presumption that managers cannot be trusted (Caplan 1966; Carmichael 1970), thus potentially allowing the avoidance of the costs of obtaining and maintaining trust. Also, the existence of reasonably clear, quantifiable and often money-

14   *Managment Control in a Voluntary Organization*

based performance criteria in such firms enable accounting to act as a substitute for trust. Therefore, the significance of accounting in capitalist firms may be related to its cost effectiveness as a substitute for trust in an environment with certain features that may discount the relevance of trust as a basis of manager relations.

In contrast, the non-calculable ideals of voluntary organizations would not be expected to provide similar support for economic incentives over trust. Indeed, one of the basic distinctions of voluntary organizations, discussed in the next section, is the commitment of both members and managers to such ideals (Handy 1988). Further, Rothschild-Whitt (1979) argued that the basis of control in voluntary organizations was personalistic and moralistic appeals to these shared values. Trust, therefore, may be assumed to be a more highly valued component of managers' relations in voluntary organizations. Also, for the same reasons it follows that trust may be cheaper and easier to obtain and maintain in such organizations. In voluntary organizations, therefore, it would be expected that there are disincentives associated with substituting management control systems for trust. In these circumstances, the relevance of accounting practices is thus reduced, and they may even be perceived as antithetical to the values of such organizations. In addition, the performance criteria of voluntary organizations are often vague and usually difficult to quantify, especially in monetary terms, thus making it more difficult for accounting practices to substitute for trust even if there were incentives to do so. Overall then, the pattern of incentives in voluntary organizations favours trust over the use of accounting and other management control technologies. Indeed, resistance to the use of such control systems may be expected as they clash with the values of such organizations.

The potential strong resistance to the processes of rationalization and the associated possible lack of relevance of accounting in voluntary organizations, based on their differences in dominant ideals and structural characteristics to capitalist firms, make them suitable empirical sites for assessing the limits of the skeletal model of the significance of accounting in organizations. As 'negative' (Glaser and Strauss 1967) or 'deviant' (Mitchell 1983) or 'extreme' (Scapens 1990; Yin 1989) cases, such sites may be the most fruitful for increasing the understanding of the purposefulness of accounting as;

Background and Rationale

i) the relevancy of the characteristics of accounting may be more open to question,

ii) the ability of rational calculation to address 'the organizing problems' of the organization may be less clear,

iii) the differences between the occupational groups in terms of expertise and 'solutions' may be more extreme (for example, between social workers and accountants in a welfare agency) and thus

iv) open resistance to, and even rejection of, accounting may be closer to the surface.

In Laughlin's (1990a) terms, they should be rich empirical sites for 'fleshing out' the basic 'skeletal models' of the purposefulness of accounting provided by the existing literature. Voluntary organizations, therefore, are selected as the focus of this study.

The selection of voluntary organizations is also justified because they form part of an increasingly important sector of modern industrial societies (Harris 1990; Kramer 1990). In the Australian context, it has been recently estimated that 6% of work places are voluntary organizations and that they employ about 221,000 people, approximately 5% of the workforce (Callus et al 1991, chapter 2). Despite the significant size of the voluntary sector, it has been relatively ignored in the organizational literature (see Harris 1990 for a review). Harris concludes that "...we remain desperately short of descriptive and analytical studies of how groups and organizations within the voluntary sector carry out their work" (1990, p.138). The same is true of the accounting literature, most of which has focused on capitalist firms. Also, in recent years state-based organizations have received increasing attention, particularly over the issue of the penetration of accounting into their management (for example, Berry et al 1985; Chua and Degeling 1989; Hopper et al 1986; Hopwood and Tomkins 1984; Nahapiet 1988). In contrast, little attention has been given to voluntary organizations such as trade unions, religious organizations and non-state based welfare agencies, particularly to detailed studies of accounting in action[5]. A notable exception is Laughlin's (1984, 1988, 1990a) work on the Church of England.

Having selected voluntary organizations as the focus for this study, the problem still remains of what type of voluntary organization best meets the criteria of a negative or deviant case. To do this requires the development of a typology of voluntary organizations.

16   *Managment Control in a Voluntary Organization*

III.   A TYPOLOGY OF VOLUNTARY ORGANIZATIONS

What precisely are voluntary organizations? Handy (1988) states that such organizations are most often defined by what they are not; they are not profit-seeking, they are not government-run. He sets out five overlapping types of voluntary organizations; service providers (e.g. Red Cross), research and advocacy (e.g. People for Nuclear Disarmament), self-help groups (e.g. Alcoholics Anonymous), clubs and societies for leisure interests (e.g. a local origami society), and intermediary bodies (e.g. Australian Council of Social Services). What features do all these types have in common? While this issue is considered in more depth in chapter 2, some major characteristics are summarized in Table 1.1.

1. Membership is voluntary. It is based on belief in the goals of the organization and a commitment to the values of community and democracy.
2. Members generally do not gain direct material rewards for their involvement in the organization; that is, the organizations are normally nonprofit.
3. Also, there is a tendency to minimize the wage relationship. This can occur in two ways. First, members may provide volunteer labour, replacing the need for paid-staff. Second, where paid staff are used they are often involved with the organization because of personal commitment to its goals, not just the receipt of a wage.

Table 1.1: Major Characteristics of Voluntary Organizations

The key distinction of voluntary organizations is that the "...people are there because they want to be there" (Handy 1988, p.2). Members join and stay with the organization primarily because they have a personal commitment to its goals. Thus, the members of the People for Nuclear Disarmament and a local origami society both form and continue their organization because of this personal belief in the specific ends of each. Rothschild-Whitt (1979) also emphasized the importance of voluntary membership, adding that this was generally associated with a commitment to the ideal of community. While the specific goals of voluntary organizations may differ, all are similar in their commitment to the idea that authority resides with the collectivity as a whole. This commitment emphasizes the values of free association, co-operation and consensus. Voluntary organizations,

Background and Rationale   *17*

therefore, are primarily characterised by a membership who adhere to broad social values of community and democracy.

This voluntary association also means that members generally are not paid or receive no material rewards for their involvement in the organization, unlike a basic reason for most involvement in capitalist firms. This does not mean that a voluntary organization cannot advance its members' material interests, as in trade unions for example, but that this reason is more a special characteristic of some voluntary organizations rather than a primary characteristic of all. A key implication of this is that the most important relation of members to the organization is not money-based. Therefore, the use of rational calculation is less obviously relevant to the satisfaction of members' ends.

This form of involvement also tends to distinguish members from the paid-staff who may carry out the day-to-day running of the organization. One major implication of this is that the organization is often dependent on its membership for either the labour force to fulfil its goals and/or the raising of funds to finance goal achievement. Also, the relationship between staff and members may be complex and sometimes in conflict (Billis 1984, 1989; Handy 1988; Morgan 1990). Professional staff in particular may espouse values which challenge the values of the organization. However, this problem is often reduced by either the deliberate hiring of staff who support such values or the fact that such staff are often attracted to such positions because of their personal beliefs. The voluntary basis of membership also, therefore, tends to permeate the nature of the relationships between members, staff and the organization.

The key features of voluntary organizations, therefore, are that their members share a commitment to the values of free association, co-operation and consensus, and that the survival of the organization is dependent on the continued support of its membership. Thus, the main organizing problem of such organizations is to maintain their membership through maintaining their basic community and democracy values and achieving their specific goals (Handy 1988; Rothschild-Whitt 1979). According to Morgan (1990), this is the key feature that distinguishes them from capitalist firms and is the main basis of their resistance to the processes of rationalization.

The construction of a typology of voluntary organizations to enable the selection of an extreme type for the exploration of the limits of rationalization, therefore, should focus on the basis of membership involvement. To the extent that the reason for involvement in the voluntary organization may be more materialistic, then there is likely to be less conflict with the use of rational calculation. This is so because the means-ends relations of the organization should be more money-based. In this vein, Morgan (1990) suggests that voluntary organizations may vary along a spectrum from the more immediately materialistic to the altruistic. This spectrum is shown in Figure 1.2. From this spectrum it is argued that churches and charities are more likely than trade unions and employer associations to resist the processes of rationalization.

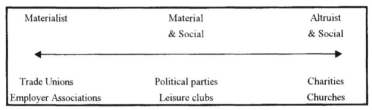

Figure 1.2: A Form of Membership Involvement Based Spectrum of Voluntary Organizations

Another characteristic of voluntary organizations which may directly affect the importance of money-based means-ends relations is the source of funding. Anthony (1978) argued that there were two main ways in which voluntary organizations raised funds. The first was either charges levied for outputs, although these charges are not usually a full market price, and membership fees. Examples are many non-profit hospitals, private clubs, trade unions and private universities. The second method was dependence on endowments, property rents, donations and grants. Examples are most health and welfare agencies and religious organizations. These two methods can be viewed as two extremes from which the total funding of the organization can be obtained. This funding source spectrum is shown in Figure 1.3.

At the direct charges end of the funding source spectrum there is a direct relationship between the provision of benefits by the organization and the funding it receives. This tends to enable at least some of the means-ends relations of the organization to be constructed as money-based. They are thus more amenable to management by

Background and Rationale 19

rational calculation and the use of financial criteria of success (see Anthony and Young 1984). At the other end of the spectrum there is only an indirect relationship between those receiving the outputs of the organization and those providing the funds. This funding arrangement breaks down the money-based nature of the means-ends relations of the organization, and thus the applicability of rational calculation and financial criteria of success. The funding sources spectrum also, therefore, supports the selection of churches and charities as extreme cases.

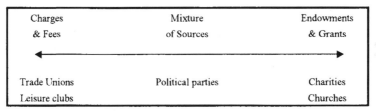

Figure 1.3: A Funding Source Based Spectrum of Voluntary Organizations

The two spectrums of voluntary organizations along the dimensions of form of membership involvement and funding source, therefore, give a typology of the relative importance of money-based means-ends relations in such organizations. This typology identifies churches and charities as the types of voluntary organization where the processes of rationalization are likely to meet the most resistance. An analysis of the uses of accounting in these types of voluntary organization then should provide a better understanding of the limits of the purposefulness of accounting.

For the purposes of this study churches are selected as the focal type of voluntary organization. The reasons for this choice are:
i) The typology was unable to distinguish between the altruistic and 'other directedness' of charities and churches. However, churches are intuitively appealing cases of the most extreme organizational site of a non-calculable basis of the legitimation of actions. As Thompson argued:

> "...perhaps more than most organizations, religious bodies have a strong ideological commitment and concern that extends to the point where even the rationality, according to which they evaluate their organization, may stress criteria of symbolic-appropriateness rather than of calculable efficiency" (1975, p.2).

20 *Managment Control in a Voluntary Organization*

Further, the 'symbolic-appropriateness' stressed is fundamentally transcendental. It appeals to the "...essential element of religiosity, i.e. God, eternity, etc. ...[which]... defies rational proof and calculation" (Morgan 1990, p.152). Churches, therefore, are felt to be potentially more fruitful sites than charities.

ii) Laughlin's (1984, 1988) work on the Church of England in the United Kingdom has demonstrated the potential of the study of churches for a better understanding of the purposefulness of accounting (see Booth 1993 for a fuller discussion of this issue). His work is considered further in chapter 2, but one of his main arguments was that churches have a set of key social dynamics involving the interaction of the sacred and the profane, with the former dominating. The sacred world is concerned with spiritual issues, and the profane with the material world. Accounting was analysed as linked with the profane and consequently key limits were placed on its use in the Church of England because of the social dynamics between the sacred and the profane.

iii) Churches have received relatively very little attention in the accounting literature[6]. Also, most of that which does exist either merely normatively or uncritically seeks to prescribe 'appropriate' accounting practices or provides traditional historical analyses of the uses of certain accounting practices by specific churches. Little critical analysis of accounting in action exists (see Booth 1993).

iv) Finally, churches are significant organizations. They have a large number of the population as adherents, they are channels for large sums of financial and other resources, and they provide a significant proportion of health and welfare services through a wide range of church affiliated agencies (Kaldor 1987).

Churches, therefore, are an important part of society and a potentially interesting site for the study of rationalization and the purposefulness of accounting. Laughlin (1988) goes as far as to argue that an understanding of churches may also give us insight into a wide range of other organizations. He states that in secular society many forms of behaviour still evidence quasi-religious overtones by being orientated to new 'sacred' foci; for example, clinical freedom claims of doctors in the National Health Service (Bourn and Ezzamel 1986a, 1986b) or academic freedom in universities (Bourn and Ezzamel 1987). An understanding of the purposefulness of accounting in churches may

Background and Rationale 21

therefore provide a strong basis for generalization to many other organizational types.

It has been argued in this section that the key characteristics of voluntary organizations, particularly their commitment to the values of community and democracy, create a setting in which the legitimacy of rationalization is open to challenge. The relative extent of the potential for such challenge was rated along two dimensions of voluntary organizations which were argued to affect the relevance of money-based means-ends relations. These were form of membership involvement in the organization, from materialistic to altruistic and social, and the source of funding, from direct charges and fees to endowments and grants. Both of these dimensions identified charities and churches as the main types of voluntary organizations where rationalization would be least legitimate. Churches were then selected as the focal type of voluntary organization for this study primarily because they were felt to have the most non-calculable legitimation basis in their commitment to the essential elements of religiosity.

IV. OVERVIEW OF FINDINGS

The major findings of this study can be summarized under two aspects, the level of significance of accounting within the Northern Division of the Mainstream Church and the form of explanation provided for this finding. These are briefly overviewed below.

Overall, it was found that accounting had a variable significance in the Northern Division using a variety of technical sophistication, quantitative process, and qualitative outcome measures. The accounting systems of the Division were sophisticated, but the extent of their impact on its management appeared limited. Within the main religious orientated operational units, accounting had little impact, and where used it was treated as secondary to the sacred religious functions of these units. Accounting was more significant in the main administrative support unit, but still the subordinate position to sacred activities appeared to exist. The clergy and other religious orientated managers were the strongest promoters of the dominance of sacred functions. While accountants also appeared to accept this position, they promoted a more active role for accounting as a necessary support function for sacred activities. Therefore, the tendency was for accounting to play a limited and subordinate role in

22   *Managment Control in a Voluntary Organization*

the management of the Division. However, there were two partial exceptions to this tendency, details of which are provided in chapters 5 and 6.

A control processes explanation (Bray and Littler 1988; Clegg 1990) is offered for this overall limited, but variable, significance of accounting within the Northern Division. In doing so, competing explanations based on efficiency arguments (Chandler 1977; Donaldson 1987; Williamson 1983) and cultural diffusion (DiMaggio and Powell 1983; Meyer and Rowan 1977) are rejected as they provide only partial understandings of the findings. A critical structuralist variant of a control processes explanation for churches is developed from the work of Armstrong (1984, 1985, 1986, 1987a) on business organizations. This stresses the importance of the different control problems of churches, particularly the tension between dominant sacred religious values and goals, and more secular coordination and administrative support functions, the actions of competing occupational groups, particularly conflict between the occupational views of the clergy and accountants, and the opposing prioritizing effects of sacred and secular crises in providing a means of understanding the use of accounting within churches.

V. CHAPTER SUMMARY

This chapter has outlined how this book is concerned with the study of accounting as a situated practice. As such it seeks to add to the rapidly growing research on accounting in its social and organizational context. This contribution is attempted through a critical structuralist framework applied to a case study of the uses of accounting in the Northern Division of the Mainstream Church.

The general problematic proposed to guide the study was - how does accounting achieve and maintain a position of organizational significance? The importance of this problematic was based on the premise that it is a generally irrefutable fact that accounting has obtained and continues to maintain a significant position in the affairs of a wide array of modern organizations. This position was problematized by arguing that the purposefulness of accounting is socially constructed, and that therefore there is no self-evident answer to the prominence of accounting in modern organizations. This problematic draws attention to the dynamic and diverse roles that

Background and Rationale 23

accounting serves in and across organizations. Therefore, research must question the various uses of accounting that exist, the forms of rationality to which they are linked and the nature of the settings in which this takes place.

To provide some focus for this problematic, a basic set of boundary conditions were argued as a 'skeletal' model to allow more specific questions to be formulated about the factors and conditions that may be potentially important for the purposefulness of accounting. This model proposed that accounting has certain characteristics which enable a particular form of visibility into and of economic (money-based) means-ends relationships in an organization. This is potentially useful as a way of understanding, addressing and formalizing the management of such relationships, which is a central organizing problem for capitalist firms. However, accounting is not the sole, or even obviously the 'best', way in which economic means-ends relationships may be managed. Other managerial occupational groups may possess alternative solutions. Therefore competition between various occupational groups may affect the significance of accounting in organizations. However, the scope of this competition may be limited by accounting constraining the ability of managers to use other ways of thinking and acting to the extent that it penetrates and dominates these alternatives. This may happen through the involvement of accounting in the construction and propagation of restricted views of rationality and moral orders in the organization, including the nature of trust relations between managers and others. The potential for the purposefulness of accounting, therefore, may be a complex construction of its particular characteristics, the organizational type within which these characteristics are relevant in some way, the occupational groups which may use and/or promote and/or resist this relevance, and the dual positive and negative effects that may result from the use of accounting.

It was then argued that these processes of rationalization were increasingly penetrating organizations in the State and civil society, but that there were many forms of resistance to this tendency. In particular, the commitment of voluntary organizations to the values of community, democracy and trust represented a non-calculable basis of organizational legitimation which was a direct challenge to processes of rationalization. Voluntary organizations, therefore, were selected as extreme cases that would enable a clearer conception of the limits of

24   *Managment Control in a Voluntary Organization*

the processes of rationalization and the potential purposefulness of accounting to be developed. Also, the selection of voluntary organizations was justified on the basis of their increasing significance in modern industrial societies and that they have been relatively ignored by accounting and organizational researchers.

Having selected voluntary organizations, a typology was then argued to enable the selection of a most extreme case. This typology was based on two dimensions of voluntary organizations which were argued to affect the relevance of money-based means-ends relations; the form of membership involvement, from materialistic to altruistic and social, and the source of funding, from direct charges and fees to endowments and grants. From these dimensions churches were selected as the form of voluntary organization where rationalization would be most contested, particularly because their commitment to the essential elements of religiosity provides a very non-calculable basis of organizational legitimation.

This sequence of arguments, then, sets out a basic framework of ideas for the conducting of this study. They problematize the significance of accounting in organizations, suggest general factors that may be associated with the social construction of this significance, and use these to identify potentially rich sites for empirical study.

The next chapter develops the basic framework of a control processes explanation of the significance of accounting in voluntary organizations, and churches specifically. It reviews the basic arguments of a critical structuralist approach to the understanding of the variety of management control strategies in business organizations and its applicability to the study of accounting. These ideas are reformulated to the specific case of churches, first by considering the nature of management control in voluntary organizations generally, and then adapting these to the case of churches.

Chapters 3 to 6 detail the case study of the Northern Division of the Mainstream Church. Chapter 3 deals with research method, justifying the selection of the case organization, describing some basic features of the organization and detailing the data collection methods used. Chapter 4 analyses the formal attributes of the Division accounting systems and considers how the financial dynamics of the Division may have affected their use. Chapter 5 evaluates the use of the accounting systems by sacred and secular occupational groups within the Division during 1987. The formulation of the 1988 Division

Background and Rationale

Budget is considered in depth in chapter 6, including the historical dynamics of Division budgeting processes.

Chapter 7 summarizes the major findings and compares the control processes explanation offered to other competing explanations. The final section of the chapter attempts to assess the generality of the findings by considering major trends in management control in voluntary organizations. The study concludes by proposing that a control processes analysis may offer a useful way to understand the dynamics of management control in voluntary organizations.

Notes

[1] There is wide acknowledgment that accounting rules are incomplete, inconsistent, and lacking in 'representational faithfulness' (for example, Tricker 1979). It is proposed in this study that these features inherently flow from the interpretive basis of accounting as one form of social rule system (see, Cooper et al 1981; Hines 1988). Social rules systems tend to be indexical in nature, that is that their meaning depends on the context in which they are used (Barnes 1986; Clegg 1975; Schwartz and Jacobs 1979). Social rules, of which those of accounting are one form, "...can never provide for their own interpretation. Issues of interpretation are always implicated in the process whereby ...[people]... instantiate and signify rules. Ruling is an activity" (Clegg 1989). The indexical nature of accounting rules, therefore, expands the ways in which accounting practices may act as useful forms of written communication.

[2] See also Cooper and Hopper (1987) for a more detailed discussion of what functions accounting may fulfil for capitalist firms.

[3] It is not the intention to assert that this simple proposition fully explains the way in which accounting historically grew to prominence in capitalist firms. As many different studies have shown (for example, Armstrong 1987a; Chandler and Deams 1979; Johnson 1983; Loft 1986; Miller and O'Leary 1987), the continuities and discontinuities of, and conditions influencing, the rise of accounting were much more complex. However, it is felt that the proposition here is generally consistent with these more detailed accounts, and forms an important basic condition for understanding the possibility of the purposefulness of accounting.

[4] That accounting can have both objective and subjective effects on the actions of managers has been a contested issue. The traditional accounting literature has concentrated on the objective effects of accounting. In simple terms, accounting was seen as a source of 'facts' which mirrored some aspect of the activities of organizations. Correct measurement and 'reading' of these facts allowed managers to take 'correct' actions to achieve the goals of the organization. The more recent critical and interpretive accounting literature has questioned the validity of these objective effects and

concentrated on its subjective effects. Again in simple terms, accounting was seen as a meaning construction process through which 'reality' was created rather than mirrored. Thus facts were not there to be read and acted upon, but to be interpreted and to provide a way for managers to rationalize and attach meaning to past, present and future actions (see Chua 1986a, and Hopper and Powell 1985 for reviews of both approaches). The confrontation of these two positions has a tendency to lead to the creation of a false dichotomy. Instead, the position adopted here is that accounting can have both objective and subjective effects (Boland and Pondy 1983; Chua 1988).

In proposing this duality, that accounting is fundamentally an interpretive process is accepted. In Morgan's (1988) terms, "...the basic subjectivity of accounting..." must be accepted. However, while this rules out the objective view of accounting as mirroring reality, it does not rule out that there may be some objective effects. The view offered by accounting numbers may give some insight that managers can use. For example, as Stinchcombe (1974, Ch 1) argued, if managers have to determine how to increase the productivity of an interdependent technological system then fundamentally they must have some way of monitoring the system in terms of the likely actions that have to be taken to change it. If one of these is cost, then accounting numbers can give the managers a view of that system that both enables their intervention and their monitoring of its effects. This is not to argue that accounting numbers give 'a true and objective' view but merely a view that reflects something about the activity that is measured. It is in this sense that it should be emphasized that accounting is still fundamentally a measurement and communication system and thus can have objective effects for managers.

[5] There is a large literature on accounting in various forms of not-for-profit organizations. However, much of this literature either deals with state organizations or concentrates on technical financial reporting issues (see, for example, Hay 1980; Henke 1986).

[6] Churches have also received little attention in the organization theory and sociology of organizations literatures, the emphasis of study being on work organizations (Thompson 1975).

Chapter 2
A Critical Structuralist Framework

I.   INTRODUCTION

This chapter develops a critical structuralist framework for the analysis of the processes of rationalization and the significance of accounting in voluntary organizations. Particular emphasis is given to churches as a special case of such organizations. In this endeavour, this chapter seeks to build on the arguments presented in general form in chapter 1 that attention must be paid to the form of organizing problems faced by organizations and the roles of various occupational groups. The aim is not to propose a full explanatory model for an understanding of the significance of accounting in voluntary organizations. Instead, the critical structuralist framework proposed is presented as a general organizing structure within which the specific details of the Mainstream Church case study can be coherently evaluated.

The chapter is organized into three major sections. The first section draws upon the work of Armstrong (1984, 1985, 1986, 1987a, 1989a) to set out the major elements of a critical structuralist analysis of management control in the context of business organizations. This emphasizes the importance of control processes in understanding the variety and development of management control strategies in organizations. The relevance of such an approach for understanding the significance of accounting in organizations is also considered. While this literature is only indirectly related to the context of voluntary organizations, it is necessary to consider the case of business organizations in some depth as the extant literature on management control has concentrated heavily on profit-making, particularly manufacturing, organizations. The second section overviews the more

28   *Management Control in a Voluntary Organization*

limited literature on the nature of management control issues in voluntary organizations. The relevance of a critical structuralist approach for this context is evaluated and necessary adaptations from the context of business organizations identified. The third section then develops the specific arguments adapting the critical structuralist approach to the case of churches. The chapter concludes with a summary of the major points.

II.   A CRITICAL STRUCTURALIST ANALYSIS OF MANAGEMENT

The aim of the discussion in this section is to outline the basic parameters of a critical structuralist analysis of management practices in organizations. This draws upon the contribution of Peter Armstrong to the labour process debate (Armstrong 1984, 1985, 1986, 1987a, 1989a). In doing so, attention is focused on issues of management control raised in this debate rather than the labour process per se. A critical review of the whole labour process debate is beyond the space available here (for useful reviews see Littler and Salaman 1982; Morgan 1990; Thompson 1989). More importantly, as the approach to this study focuses upon the relation of accounting to management practices and control in organizations, it is only that part of the labour process debate that deals with managerial strategy and control that is relevant. This analysis of management control in capitalist organizations is proposed as a general framework which can be adapted for understanding the operation of this process in other types of organizations.

The first subsection outlines the basic arguments of a critical structuralist understanding of management control in capitalist organizations. The next subsection reviews the specific relevance of this method of analysis for the understanding of the significance of accounting in such organizations. The final subsection summarizes the arguments in terms of the major points of a critical structuralist framework.

The Management Process and Inter-Professional Competition

There has been a great deal of attention given in the industrial sociology and organization theory literatures with the growth in the size and complexity of modern organizations and their control strategies. Clegg (1990) argued that a major approach to explaining this which has held great sway is based on efficiency arguments, either in terms of the market failures approach (for example, Chandler 1962, 1977; Williamson 1975, 1983) or responses to strategic contingencies (for example, Donaldson 1985, 1987). The general tenor of such arguments is that the development of modern organizations and the changes in the control strategies they use result from efficient adjustments to either failures in the conditions for efficient markets or from changes in strategic contingencies. The range of management control strategies found, at least in the longer term, exist because they are the most efficient ones for solving the uncertainties faced by modern organizations in particular periods.

The problems with the market failures argument are well known and have come from both within its own camp (Robins 1987) and from external commentators (Bray and Littler 1988; Clegg 1990; Perrow 1986). For example, it ignores the dynamics of change, trivializes human agency, ignores distributional inequalities in power and resources, and has circular logic. Overall, the market failures approach adopts an overly narrow economic conception of organizational action. Similarly, the strategic contingencies approach has been extensively criticised, even in its recent more sophisticated formulations (Clegg and Dunkerley 1980; Hinings et al 1988; Starbuck 1981; Wood 1979). As Clegg states, its "...organizations are somewhat bloodless - one has no sense of them as arenas peopled by potentially plural agencies with multiple and conflicting conceptions of their own and other interests, conceptions which, often in the messiest way, can obstruct the pressure of efficiency" (1990, p.73). One way of avoiding these problems is to adopt a perspective where control processes in organizations, at least in part, are the focus for explaining the historical development of their structures.

The publication of Braverman's *Labor and Monopoly Capital* (1974) sparked a resurgence of the debate on the nature of the labour process and control processes in organizations. Braverman was

30　　　　　　　*Management Control in a Voluntary Organization*

concerned with the form of the labour process, the means by which humans reproduce the material means of their existence, under the capitalist mode of production. A key feature of this process is the problem for the capitalist of converting *potential* labour power into a profitable surplus. As Hopper et al put it:

> "The basic and recurrent problem for the employer (or manager) of a capitalist enterprise therefore is to organize and control the labour process (and the market) to ensure that a surplus value over and above the costs of production is in fact extracted from the productive activity of the purchased units of labour" (1987, p.445).

According to Bray and Littler (1988), consideration of this issue has followed three major themes; the importance of deskilling and the development of a model of skill changes, the understanding of capitalist labour markets, and explanations of changes in managerial strategy and control. While all three overlap, it is the latter which is considered here.

For Braverman, the main way in which the capitalist gained control of the labour process was through systematic deskilling, the epitome of which was the development of scientific management, or Taylorism. While Taylorism, in its pure form, may have had a short historical reign, to Braverman it represented an ideal type of all the modern management techniques that followed it and persist to this day. The focus, therefore, was upon the systematic reorganization of management practices by capitalists and managers to deskill work to "...render it more transparent to management *control*, thus facilitating the extraction of surplus value" (Armstrong 1986, p.20, emphasis in original). Since Braverman the labour process debate has critiqued the dominance of the deskilling hypothesis and explored the variety of control strategies used by management. Major contributors to the debate have been Burawoy (1979), Clawson (1980), Edwards (1979), Friedman (1977), Gordon, Edwards and Reich (1982) and Littler (1982). These authors, and others, point to the variation in control problems across time, nations, industries and individual capitalist enterprises, and to the similar variation in the solutions sought to these problems. As a result, the labour process debate has led to a critical re-assessment of the nature of the control relationship in capitalist organizations.

The general formulation of the explanation of the changes in management control strategies associated with the development and growth of capitalist organizations presented has been that the rationalization of management control practices was a response to the

A Critical Structuralist Framework

31

failure of first craft traditions and internal contract systems and then piece rates to sufficiently increase work intensification in the face of increased competition brought about by economic slumps (for example, Edwards 1979; Friedman 1977; Littler 1982). The conclusion was that the need by employers and managers to 'combat effort regulation' led to the direct intervention by managers in the process of production and the deployment of a range of control strategies.

In a series of papers, Armstrong (1984, 1985, 1986) argued that these accounts have several deficiencies. The explanations "...are essentially functionalist in that the appearance of new strategies tends to be accounted for in terms of the problems which these solve" (Armstrong 1986, p.21). They do not provide a convincing explanation of the origins and nature of these particular solutions to the problems confronted by capital, particularly in light of comparative international evidence (Littler 1982). In addition, they also have difficulty in offering convincing explanations of the periodisation of changes in control strategies via economic crises. The "...problem here is that there are *always* crises somewhere in capitalist economies; nor is it established that the search for a competitive edge is absent when and where there is no crisis" (Armstrong 1985, p.131, emphasis in original). Thus, Taylorism was introduced in the USA under boom conditions while its derivative, the Bedaux system, was introduced in the U.K. during a slump (Littler 1982). The standard labour process account of the rationalization of management control, therefore, is deficient in i) the reasons for its advent, ii) the precise nature of the solutions adopted, and iii) their location historically.

In contrast, Armstrong offered Layton's (1969) account of Taylorism as a product of the ideology of American engineers and as a reaction against their subordination within capitalist enterprises that occurred at that time. Engineers found themselves reduced to minor positions in the growing bureaucratic organizations of the time, whereas previously they had experienced significant independence in the running of small jobbing machine shops. In response, engineers developed scientific management ideas and techniques by applying previous insights from machine redesign to the design of the work process. They then actively promoted it as 'their solution' to the control problems in the emerging hierarchies in an attempt to gain a dominant position in their management. These events offer a more

32 *Management Control in a Voluntary Organization*

convincing explanation of the historical location of the rise of Taylorism. Also, its basis in the extant knowledge base of engineers offers an explanation of the emergence of this particular solution.

Armstrong proposed that a more general and satisfactory explanation of the development and variety of management control strategies could be based upon a combination of Layton's focus on the actions of a professional group and the more standard labour process accounts of the control problems of organizations and the effects of economic crises. With the elaboration and differentiation of management under modern capitalism, what Carchedi (1977) referred to as the assemblage of roles making up the 'global function of capital', there has been an associated development of occupational specialisms within management, eg. accounting, personnel, engineers, marketing and general management, which in some cases are aligned with professional groups. A key point arising from this differentiation of management is that there is no preordained reason why any particular occupational specialism should hold the dominant positions within the management hierarchy. Capitalist management, therefore, "...beyond a certain level of differentiation, ... can be seen as a collection of relatively self-conscious specialisms which compete at a group level for access to the key positions of command" (Armstrong 1985, p.133).

The basis for achieving a 'key position of command' within management is the possession of solutions to the control problems of capitalist organizations. The initial step is the identification of a key problem for which the occupational group can offer a reduction in the uncertainties faced by the organization. For capitalist firms, three key general areas of uncertainty are the extraction, realization and allocation of surplus value (Armstrong 1987a). Extraction requires control of the labour process. Having extracted a surplus, which is now embedded in a service or commodity, it must be converted into money, or realized. When realized, problems may also be encountered in allocation internally in terms of reinvestment in the production process and between functions within the 'global function of capital' that have some claim, eg. managers, investors, creditors and the state. To increase its claim to a position of dominance in management, an occupational group needs to develop solutions to one or more of these problem areas and promote them as 'better' than any existing solutions. As part of this process a group may ideologically stress the

A Critical Structuralist Framework

importance of the problem, and the failure of previous solutions. In addition, the opportunity for an occupational group to promote solutions may be enhanced by associated economic crises as they increase the level of, at least perceived if not actual, uncertainty surrounding the control problem. However, the actions of an occupational group are not dependent on such crises occurring.

In developing solutions to key control problems it is likely that an occupational group will draw upon its existing body of knowledge and specialised techniques. Such knowledge and techniques may be adapted to and deployed in totally different spheres from those in which they were originally developed, as was the case for the development of Taylorism from engineers' knowledge of machine design. It is also possible that solutions may be 'borrowed' from other specialisms, eg. the 'takeover' by the accounting profession of costing techniques originally developed by engineers. Whatever the source, for a solution to be successfully used to gain dominance, an occupational group must be able maintain "...a certain mystique and indeterminacy about ...[the solution]... so that the strategy can be operated only by themselves" (Armstrong 1985, p.134), and thus they can retain control over its deployment. This is more likely if the solution is developed from the existing knowledge base or if borrowed solutions can be successfully integrated with this knowledge base. However, it is not necessary that all the knowledge or activities of the occupational group be surrounded in 'mystique and indeterminacy'. A group may be internally differentiated, with higher levels retaining control over core indeterminate elements and more codifiable aspects being performed by lower levels on a more routine basis. Also, the existence of such a group 'elite' is more likely to provide the prestige and management experience base from which access to high levels of management hierarchies can be more easily obtained.

Armstrong's argument, therefore, is that the actions of occupational groups competing for dominance within management are important in explaining the specific nature and timing of the development and variety of management control strategies in organizations. Attention should be directed to the development and promotion of solutions by such groups to the uncertainty surrounding key control problems of organizations, their success in securing the adoption of the solutions and in retaining discretion over their deployment, and the associated role, if any, of economic crises in

34 *Management Control in a Voluntary Organization*

prioritizing areas of uncertainty and the relevance of particular types of solutions. This argument is a useful contribution to understanding the development of management control strategies because it retains the strengths of the previous structuralist labour process explanations and extends them with a critical understanding of the agency of occupational groups.

Armstrong's critical structuralist framework provides an approach to understanding the relationship between management practices, the actions of accountants and other occupational groups, and the significance of accounting argued in chapter 1. However, control is not the basis of the relationships between managers in organizations. Armstrong (1989a) has rightly stressed that the basic nature of the relations between managers is one of agency[1]. Superiors have to delegate responsibility to subordinates, creating an accountability problem - how to ensure that subordinates act in the interests of superiors? Armstrong (1989a, see also 1987b, and Simon 1990) argued that the essence of this accountability relationship is one of trust between managers.

Fox (1974) argued that trust and distrust become embedded in the roles and rules of organizations and in relations between managers. The normal case for managers, particularly more senior ones, is high levels of institutionalized trust. Accountability relations are thus characterized by the assumption that a commitment is shared to organizational goals and values, close supervision and tight rules are inappropriate, and communication should be open and unfettered by hierarchical distinctions. Given this, apparent failure to meet delegated responsibilities is not assumed to be due to wilful negligence or other 'dysfunctional behaviour', as it would be under economic conceptions of agency relations (for example, Baiman 1982, 1990), but to require either an improvement in the ability of managers to perform or their replacement. However, Fox argued, the basic emphasis of management control systems is the opposite. They are designed on the premise that managers cannot be trusted and that therefore standards and rules for their performance of delegated responsibilities must be laid down and/or close supervision take place, actual performance monitored and 'objective' performance evaluations given to superiors. Control systems then are characterised by an assumption that subordinates are not committed to organizational goals and values and that failure to perform is due to careless indifference or wilful negligence. The

A Critical Structuralist Framework

appropriate response is punishment to ensure future compliance. Fox, therefore, shows that trust and management control systems are conflicting alternative mechanisms for solving the agency problem.

The rationalization of management therefore acts against the preferred basing of management relations on trust. Armstrong (1989a) argued that this contradiction existed because trust was expensive to obtain and maintain. One way of ensuring commitment is the socialization of managers. This requires expensive training programmes and the provision of significant higher rewards for loyalty. Also, requiring commitment may mean that search and selection processes are more expensive as they must be more extensive and particular. Finally, ensuring commitment is time consuming in both enculturation efforts and experimental tests of its existence. It may be that control systems could be much cheaper alternatives than trust in some settings. The economic nature of the key control problems in capitalist organizations mean that managers may have positive incentives to find more cost effective solutions to the agency problem. Also, managers may have additional incentives to implement control systems for their subordinates if these are seen as ways of proving their own trustworthiness to superiors. Relations between managers in organizations, therefore, can be expected to involve a trade-off between trust and management control systems.

These choices on trade-offs between trust and control systems, therefore, also can be expected to be relevant to explaining the development and variety of management control strategies within organizations. This is likely to be particularly relevant for accounting as its approach to control is strongly based on ideas of distrust (Caplan 1966; Carmichael 1970). This comes out strongly in Argyris' (1952) early behavioural work on budgets where operational managers resented the use of such controls and accountants acted as if operational managers were shirkers. A similar theme can be seen in Berry et al's (1985) more recent work on the National Coal Board. Also, Armstrong (1989b) has argued that the primary focus of accounting control systems is the delegation of blame, hardly a scenario for fostering trust (see also Argyris 1952). Therefore, it is proposed that the critical structuralist framework for explaining the development and variety of management control strategies in organizations should be expanded to include the contradictory nature of trust and control within managerial relationships.

36   *Management Control in a Voluntary Organization*

In summary, in this subsection it has been argued that the development and variety of management practices in organizations should be understood from primarily a control processes stance. The general trend of management control strategies in organizations has been towards the increasing rationalization of management techniques, which is discussed further below. A framework for examining this process of development based on the critical structuralist work of Armstrong was proposed. This framework emphasized the importance of the control problems faced by organizations, their possible prioritization by economic crises, and the role of inter-professional competition in developing and promoting solutions to these uncertainties in order to gain access to key positions within management. It was also argued that the dynamics of the relationship between managers, and thus also that between competing occupational groups, should acknowledge the inherent contradiction and trade-offs between trust and control. Together, these ideas provide an access to the complexity of management control practices in organizations. However, it should be stressed that a limitation of these arguments as presented here, and in the literature that they draw upon, is that they are related only to management practices and relations in profit-making organizations. This restriction is addressed later in the chapter.

Accounting and Management Control

The aim in this subsection is to demonstrate the potential of the critical structuralist framework outlined above for explaining the significance of accounting in organizations. This is attempted in two ways. First, a brief overview of Armstrong's historical analysis of the rise of accountants and accounting control in British capitalist enterprises is given. This illustrates the empirical potential of a critical structuralist approach. Second, some more general arguments about the advantages of such an approach are considered. Together these two sets of arguments show that a critical structuralist framework has potential utility for the concerns of this study.

Armstrong (1987a) set out to explain the apparent dominance of accountants and the significant use of accounting and financial controls in the management of modern British capitalist enterprises. A simple appeal to the inherent utility of accounting and accountants for

A Critical Structuralist Framework 37

such tasks was rejected because of comparative evidence that German and Japanese firms succeed without such levels of accounting dominance, and that there have been significant attacks on the actual efficacy of accounting for the control of organizations. Instead, he sought to examine the actual pattern of historical events that seemed to be associated with the rise of accounting in Britain.

In the early part of the 19th century there had been sporadic development of cost accounting techniques in individual capitalist firms. Further impetus to such developments seemed to have come from the search for better pricing methods associated with the economic slump of the 1880s, and increasing overheads, product diversity and competition on tendering. Costing was thus used to address a realization problem for the firms. However, its adoption was still very slow, partly because costing techniques had no clear competitive advantage in the solution of this problem. However, while this indicated some increase in the use of accounting controls there was little interest evidenced in such concerns by the accounting profession of the time. Most of the development that occurred was carried out by engineers. This scenario led Armstrong to conclude that "...the future of cost accounting as a body of knowledge was, at this time, open" (1987a, p.419). Yet by the 1970s accountants and techniques of financial control and cost accounting had achieved a significant foothold in British organizations.

Armstrong (1987a) then presented an analysis of the control problems, associated crises and actions of accountants that seemed to explain this change in the management control systems of British organizations. While in terms of historical detail this analysis was fairly general, it is still too extensive to review in full detail here. A summary of most of the major sequences of the analysis[2] is presented in Table 2.1. The discussion that follows concentrates on the structure of the argument rather than the supporting evidence.

Armstrong (1987a) argued that two conditions were necessary for the commencement of the rise of accountants and accounting controls in British organizations. First, the accounting profession had to rise to a significant position within the global function of capital. As Table 2.1 shows, this occurred during the 19th Century from solutions offered to problems associated with the allocation of surplus value via the handling of bankruptcies and audits. By the turn of the century the accounting profession had established two key positions within the

38 *Management Control in a Voluntary Organization*

sphere of allocation - insolvency management and external audit. The second necessary condition was the integration of costing techniques in the knowledge and skills base of the accounting profession. This occurred through the use of accountants by the State during WWI to assist in the regulation of prices for war industries. The result was an increase in the status of costing within the profession and its integration within the insolvency and auditing knowledge base of the profession (see also Loft 1986). These two series of events created the potential for further extension of the prominence of accounting within management.

However, this potential was not realized until the inter-war slump. This economic crisis was associated with the appointment of accountants to address the financial control problems of firms, and their consequent restructuring around more centralized financial control over internal investment and more centralized oversight of operations through budgetary control and monitoring systems. These solutions were based on a combination of the profession's existing auditing and costing knowledge and techniques. They provided, an admittedly crude, means of financial overview of the whole firm, and thereby "...a major incursion by the accounting profession into the function of the extraction of surplus value from the labour process" (Armstrong 1987a, p.425) and an increased demand within firms for accountants to implement and operate these new financial systems. Further impetus in both directions was received from the mergers activity of the 1920s and 1930s. In particular, the recommendation by accountants of a holding company format increased dependence on financial oversight as part of internal management control by adaptations of existing accounting surveillance tools developed for investors. Therefore, by the time of WWII the movements towards a greater financial emphasis in the management of capitalist enterprises and a clear space for the greater development of management accounting controls had been created.

The advent of WWII and State regulation of profits and prices again created the opportunity for the greater prominence of cost accounting and accountants within the war ministries and firms. After the war, some impetus for this prominence continued with concerns by the Labour government over increasing exports and controlling inflation. The involvement of accountants on the wide range of boards, councils and committees used by the State in their attempts to plan the

A Critical Structuralist Framework

economy increased the significance given to financial control systems. From this time, while more sophisticated systems such as standard costing were still rare, costing based controls and headquarters financial monitoring systems were firmly entrenched in British firms.

Control Problems	Crises	Outcomes
19th Century		
Allocation uncertainties surrounding organizational failures.	Increase in firm failures in third quarter of century.	Growth of accounting profession to perform financial duties of bankruptcies.
Also uncertainties about allocation of capital.	Reliance of British capital on equity finance due to banking arrangements.	Profession gained control of some of the rules by which capital allocation managed via financial reports and audit. Trust built up by profession may also have been significant.
World War I		
State regulation of profits and prices increases uncertainty about acceptable costs.	Munitions crisis of 1915. State places restrictions on strikes and dilution of skilled trades. Trade-off is limit on profits.	Large number of accountants recruited into the war ministries. Result is integration of costing knowledge into knowledge base of profession.
Inter-War Years		
Firms experience profitability and liquidity problems.	Financial problems heightened by inter-war economic slump.	Accountants appointed, often by creditors, to solve problems of financial control. Impose centralized budgetary control and monitoring systems. Based on a combination of auditing and costing knowledge.
Merger activity in 20s and 30s. Possibly related to search for solutions to above financial problems.	Heightened competition and excess capacity.	Accountants involved in recommending on control structures for mergers. Used holding company form which heavily relied upon financial headquarters control. Also some importation of ideas from US via takeovers and trade visits.
World War II		
Realization and allocation problems again associated with need for costing controls.	Early in war State regulated production and prices.	Accountants again recruited into war ministries (accountancy a reserved occupation). Elite of profession gain positions of significant power in ministries. Also incentives for industry to hire accountants to ensure their costs are not understated. Many stay on after war.

Table 2.1: A Summary of Armstrong's Analysis of the Rise of Accounting Controls in British Capitalist Enterprises

Control Problems	Crises	Outcomes
Postwar Reconstruction		
State concerned over allocation of materials and price levels.	Need to increase exports and control inflation perceived by State.	Accountants play part in State regulatory boards (flow on from wartime positions).
Also concerns with low levels of productivity in firms.		Productivity teams visit US, accountants impressed by budgetary control and standard costing systems. Spread to industry very slow.
Post 1950		
Growth of industrial concentration. State promotes mergers. Also used by firms for growth by acquisition. Result is focus on search for profitability by a financial logic.	Balance of payments problems. Believed to be related to small, uncompetitive firms in British industry.	Accountants involved in assisting merger activity.
Adoption of divisional organizational form increases internal allocation and extraction problems in firms.		Where divisional form adopted, greater emphasis is given to financial allocations controls and budgetary control systems and financial performance measures.

Table 2.1: A Summary of Armstrong's Analysis of the Rise of Accounting Controls in British Capitalist Enterprises - Continued

After 1950 the spread of more sophisticated financial control systems was aided by concerns in such firms with attempts to increase their profitability via a financial rather than production logic, particularly via increased merger activity. This was supported by actions of the State and concerns over the competitiveness of British industry. The greatest impetus for more financial control systems came where the divisional organizational form was adopted. The result of these series of changes was the increasing subordination of operational managers to their financial counterparts, "...the headquarters accountant/executive" (Armstrong 1987a, p.430).

Armstrong's (1987a) analysis illustrates how the rise of accounting controls in British capitalist firms can be understood as arising from a combination of the actions of the accounting profession to promote their prominence within the global function of capital and the particular historical circumstances of the development of capitalism in Britain. The rise in prominence of accountants was because they were able to offer solutions to first various realization and allocation, and then extraction problems faced by management. Often the potential for this to occur was increased by various economic or other crises. Also, it seems that accountants were able to develop and maintain a monopoly over the application of such solutions. This pattern of actions by accountants appeared to be inextricably intertwined with the development of capitalism in Britain over that time period. However, determinism is avoided in the analysis as the potential always existed for other solutions or developments to take place. The explanation of the specific pattern that did occur is based in the specific historical actions of accountants and other major players, notably the State, creditors and management.

However, the breadth of history and the complex issues covered by Armstrong in a single journal article result in many of the historical details not being clear. For example, there is no complete explanation of how accountants came to dominate insolvency practice, there are competing explanations for the development of the dominance of auditing, and that accountants achieved a monopoly over the accounting solutions deployed is demonstrated but an explanation of how this occurred is missing. Thus, there are lacunae in the how and why of some of the developments that took place.

In part, these gaps may also be attributed to the focus of a critical structuralist framework. The concern with explaining the development of management control strategies and the significance of accountants within management means that less emphasis is given to many of the dynamics of the development of the accounting profession. For example, the analysis of the development of the accounting profession in Britain by Willmott (1986) uses a similar critical framework but concentrates more on the relationships between professional bodies, the state and the economic context. The critical structuralist approach, therefore, should not be seen as a total explanation of the relationship between accounting, accountants and their social context, but rather one that focuses attention on this relationship in connection with the development of management control process within organizations.

42   *Management Control in a Voluntary Organization*

What advantages then does such a critical structuralist framework have for the understanding of accounting? Many have already been alluded to in the discussion so far, but it seems worthwhile to consider them more systematically to conclude this subsection[3].

First, a critical structuralist framework provides a useful basis for a social contextualization of an understanding of accounting. For the case of capitalist enterprises, attention is drawn to the importance of the social relations between capital and labour in this context, which has been significant for the development of accounting practice as we know it in relation to the development of management control strategies. An understanding of the latter points to the roles of many accounting practices in the direct subordination by managers of labour or other managers, or in assisting with subsidiary problems of realization or allocation of surplus value. An analysis of accounting, therefore, is linked to how it is fashioned to serve particular dominant interests (see also, Booth and Cocks 1990; Cooper and Sherer 1984; Tinker 1985). However, the limitation of such arguments so far to this particular organizational context should be emphasized.

Second, as an extension of the first advantage, a critical structuralist framework locates the study of accounting in its historical context. An understanding of the social context of the mode of production and the problem of the control of the labour process necessarily require an appreciation of how the history of modern Western industrial societies is related to the significance of accounting. This not only has the advantage of better understandings of the continuities and discontinuities of the development of accounting techniques, as in the illustration above, but also in providing an historical context for more contemporary studies of accounting practices. However, this is not to assert some form of simple historical determinism of current practices as we must always be aware of the potential for and actuality of change (Hopwood 1983).

Third, the critical structuralist framework provides a means of explicitly linking the development and uses of accounting practices to the actions of accountants and other managerial groups. Often in the traditional and interpretive approaches to the study of accounting there is a tendency to place too much emphasis on the treatment of accounting as a disembodied technology. The critical structuralist approach requires that the relation of accounting practices to interests

A Critical Structuralist Framework 43

be addressed. This is partly achieved by the linking of accounting with the control problems of management discussed above, but is even more emphasized by its linking with the interests of occupational specialisms competing for key positions within management. This is especially important for accounting as it links its understanding with the actions of accountants and the accounting profession more broadly; a relatively neglected area in the study of accounting (Burchell et al 1980; Willmott 1986). An understanding of accounting, therefore, is also linked to issues of human agency.

Finally, the overall effect of the above points is the rejection of the study of accounting based on a initial premise of its neutral, inherent purposefulness. The critical structuralist framework emphasizes how accounting serves and legitimates the interests of management and the occupational groups that compete for its dominance. Accounting is seen as both a medium and outcome of the social relations of production, not as some separate objective reflector of such relations. Also, this view negates the definition of resistance to accounting practices by some workers and managers as a form of 'social deviance'. Rather it may be theorized as a consequence of the social relations within which the accounting practices are developed and deployed. In other words, the critical structuralist framework situates accounting as a social practice.

Overall, the critical structuralist framework offers a method for the study of accounting practices in organizations that is thoroughly embedded in a critical understanding of social context but also attempts to avoid being deterministic and overly structuralist by attending to the "...interpretive and dialectical nature of social reproduction" (Hopper et al 1987, p.454).

Summary of Major Points

This section has outlined the major features of a critical structuralist approach to the understanding of management control in organizations. This approach provides a social and historical contextualization of the analysis of the development of the processes of rationalization and the significance of accounting. To do so, the explanation offered is firmly based in an understanding of the effects of the social structure, but is also adequate at the level of human agency via its consideration of the role of various actors in the production and reproduction of this social structure. The major points developed in this section are summarized below.

First, within a critical structuralist approach the processes of rationalization and the variety in management control strategies are understood in relation to the development of the processes of control in organizations, not as the outcomes of searches for more efficient organizational forms. A control focus gives attention to both issues of structure and agency. Action in organizations is not treated as some overly rational adaptation process, but as a complex social production. However, the critical structuralist ideas outlined to this point have been developed only within the context of private sector capitalist organizations. Their applicability to the context of voluntary organizations still needs to be considered. The remainder of this chapter addresses this issue.

Second, economic or other crises of various forms may provide extra impetus for seeking solutions to particular control problems at specific points in time. That is, crises may prioritize a control problem and even construct its understanding in a particular way. In addition, the relevance and nature of crises may be ideologically emphasized by competing occupational groups to promote their own interests. Thus, the potential may be created for particular types of solutions to appear more relevant. However, what strategies are actually used is still left open, they are not determined by the nature of crises. These issues are elaborated further in the remainder of the chapter.

This leads to the third point; the types of solutions deployed are related to the actions of occupational groups competing for the key positions of command in the management of organizations, in inter-organizational relations and also in the relations between organizations and the state. To further these interests, occupational groups construct solutions to problems faced by organizations based on their extant knowledge base and specialist techniques. Note that it is not necessary that these solutions be totally effective for the specialism to acquire dominance. The contradictions within capitalism and the complexity of economic and organizational relations means that effectiveness usually will be ambiguous. Finally, for dominance to be achieved and maintained the solutions developed must also be sufficiently indeterminate and surrounded by an occupational group mystique so that they can retain a monopoly over their deployment.

A Critical Structuralist Framework 45

Thus, as Armstrong (1987a) has argued, accounting may become significant in organizations because it offers solutions to continuing control problems. It may be particularly powerful in this regard because it potentially offers a common view across problems by focusing on or at least creating the impression of their having a core monetary dimension. These solutions have been promoted by the accounting profession to increase its prominence within the global function of capital. The rise of accounting and financial controls and the rise of the accounting profession thus need to be seen in the overall context of the emergence and development of management control.

III. MANAGEMENT CONTROL IN VOLUNTARY ORGANIZATIONS

It was argued in the previous section that the significance of accounting in organizations could be analysed using a critical structuralist approach within the context of the emergence and development of management control. How relevant is such an argument to voluntary organizations, the general focus in this study? This section overviews issues of management control in voluntary organizations and assesses the applicability of the critical structuralist framework to this arena. This provides a general platform on which the more specific arguments developing a critical structuralist framework for the analysis of the significance of accounting in churches, the specific focus in this study, can be based.

A limitation of this discussion is that there is little extant knowledge of management control in voluntary organizations (Harris 1990). Various aspects of volunteers and their role in social welfare have been studied for some time (for example, Gidron 1978; Katz 1970; Sills 1957). However, studies at the organizational level have been more sporadic and have generally concentrated on specific voluntary organization types, with little effort being directed at theorizing management issues in voluntary organizations as a whole (Billis 1984, 1989). Also, many of the attempts that do exist have been normatively rather then empirically based (for example, Ramanathan 1985). Compared to the literature on industrial and government organizations, there is little systematic knowledge about management control in voluntary organizations (Milofsky 1988a; O'Neill and Young 1988a; Ware 1989). The arguments in this section, therefore,

46   *Management Control in a Voluntary Organization*

should be seen as indicative of the current understanding of management control in voluntary organizations rather than a definitive statement of such issues.

The discussion commences with an assessment of what constitutes the voluntary sector. How rationalization and management control ideas from capitalist organizations may have permeated this sector is then reviewed. The next subsection considers the distinctive features, if any, of management control in voluntary organizations. The section concludes with a statement of the major distinctive features of voluntary organizations and an assessment of the applicability of the critical structuralist approach.

What is the Voluntary Sector?

Defining the voluntary sector is fraught with difficulties (Harris 1990). There is no agreement internationally on the nomenclature covering this arena. It may be variously named the voluntary sector, third sector, intermediate organization sector and not-for-profit sector. This is more than just a semantic problem as slightly different activities and organizations may be included under each title. Also, the boundaries between this sector and the government and commercial sectors are permeable and blurred (Billis 1989). An additional problem linked to these ambiguities is that the voluntary sector is often defined residually (Harris 1990; Van Til 1988). This is an unsatisfactory approach as it only enables the specification of features that the voluntary sector does not have rather than the distinctive features that a positive definition should highlight. Recent work by Van Til (1988) has gone some way to addressing this problem by emphasizing that a definition should be based in the centrality of volunteers and voluntary action to the distinctive nature of labour relations in this sector. Using this as a starting point, it is proposed that the concept of voluntary labour suggests a distinction between coerced and uncoerced activity, with the voluntary sector based in the latter. Further, uncoerced labour can be conceptualized as a continuum from total wage labour to total non-wage labour. The voluntary sector is concerned with activity towards the non-wage labour end. Even where wage labour is used, it is often acknowledged that lower rewards are accepted because of commitment to the voluntary ideals of the sector (Gerard 1983; Vladeck 1988). The voluntary sector, therefore, can be broadly stated

A Critical Structuralist Framework

to be that area of social activity where people, individually or in more organized forms, are involved in uncoerced non-wage labour, or at least the ideal of non-wage labour.

Within this broad sector, this study is concerned specifically with voluntary labour conducted within more structured arrangements, that is voluntary organizations. Given the difficulties of precise definition, the three key defining features put in chapter 1 are taken here as an operational definition of voluntary organizations. A voluntary organization has (i) uncoerced membership based on commitment to the goals of the organization and the values of community and democracy, (ii) direct material rewards for members have little to do with this commitment or involvement, and (iii) there is a tendency to minimize the wage relationship either through the use of volunteer labour or the commitment of paid staff to the goals and values of the organization.

What the voluntary sector is not, therefore, is involvement in business, for-profit activities or public sector government activities. Also, outside the bounds of the sector, but less clearly, are the less organized areas of kin and communal networks (Harris 1990). This provides some boundaries for the activities included within the voluntary sector and voluntary organizations, but the possible internal variety of activities is still large, for example, mutual benefit activities such as clubs and co-operatives, service provision activities such as the Red Cross, and coordination activities such as peak social service organizations. In addition, the scale of activities may vary considerably, for example, from a neighbourhood social club to the Catholic Church.

The key feature of all voluntary organizations must be the voluntary participation of its membership. This gives it a distinctive focus on the common values that bring these members together. Generally, these values emphasize the importance of free association, co-operation and consensus. How members are involved in the organization may vary considerably. They may form the total work force of the organization. At the other extreme they may only be involved in management committees and paid staff may carry out all tasks. Some argue that the primary function of volunteers in most voluntary organizations is to act as fund raisers (Kramer 1981). However, whatever the type of involvement, the key issue is that the organization exists to serve the values that attracted its membership.

48   *Management Control in a Voluntary Organization*

Voluntary organizations therefore must manage their relations with their membership through maintaining their basic community and democracy values (Handy 1988; McGregor et al 1982; O'Connell 1988; Rothschild-Whitt 1979).

Other distinctive features that follow from this key feature are the involvement of volunteers in the work of the organization and their interaction with paid staff (Kramer 1981; McGregor et al 1982; Milofsky 1988c; Vladeck 1988). The significant involvement of volunteers in task execution is somewhat unique to voluntary organizations. Volunteers predominantly participate for psychological and social, not material rewards. This adds a different emphasis to their integration within the organization from normal employment relations. Also, there is potential for conflict with paid staff, who are often professionals. The latter may regard volunteers as amateurs interfering in their professional domain, or find it difficult to integrate with those who have only an irregular involvement with the organization. There is a tendency, therefore, for voluntary organizations to have different 'employment' relations than other organizations.

The specific goals of voluntary organizations must also be emphasized (O'Neill and Young 1988b). These can vary widely within the voluntary sector through various forms of direct service provision, fund-raising, various mutual benefit activities, research, advocacy and co-ordination (Harris 1990). The distinctive features of these goals overall are that they are not materially based (altruistic), qualitative and often intangible, generally people orientated and non-monetary (Gerard 1983; Kramer 1981). These types of ends, in association with the voluntary values discussed above, mean that goals are more critical in determining how voluntary organizations function than in other sectors. The "...particular activities that business and government organizations undertake are *instrumental* to achieving their overall objectives. For ...[voluntary organizations]..., the particular service or the given constituency or the articulated cause is of *primary* concern, not subservient to an overriding financial or political bottom line" (O'Neill and Young 1988b, p.4). Voluntary organizations therefore must also manage their relations with their membership by adhering to and achieving their specific goals.

Another distinctive feature following from the general nature of voluntary organization goals is their ambiguity and a consequence lack

A Critical Structuralist Framework 49

of clear performance measures (DiMaggio 1988; Mellor 1985; Milofsky 1988c). The goals of voluntary organizations are often set at high levels of abstraction and consequently can often be unclear, seeming to support many plausible courses of action. This tendency is exacerbated by their qualitative, intangible, altruistic nature. The net effect is that the setting of clear performance criteria is difficult and it is therefore challenging to formulate performance measures for voluntary organizations.

The voluntary sector, and voluntary organizations within it, therefore, have distinctive features from the capitalist organizations context discussed in the previous section. The central emphasis on membership values of democracy and the commitment to, and nature of, the specific goals of the organization make the values dimension of voluntary organizations more critical. These are associated with other distinctive features in terms of relations with volunteers, paid staff and the availability of performance measures. From the arguments developed previously, what is particularly relevant about the importance and nature of the values of voluntary organizations is that it is difficult to reduce them to rational calculation, unlike the profit and monetary focus of capitalist firms. However, even if voluntary organizations are distinctive in themselves, it does not necessarily follow that they have distinctive management control issues. The remainder of this section considers this question.

The Dynamics of Diffusion to the Voluntary Sector

One reason that voluntary organizations may not have distinctive management control issues is that control practices from the business sector may have permeated organizations in the voluntary sector. It was one of Weber's (1927, 1947) major themes that rationalization was an increasing feature of modern Western societies. Much attention has been given to the increasing rationalization of professions and organizations in the state and civil society (DiMaggio and Powell 1983; J. Meyer 1986; M. Meyer 1987; M. Meyer and Brown 1977; J. Meyer and Rowan 1977; Morgan 1990). DiMaggio and Powell (1983) point to the increasing homogeneity of organizational forms in modern societies. They also outline examples of the increased standardization and formalization of operating procedures in various types of voluntary organizations; social service

50   *Management Control in a Voluntary Organization*

agencies, local neighbourhood collectives and alternative schools. In a similar vein, the work of M. Meyer (M. Meyer and Brown 1977; M. Meyer 1987) points to the increased bureaucratization of state agencies over time. In both cases, the end result is the increased formalization and rationalization of the management of organizations in all sectors of modern societies.

According to DiMaggio and Powell (1983), this increasing homogeneity of organizational form is the result of institutional isomorphism. That is, the constraining process which forces an organization to become more like the other organizations that make up its environment and compete with it for resources, power and legitimacy. Institutional isomorphism acts through three mechanisms:

> "1) *coercive* isomorphism that stems from political influence and the problem of legitimacy; 2) *mimetic* isomorphism resulting from standard responses to uncertainty; and 3) *normative* isomorphism, associated with professionalization" (DiMaggio and Powell 1983, p.150).

These mechanisms lead to increasing rationalization through formal and informal pressures on organizations; to adopt the procedures of organizations on which they are dependent, eg nonprofits prepare accounts to meet the requirements of funding agencies (Kramer 1981); to meet cultural expectations about appropriate practices, eg. collectivist organizations develop nominal authority figures to handle contact with hierarchical organizations (Rothschild-Whitt 1979); and by the adoption of available solutions to address ambiguous problems, eg. adoption of PPB by government agencies in America during the 1960s (Jablonsky and Dirsmith 1978). Also, the formal education and inter-organizational networks of various professionals employed by organizations act as a means of the dispersion of a pool of common ideas across them. Similar views are developed in the institutional theory of organizations based on the work of J. Meyer and Rowan (1977). This theory proposes that organizational structure is based more on institutionalized beliefs about legitimate organizational forms, a control processes argument, than any search for greater efficiency or effectiveness (see Zucker 1983, 1987). Their consideration of the process of institutional isomorphism leads DiMaggio and Powell to conclude that:

> "Rational administration pushes out non-bureaucratic forms, schools assume the structure of the workplace, hospital and university administrations come to resemble the management of for-profit firms, and the modernization of the world economy proceeds unabated" (1983, p.156).

At a more macro level of analysis, J. Meyer (1986) argued that "...beyond rationalization at the level of specific organizations ... the really important effects result from the rationalization of whole institutional sectors and societies" (p.348). Thus, in recent years there has been increasing rationalization in, for example, hospital management, the psychology of job satisfaction and the management of the environment on an almost world-wide level (J. Meyer 1980). J. Meyer refers to this broader process as cultural rationalization. One element of this process is the standardization of the meanings of the components of social activity, eg. actors, objects and actions. A second element is the reduction of standardized elements to a common yardstick of measurement, eg. monetarized measures of work or grade point averages of student performance. Finally, monetarization can lead to the construction of notions of the causal integration of exchange or production. This involves the conception of the tracking of the money value of standardized elements through an exchange or production process. These three elements are produced by, and act to reproduce, the social organization of value around means-end relationships, which primarily occurs in the form of monetarization.

> "Thus, everything in a local setting, or now a whole society and most of the world, can be conceived to be property with a certain monetary value. It enters into social life as resources and costs. Much human action enters in, analyzed as productive, with a definite value. The products have value too, and now the concept of a GNP or even a world product is given meaning. All together it makes up wealth, and a conception of the total monetarized value of the world is not too difficult to work out. Thus the world can be seen as a web of means-ends relations" (J. Meyer 1986, pp.348-49).

J. Meyer (1986) argued further that this conception of value is based upon, and reinforces, the "...social construction of reality in a grand control structure" (p.349). That is, a rationalized mapping of the entities that enter into the means-ends relations of value. This process involves the construction of ideas about natural resources, the legal conception of things as property, of individuals, corporations and the state. The creation and standardization of these entities and their linkage via rules of property and membership enables them to be included in the web of means-ends relations, thus making this web possible. Overall, therefore, J. Meyer's argument points to the rationalization of Western societies on a very broad and pervasive level. Indeed, his argument presents rationalization as a very basic element of such societies as we know them.

52   *Management Control in a Voluntary Organization*

The arguments above point to the spread of management control strategies developed in business organizations to other organizational types in the state and civil society. Whether from the process of institutional isomorphism, or as part of wider social processes towards rationalization, or both, the use of control systems, including accounting systems, which focus managerial strategies on measurable characteristics of work performance and measure success or failure in terms of quantifiable, often financial, criteria have become a powerful image in modern organizations (Morgan 1990). As part of this, accounting has become an institutionalized component of management control (Hopwood 1983). Accounting practices have been implicated in the creation of new forms of visibility into money-based relations and in the penetration of and dominance of these restricted forms of visibility into spheres where their relevance is less clear (for example, Hamburger 1989; Hopwood and Tomkins 1984; Miller 1990; Preston 1990; Rosenberg et al 1982). Particularly important in this spread may be the monetarization of means-ends relations. All organizations - government agencies, hospitals, churches - come to have some form of economic linkages both internally and externally. These means-ends relations enable the deployment of legitimated ideas of calculability and rationalization from business organizations. Therefore, the "...structure of rationalized relations in capitalist organizations are imposed on other money-based forms of organization" (Morgan 1990, p.125).

Voluntary organizations have not been exempt from this process. There has been much effort directed at developing and implementing 'objective' and quantified performance measures for a wide range of voluntary organizations, particularly those using government funds (for example, AAA 1989; Theobald 1985). Broader efforts have also been directed at improving the 'professionalism' of their management, including the adoption of more commercial management techniques, structures and the hiring of managers with business experience (for example, Anthony and Young 1984; Griffiths 1988; HMSO 1989; O'Neill and Young 1988a; Wilson 1989; Woodfield et al 1987). Overall, there is considerable evidence of the rationalization of management practices in voluntary organizations and the tendency for them to become more like business organizations. Many of these pressures can be expected to continue into the 1990s (Kramer 1990).

A Critical Structuralist Framework 53

It could be assumed from such arguments that there are either very few distinctive features of management control in voluntary organizations, or that what there are are fast disappearing. However, this would be to consider rationalization a fait accompli rather than a social tendency. In chapter 1 the importance of recognising the resistance to the processes of rationalization was stressed. Even within business organizations, labour does not meekly acquiesce to the control strategies of management, and contending occupational groups may resist the deployment of each others' solutions to control problems; that is, following Foucault (1979, 1980), the power-knowledge relations that underlie the processes of rationalization continually give rise to forms of resistance and non-compliance. In addition, the non-calculable values that dominate activity in voluntary organizations are a particularly strong basis of resistance to the use of rational management and accounting practices (Morgan 1990). Thus, it should not be expected that cultural rationalization of management practices will be complete, especially for voluntary organizations. The distinctive nature of these organizations may mean that distinctive management control issues still exist, even though there is a tendency towards the adoption of business practices and control systems.

Managing Voluntary Organizations

From a critical structuralist perspective, the arguments on the distinctive features of voluntary organizations and their relation to resistance to rationalization point to a different order of control problems in voluntary organizations. Conceptually, these may be divided into two types; those related to the voluntary values orientation, which affects all voluntary organizations, and those related to the specific goal orientation of individual or groups of organizations. As the former may affect different voluntary organizations to different extents and given the diversity of the latter, it is impossible in the brief exposition here to explore the actual variety of control problems in voluntary organizations. However, all that is necessary for the purposes of this section is a discussion similar to an 'ideal type' analysis of the general tendencies towards a different order of control problems in all voluntary organizations. In addition, organizational size has been argued to affect the complexity of management in voluntary organizations (Cook 1988; DiMaggio 1988),

54   *Management Control in a Voluntary Organization*

but whether the nature of control problems is really any different is disputed (Cook 1988). As most of the available literature deals with organizations of reasonable size, at least a moderately large organization is assumed in the following discussion.

Milofsky (1988c) argued that the primary problem affecting the survival of voluntary organizations is the management of membership. Every voluntary organization must attract a sufficient following to legitimate its existence and provide the resources support, either directly or by donation, for it to carry out its tasks. This includes the integration of volunteers within the employment relations of the organization. Beside focusing on its specific goals, a critical factor in achieving this is to satisfy the values that attract members to voluntary organizations, those of community and democracy (Leat 1988; O'Connell 1988; Rothschild-Whitt 1979). According to Gerard (1983), 65% of British charities had consultative or fully participative management structures. A similar pattern could be seen in Kramer's (1981) study of welfare agencies across four nations. Thus, there is a tendency for voluntary organizations to emphasize participatory democracy, dispersion of power and consensus management (O'Connell 1988).

This values orientation conflicts directly with the dominate hierarchical, bureaucratic management structures of business organizations (Billis 1984; DiMaggio 1988; Milofsky 1988b, 1988c; Rothschild-Whitt 1979; Scott 1981). Stanton's (1989) description of collective management in a welfare agency emphasizes this point. The staff of the agency argued that their relations with clients stressed working together and self empowerment, and that it was highly inconsistent for their own internal work relations to be based on hierarchy and delegated responsibilities. Similarly, Scott stated that bureaucracy "...was an anathema to people committed to maximum participation" (1981, p.38). It would seem from the discussions in the literature that the need to manage issues around the values of community and democracy give rise to a different order of basic control problem than those discussed for business organizations previously in this chapter. This difference is emphasized by the different solutions adopted and the resistance offered to those used by business organizations.

This theme of difference continues when the general nature of the specific goals of voluntary organizations are considered. Their

A Critical Structuralist Framework 55

goals are altruistic, qualitative, intangible and non-monetary (Gerard 1983; Kramer 1981). Such goals are difficult to reduce to 'objective' performance measures (DiMaggio 1988; Leat 1988; Mellor 1985; Milofsky 1988c). This means that managers must give more attention to the symbolic appropriateness of actions than rational calculation of options and outcomes (Leat 1988; DiMaggio 1988). Thus, it is commonly stressed that 'successful' voluntary organization managers need more 'people skills' than technical management knowledge (O'Connell 1988; DiMaggio 1988; Vladeck 1988). Overall, the non-calculable nature of the goals of voluntary organization lead to a different nature of control problem than for the goals of business organizations. The emphasis on the implementation and achievement of non-calculable, altruistic goals offers resistance to managerial control strategies based on measurable characteristics of work performance and the measurement of success in terms of quantifiable, often financial, criteria (Leat 1988; Morgan 1990).

The perceived different nature of the control problems of voluntary organizations results in a view that senior managers need a background in the service or specialist area of the organization (DiMaggio 1988). The importance of staff being committed to the goals and values of voluntary organizations comes out more strongly in the relations between the two major types of occupational groups involved in their management. These are the professional staff groups involved in direct goal accomplishment, for example, welfare officers, counsellors, etc., and the groups involved in administrative activities, for example, accountants, personnel officers, executive officers. The former are argued to be strong supporters of the values and specific goals of voluntary organizations (Harris 1990; Kramer 1981). Weiss (1988) argued that 'professional staff' will have occupational views about how the voluntary organization's tasks should be accomplished and will resist any "...programmes that interfere with their ability to do their job as they see fit" (p.104). In particular, she stated that their alignment with the values of voluntary organizations will lead to resistance to any increase in management control strategies that do not seem to support their service goals. This is also seen in the work of Stanton (1989). There is thus the potential for conflict between professional and administrative staff over the deployment of occupational solutions to the management of voluntary organizations. Also, the indication is that professional staff hold the dominate

56   *Management Control in a Voluntary Organization*

position because their solutions are argued to be more relevant to the particular nature of control problems in voluntary organizations.

The same arguments could be applied to relations between professional staff and the members of voluntary organizations (Harris 1990; Kramer 1981; Mellor 1985). Values could be expected to be more aligned here, but professional staff may have biases from their particular occupational interpretation of goals and values. Therefore, there could be conflict also between profession staff and members over solutions to control problems, but this is less likely than for that between professional and administrative staff.

Variety in occupational views may also be a source of conflict within the professional staff category. Weiss (1988) points out that many voluntary organizations will have several different occupational groups represented within their professional staff. "Each professional group has been trained to understand and treat problems in its own way, and each specializes in certain kinds of clients and certain kinds of problems. ... In spite of obvious overlap, such differences make close cooperation difficult" (Weiss 1988, p.104). Therefore, while professional staff may dominate, there will still be competition between different occupational groups on appropriate solutions to control problems. Also, the qualitative and ambiguous nature of the goals may facilitate the scope for such competition.

The preceding discussions of the values orientation of voluntary organizations and the commitment of most occupational groups and organizational members to these values highlight the different nature of the managerial agency relationship in voluntary organizations. Accountability between different managers and between managers and members places more emphasis on trust in voluntary organizations (Leat 1988). This 'ideal of trust' is reinforced by the existence of non-calculable goals and the difficulty of deploying quantitative performance measures. The giving of 'satisfactory accounts' in voluntary organizations must therefore rely more on persuasion and appeals to shared values and norms than reference to 'objective' standards and measurable outcomes (Day and Klein 1987; Leat 1988). This indicates that trust may be easier, and thereby cheaper, to obtain and maintain in voluntary organizations. Therefore, there would appear to be a tendency towards economic and values disincentives associated with substituting management control systems for trust as

A Critical Structuralist Framework 57

the dominate basis of the agency relationship in voluntary organizations.

However, this tendency may not be equal across all occupational groups, particularly the 'professional' and 'administrative' categories. Some of the latter, such as accountants, may place less emphasis on trust and more on the supposed cost effectiveness of management control systems. Differences in views on the nature of the managerial agency relationship in voluntary organizations and the associated relevance of management control systems, therefore, may be another source of conflict between professional and administrative occupational groups.

The indication then is that the central control problems of voluntary organizations are of a different order to business organizations. They focus more on altruistic values, qualitative, non-monetary goals and managerial relations based on trust. Also, these problems seem to require, at least symbolically, different types of managerial control strategies. In particular, their non-calculable nature makes the application of quantified measures of work performance and success difficult. Indeed, the application of business control strategies is more than difficult, it may be considered an anathema to the whole context of voluntary organizations. It would appear, therefore, that a critical structuralist approach has to be amended in the case of voluntary organizations to allow for these different uncertainties and the control strategies that appear relevant. Also, the concept of the actions of occupational groups still appears relevant in the context of voluntary organizations. The only adjustment that may be necessary would be to extend the concept of 'occupation' to include volunteers.

While the above discussion stresses the differences in managing voluntary organizations, it should also be noted that they have some similarities to business organizations. Like all organizations they face general issues of co-ordination and resource renewal. With the effects of cultural rationalization, many of these issues become expressed in terms of monetarized relations (Milofsky 1988c). Rationalization pressures also become expressed in greater concerns with efficiency and effectiveness in voluntary organizations (DiMaggio 1988; Wilson 1989; Wolfenden Committee 1978). Gerard (1983) reported that charities in his survey were preoccupied with operating constraints, particularly human and financial resources. Vladeck (1988) also argued that scarce finances was a major issue for most voluntary

58 *Management Control in a Voluntary Organization*

organizations. Further, Kramer (1981) stated that the fiscal environment of voluntary organizations, particularly dependence on external funding sources, was involved in the formalization of their management. Another pressure for the adoption of certain control systems came from regulation by the State, often associated with funding arrangements (Harris 1990; Kramer 1981). Therefore, there are many 'business' control problems and uncertainties that voluntary organizations also have to address. However, given the discussion in this subsection, it would be expected that these control problems would be subordinated to the more central issues concerned with values and goals.

Summary of Major Points

In this section the distinctive features of the voluntary sector and management control in voluntary organizations have been reviewed. The aim of this discussion was to evaluate the applicability of a critical structuralist framework to the analysis of management control for voluntary organizations and thereby provide a platform for proposing a critical structuralist analysis of the significance of accounting in churches. The general tenor of the discussion was that voluntary organizations did have important distinctive features from business organizations that must be taken into account in understanding management control, but that a slightly modified critical structuralist framework was still potentially useful. The remainder of this summary sets out the major points of such an analysis.

First, voluntary organizations tend to have a different order of primary control problems than business organizations. These are centred around the altruistic and social values and qualitative, non-monetary goals that usually dominate in such organizations. From a critical structuralist perspective, the key feature of these different control problems are that they are antithetical to the management control strategies commonly used in business organizations. The control problems of voluntary organizations emphasize different types of solutions based on maintaining the values of the organization and higher levels of trust in management.

Second, however, voluntary organizations also have secondary control problems similar to business organizations in the sense that

A Critical Structuralist Framework 59

they also have to deal with problems of co-ordination and resource allocation. Also, cultural rationalization, particularly through pressures for greater efficiency and effectiveness, has a tendency to increase the use of business based management control strategies in voluntary organizations. The conflict of these secondary control problems and their solutions with the dominant control problems and their solutions is central to understanding the variety and development of management control in voluntary organizations.

Third, the actions of various occupational groups in promoting and resisting various control strategies is also potentially relevant in voluntary organizations. Members and professional occupational groups directly involved in service delivery or other core activities of the organization would be expected to support the dominant control problems and to promote 'appropriate' solutions. While there may be competition between these groups over what are 'appropriate' solutions, based on their own occupational ideas, the general tendency for all of them is to resist encroachment of business based management control strategies, particularly where they seem to directly impinge on their area of activity. However, other occupational groups involved in the administration activities of voluntary organizations may be expected to be more structurally concerned with the secondary control problems and for their occupational solutions to be based on business control strategies. The conflict between the dominant and secondary control problems and their 'appropriate' solutions, therefore, can be expected to be related to competition between members, 'professional' occupational groups and 'administrative' occupational groups.

Finally, the relevance of control problems and the solutions of occupational groups may be affected by various crises. The major types of crisis that would seem relevant to the dominant control problems are either failure to maintain the commitment of members or 'professional' groups, or shortages in resources, particularly funding. There were strong indications in the literature that problems in the area of finances have been a major influence on the increasing rationalization of voluntary organizations in the last two decades.

IV.   A CRITICAL STRUCTURALIST FRAMEWORK FOR CHURCHES

Writers on the secularisation of society have commented on the rationalization of religious organizations (for example, Berger 1963; Berger and Luckman 1966; Wallis 1984; Wilson 1961, 1969; for a contrary view see Martin 1969). A general theme of this body of work has been the taking on by religious organizations of the features of business organizations. Also, it has been suggested that there has been rationalization of the economic aspects of religious organizations in that greater attention is devoted to rational money-making activities and the control of costs (Morgan 1990). This literature suggests that there has been significant incursion of business based management control strategies into churches. However, O'Connell (1988) argued that religion is probably the largest form of voluntary behaviour in modern societies and that churches are a fundamental example of the values of voluntary organizations. Thus, as argued in chapter 1, it is proposed that churches are potentially 'ideal types' of the features of voluntary organization as set out in the previous section and thereby extreme sites of resistance to rationalization. This section develops the specific arguments of a critical structuralist analysis of the significance of accounting in churches as voluntary organizations.

Churches are strong sites of the concept of membership based on community and democracy values. This requires organizing effort to be directed to the maintenance of the values of free association, co-operation, consensus and trust (Handy 1988; Morgan 1990; Rothschild-Whitt 1979). In addition, the specific goals of churches are extreme types of the qualitative, non-monetary form found in voluntary organizations. As Thompson (1975) argued, the 'symbolic-appropriateness' of activities has to be demonstrated more in churches than any other form of organization. This means that the spiritual basis of actions must be attended to through appeals to the essential element of religiosity (Morgan 1990). The solving of these two interrelated elements of the dominant control problems of voluntary organizations via rational calculation and means-ends analysis is difficult as the ends, particularly the transcendental basis of the dominant religious focus, defy calculation and rational proof.

The importance of this different order of control problems for churches is supported by a wide range of studies within both the

A Critical Structuralist Framework   61

organization studies and accounting literatures on churches and related religious organizations. These literatures will not be reviewed in depth in this section as they have been recently discussed at length in a review and research agenda paper on accounting in churches by Booth (1993). Instead, drawing heavily on Booth (1993), a brief summary of the major thrust of the discussions in these literatures will the given. Then the major propositions from these discussions for the significance of accounting in churches will be summarized around the concept of the sacred and secular divide proposed by Laughlin (1984, 1988).

The accounting literature on churches, which has been almost exclusively concerned with accounting practices in Western mainstream churches, has two streams; a more extensive professional literature, which generally focuses on prescribing 'good' accounting practices[4], and a smaller research literature. The latter has attempted to explain accounting practices in use, but is very limited in extent, there being only three studies of churches per se. In addition to these, there are several studies which have examined accounting practices in closely related organizations such as mission agencies and early American religious sects. There have been three main ways in which the nature of accounting practices has been investigated; surveys of particular areas of practice (Rowe and Giroux 1986; Zietlow 1989), historical analyses of uses of accounting in particular organizations (Faircloth 1988; Flesher and Flesher 1979; Kreiser and Dare 1986; Swanson and Gardner 1986, 1988), and one detailed case study of accounting practices within a church (Laughlin 1984, 1988, 1990a).

The surveys of accounting practice provide some very general descriptions about what accounting practices are used by some churches, thus making it possible to get a limited insight into the penetration of accounting practices in churches. However, they offer little, if any, insight into the dynamics of such use. It is not possible to consider such questions as how, when and for what activities accounting practices are used; to identify any resistance to their use; or to understand how, if at all, accounting interacts with religious belief systems. The historical analyses attempted to bridge these gaps. The studies by Faircloth (1988), Flesher and Flesher (1979) and Kreiser and Dare (1986), which deal with the use of accounting in commune type religious sects during the early history of the USA, indicate a very sophisticated (within their time context) use of accounting practices. A

62   *Management Control in a Voluntary Organization*

similar finding came from Swanson and Gardner's (1988) study of accounting within an 18th century agency of the Church of England concerned with raising and disbursing funds to support overseas missionary activities. However, the usefulness of these studies is limited as their focus organizations may be atypical of churches in general as they had a heavy engagement in business activities and the belief systems of at least some appeared to support such activities as virtuous. Therefore, the findings of sophisticated accounting practices for the time may have reflected these specific characteristics. Another study by Swanson and Gardner (1986) was more directly concerned with mainstream churches through an analysis of the development of financial reporting in the USA Protestant Episcopal Church. Their findings present a picture of the evolution of an increasing use of accounting practices to meet the needs of the church to ensure "...its economic viability and actual survival" (1986, p.62). However, this analysis unproblematically links accounting to the changing environments and internal needs of the church, thereby ignoring the possibility of resistance to the development and use of accounting. In general, therefore, the above studies provide little significant insight into the how, who, when and why of accounting practices in churches.

A more detailed answer to such questions is provided by Laughlin's (1984, 1988) detailed case study of accounting practices in the Church of England. Laughlin examined the use of budget preparation and control, financial reporting and other accounting systems at parish, diocese and central levels of the church. Laughlin concluded that it appeared as if accounting systems were a 'partial irrelevancy' to the on-going life of the parishes as none of the systems had much impact on actions at this level. While the systems were more sophisticated in the dioceses, he also concluded that they were insignificant in ordering and developing diocese activities. The accounting systems were seen as more important to on-going activities in central church units as they were used to assist in both income generation and containment of expenditure programs. However, again they did not appear to have any directional impact on activities.

Laughlin, while recognising the impact of many specific local factors and significant actors, identified several major general explanations of the marginalization of accounting within the Church of England. Of central importance was the role of the beliefs systems of churches as the main source of resistance to the use of accounting,

A Critical Structuralist Framework 63

which was articulated in terms of the sacred and secular divide metaphor to be discussed further below. Also, the clergy were argued to play a major role in the playing out of these social dynamics. They used their position as the dominant occupational group within churches, whose structural position is to support the dominance of religious beliefs, to promote the irrelevancy of accounting. In addition, the need for the church to have secular support functions, and the importance (perceived or actual) of these functions varying with the level of financial stress experienced by the organization, were identified as important mitigating conditions of action for the working out of the social dynamics around accounting systems. Finally, Laughlin argued that resistance to the use of accounting may be reduced by allocating the function of providing the financial resources to support sacred activities to clearly 'partitioned' sections of the organizational structure. Some form of accounting system was argued to be necessary to enable this role to be carried out, but by isolating these activities from the core sacred functions resistance was potentially reduced.

While churches and other religious organizations are relatively understudied in the organization studies literature (Harris 1990; Thompson 1975), this literature[5] has considered a diverse range of topics such as the historical roles of religious organizations (Weber 1930; Miller 1983), the development of taxonomies (Wilson 1961, 1967), the role of the clergy (Ashbrook 1967; Fichter 1961), the analysis of such organizations as bureaucracies (Harris 1969; Thompson 1970), and the application of contingency theory (Hinings 1979; Odom and Boxx 1988). This literature, while not directly commenting on accounting issues, provides support for the explanatory factors identified in Laughlin's study.

First, the importance of religious belief systems[6] in understanding the management and structuring of religious organizations has been a central theme in the relevant organization studies literature (Bartunek 1984; Goldner 1979; Harris 1969; Hinings and Foster 1973; Hinings and Bryman 1974; Hinings 1979; Thompson 1970, 1975; Rudge 1968). In a review of much of this literature, Thompson (1975) argued that belief systems are a major legitimating criteria in religious organizations (see also, Goldner 1979) and argued that they act as major sources of resistance to secular intrusions into such organizations. This process of resistance was proposed as being related to the different nature of the means-ends relationships in churches. The dominant ends in such organizations are transcendental, which makes any empirical assessment of their achievement impossible. Thompson (1975) states that this makes it difficult to apply any 'rational' form of means-ends analysis, and thus difficult to apply most secular management practices. Thus, the dominance of religious belief systems for judging the legitimacy of actions and their incorporation of transcendental ends potentially provides a strong basis of resistance to secular management practices such as accounting.

However, the literature suggests that such processes of resistance are not deterministic as there is significant potential variety in religious beliefs and how they are interpreted in particular settings (Bartunek 1984; Harris 1969). Thus, the actual process of resistance or support must be demonstrated and explicated in practice even though resistance may be the normal starting premise for any analysis. As Harris argued, beliefs only "...bite when applied to a particular situation" (1969, p.171).

Second, the action of both church members and the clergy have been identified as playing key roles in the social dynamics within churches (Bartunek 1984; Harris 1969; Thompson 1970). Churches have to pay particular attention to how they relate to their members, and their internal operations and practices have to be justified to this membership. Such justifications usually draw upon religious beliefs for their 'authority. How the membership, who are most likely to be composed of groups with different interpretations of religious beliefs and to be sources of 'other interests', interprets the relation of secular management practices to their beliefs will be part of the determination of the level of resistance that is produced. In addition, Thompson (1975) has emphasized the importance of the role of the clergy in the management of religious organizations. They are the occupational group directly concerned with the maintenance of churches' religious beliefs and the achievement of their transcendental ends. In addition, Thompson pointed to the potential for conflict between the clergy and other internal occupational groups. Overall, therefore, the organization studies literature indicates that church members and the clergy would be expected to support the dominance of religious beliefs in the management of churches and to thereby be significant sources of resistance to secular management practices.

A Critical Structuralist Framework 65

Finally, the organization studies literature suggests some additional contingent factors flowing from various conceptions of the level of resources, in a broad sense, available to support organizational activities that may impact upon the above dynamics. Two conceptions of organizational resources are useful starting points for considering such contingencies; membership size and financial resources. In line with the arguments of the importance in churches of the maintenance of the loyalty of members, Hinings and Foster (1973) argued that the number of members is the most critical measure of the size of churches, which in turn has implications for the ways in which the organization may be organized and the level of other resources (eg. facilities, money) necessary to support it' (Hinings 1979; Hinings and Bryman 1974).

A strong membership position may tend to strengthen the dominance of religious beliefs and the maintenance of the status quo within the organization, including the current processes of resistance to, and support for, accounting. However, a weak membership position could be interpreted as a 'sacred' organizational crisis in the sense that the 'legitimation' for the existence, or even the survival, of the organization may be questioned. This may create more fluid conditions of possibility within which the dynamics of the processes of resistance to, and support for, secular management practices are played out. These more fluid conditions may either strengthen the calls for 'legitimate' religious solutions for 'the crisis' to be found and/or provide room for secular solutions to be proposed that may not be as acceptable under 'non-crisis' conditions. Membership size, and in particular any trend towards growth, stagnation or decline, are therefore proposed as potentially significant conditions of possibility surrounding debates over the 'usefulness' of secular management practices.

In addition, Harris (1969) argued that restricted financial resources were a significant condition of possibility surrounding to the consideration of organizational restructuring in his study. More generally, Hinings and Foster (1973) noted that many mainstream churches had experienced funding shortages in the later half of this century, leading to a tendency towards centralisation to conserve and control these scarce resources. These support Laughlin's (1984, 1988) arguments about the role of financial stress as a significant condition of possibility in reducing the extent of resistance to the use of accounting for certain purposes within the Church of England. The availability of financial resources thus has been shown to affect how management issues are perceived and responded to in churches.

Abundant financial resources may result in secular financial management issues being more likely to be seen as 'less critical' for continued operations, thereby strengthening the dominant position of religious beliefs. In contrast, financial resource shortages may create more fluid conditions of possibility. Consistent with the literature, such a condition may be interpreted as a 'secular' crisis, and may thereby prioritize secular management 'solutions', particularly accounting ones, to such 'financial management' problems. However, it is also possible that financial resource shortages may be interpreted as a 'sacred' crisis, with the opposite result on the 'legitimacy' of secular management solutions. Therefore, the level of financial resources may be a significant condition of possibility influencing the dynamics of the processes of resistance to accounting and other secular management practices in churches.

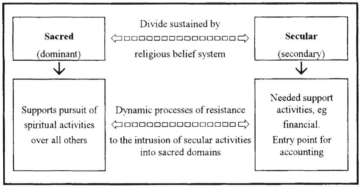

Figure 2.1: The Sacred and Secular Divide and the Processes of Rationalization in Churches

The general propositions from the above discussion about the potential factors affecting the processes of rationalization and the use of accounting and other secular management practices in churches can be summarized around the sacred and secular divide proposed by Laughlin (1984, 1988). Figure 2.1 illustrates the major features of this argument. Religious belief systems produce an underlying social dynamic in churches where the sacred concerns of these systems are dominant over secular activities such as administrative systems and

A Critical Structuralist Framework 67

accounting practices. This social dynamic sets up a powerful source of potential resistance to the processes of rationalization. Rationalization uses secular techniques and logics. Any intrusion of such practices into the central organizing activities of churches is resisted as they are not symbolically appropriate in terms of the sacred. The transcendental ends of the sacred, therefore, act to delegitimize the temporal, empirical types of ends that are the concern of rational management and accounting practices.

The particular nature of the dominant control problems in churches, therefore, should act as sources of potential resistance to the processes of rationalization. They are of a different frame of reference to the control problems of business organizations, on which the relevance of rationalization is premised. As argued for voluntary organizations above, a critical structuralist framework for churches should emphasize membership values and the dominance of sacred organizing problems. These problems require different responses from the 'managers' of churches than those of business organizations.

However, as for voluntary organizations, churches have a set of secondary control problems. The sacred and secular divide indicates that the organizing of secular support activities is still part of the management issues in churches. This may in part reflect the need of churches to determine ways of co-ordinating and structuring their various tasks. It also probably reflects the process of cultural rationalization and institutionalized ideas about appropriate organizational structures (DiMaggio and Powell 1983; J. Meyer 1986; Meyer and Rowan 1977; Zucker 1987). In addition, churches, as part of increasingly rationalized Western societies, find that many of their relations with society are monetarized. The management of these money-based relations still has to addressed, and rational calculative based means-ends forms of analysis are the dominant legitimate solutions to such organizing problems (Berger and Luckman 1966). In other words, the secular represents the intrusion of rationalization into churches through control problems similar to, but not as specific, as those in business organizations. These secondary control problems are perceived to conflict with the dominant sacred, non-calculable control problems.

A critical structuralist analysis for churches, therefore, should consider two general types of control problems to which management must find solutions; dominant concerns with the maintenance of

68 *Management Control in a Voluntary Organization*

sacred ends and membership, and secondary concerns with administrative and financial support activities. Drawing further on the discussion in previous sections and above, the timing of an impetus for solutions to both sets of problems may be related to crises that prioritize one or the other of these problems.

First, crises relating to membership or the foundations of the beliefs of a church may be expected to prioritize the sacred set of control problems. This type of crisis would be expected to strengthen the sacred and secular divide, thus favouring solutions based on sacred concerns and increasing resistance to the processes of rationalization.

Second, crises of a more economic nature, such as a declining income base or spiralling costs, may prioritize secular control problems. This may weaken the sacred and secular divide by the construction of these problems as issues that must be addressed even at the expense of the sacred, at least in the short term. When problems are constructed in such ways, the sacred may not appear to provide viable solutions, especially against the backdrop of ideas flowing from cultural rationalization. This type of crisis would increase the potential for the intrusion of rationalization into the church.

Finally, financial and membership crises may be related in practice. Harris (1969), in his study of an Anglican Diocese in Wales, identified financial shortages flowing from declining Parish membership as one of the conditions that prompted the search for new organizational structures. This interrelation of sacred and secular crises prioritizes both sets of control problems (Berger 1963) and may blur the distinctions between them. Also, it may bring sacred and secular solutions into direct competition. While the sacred and secular divide would still be expected to operate under such conditions, the actual outcomes in terms of rationalization are potentially much more indeterminate. This is consistent with Harris (1969), where more rational management techniques were both supported and resisted by different groups in the Diocese because they were argued to be both consistent and inconsistent with sacred beliefs. Various sacred and secular crises, therefore, may be expected to effect the need for solutions to sacred and secular control problems in churches.

Drawing on the final major element of the critical structuralist framework, the types of solutions deployed in response to such problems will be those promoted by various competing occupational groups. The clergy are the major occupational group engaged in the management of churches. It was argued above that their 'expertise' and relevance is based on their support of the basic religiosity of churches (see also Wilson 1969, particularly Chapter 5). Also, other occupations, such as social workers and religious educationalists, who may be expected to be involved in the running of church activities should be included as supporters of sacred control problems. These occupational groups may be expected to offer sacred solutions to sacred control problems, although these solutions may be in competition due to differing occupational views. Also, they may promote some form of 'sacredized' secular solutions to secular control problems in attempts to maintain the sacred and secular divide. For these reasons, the clergy and other sacred occupational groups would be expected to resist the solutions of secular 'administrative' occupational groups to secular and particularly sacred control problems. As suggested above, such direct competition is most likely in times of crises that mix sacred and secular problems.

Accountants fit within the 'administrative' set of occupational groups. Accountants can be argued to have a strongly developed occupational territory flowing from their position within modern industrial societies. They go through a long educational programme that is heavily concentrated on specialist accounting techniques and problem foci. Their whole occupational ideology is orientated to an accounting biased financial view of management and solutions to its problems (Booth and Cocks 1990; Hastings and Hinings 1970; Tricker 1979). Accountants would therefore be expected to focus on the financial dimensions of secular control problems and promote accounting solutions to them. However, it should also be noted that accounting has been institutionalized as part of cultural rationalization in Western societies and therefore, at least in part, its significance in any organization may become disembodied from the direct actions of accountants.

V.   CHAPTER SUMMARY

In this chapter the basic arguments of a critical structuralist framework for the analysis of the variety and development of management control strategies in organizations has been outlined. The major components of this framework were; the existence of various control problems in organizations, the actions of occupational groups

70 Management Control in a Voluntary Organization

in promoting, deploying and resisting 'relevant' solutions to these control problems, and the prioritizing effects of crises on particular problems and solutions. In the context of business organizations the central control problems revolved around the control of the labour process and the realization and allocation of surplus value. It was argued that accounting could become significant in such organizations because it offers particular forms of solutions to these control problems. Important in this were the actions of the accounting profession in promoting these solutions to increase its position within management hierarchies. Also, their actions could be aided by the occurrence of various economic crises which prioritized particular problems and solutions. It was argued that such a critical structuralist analysis was a useful approach because it presented a social and historical contextualization of the understanding of the varying significance of accounting in organizations and it linked this understanding explicitly with the actions of accountants and the accounting profession more broadly. It was thus adequate at both the levels of human agency and social structure.

This critical structuralist framework was then adapted to the different management control context of voluntary organizations and the specific case of churches. The major difference was that the dominant control problems of voluntary organization, and churches, were of a different order to those of business organizations. Their basis in the values of community and democracy and qualitative, non-monetary gaols favoured different types of solutions to the management control strategies deployed in business organizations. Specifically for churches, the sacred and secular divide was used to conceptualize these distinctions. The major occupational groups contesting the significance of accounting would be expected to be the clergy, other sacred specialists such as religious educationalists, and accountants. Finally, the occurrence of sacred and/or secular crises may prioritize particular control problems and solutions.

This adapted critical structuralist framework provides a general indication of the relationships between the processes of rationalization and the significance of accounting in voluntary organizations. While the dynamics of such relationships in any organization at any point in space and time will need to be empirically determined in relation to a complex set of organization specific factors, it is possible to propose

A Critical Structuralist Framework 71

three broad propositions to guide the analysis of the significance of accounting in churches.

First, through rationalization there will be a tendency for the increased use of rational management control strategies in churches, which will also tend to increase the significance of accounting. However, because of the sacred and secular divide, rationalization and accounting will meet with resistance. Overall, therefore, it would be expected that accounting will be seen as a secondary concern in churches and any significance that it does have will lead to tension with the sacred domain.

Second, it would be expected that there will conflict between accountants and the clergy and other sacred occupational groups over the use of accounting in churches. At the minimum, accountants would be expected to have a much weaker acceptance of the secondary position of accounting within the sacred and secular divide. Accountants would be expected to promote the greater relevance and use of accounting to the management of churches.

Third, secular crises with a financial dimension, or sacred crises that can be interpreted as having secular effects, will prioritize the relevance of accounting and allow greater opportunity for accountants to promote their solutions within churches. Also, if such solutions can be portrayed as supporting sacred problems then the resistance of the clergy and other sacred groups may be diminished. In contrast, sacred crises may have the opposite set of effects.

In the following chapters the utility of the developed critical structuralist framework and the relevance of the above propositions are considered in the context of the case of the significance of accounting within the Northern Division of the Mainstream Church.

Notes

[1] See Armstrong (1991) for a fuller discussion of the issues of trust and agency and their application to accounting.

[2] This summary excludes the final part of Armstrong's (1987a) argument dealing with the effects of company taxation and movement of company activity to investment rather than productive activity.

[3] As well as the discussion in this and the preceding subsections, the following draws upon the discussion of the advantages for the study of accounting of a labour process approach over traditional and interpretive alternatives in Hopper et al (1987).

72   *Management Control in a Voluntary Organization*

[4]   There have been three general themes in the professional accounting literature. First, there has been a concern with the inadequacies of accounting practices in churches, which have been argued to have poor internal control, primitive and inadequate accounting systems, and a lack of expertise and commitment to financial management (Ellis 1974; Keister 1974; Leathers and Sanders 1972; Prentice 1981). However, no systematic evidence tends to be presented to support these claims. The solutions advocated for these problems are generally for churches to follow 'good commercial practices'.

Second, there have been descriptions of what were considered good accounting practices within individual churches (Cunningham and Reemsnyder 1983; Floyd 1969; Harper and Harper 1988; Scofield and Milano 1984). In general, the criteria used to judge good practice have been existing commercial practices or professional accounting pronouncements. However, sometimes the need for concessions to be made to the specific requirements of churches was noted, for example the need for the accounting system to be used by non-expert volunteer labour.

Third, another prescriptive approach has argued that the differences between the 'spiritual and non-spiritual' aspects of churches need to be taken into account in designing and implementing accounting systems (Arndt and McCabe 1986; Boyce 1984; Burckel and Swindle 1988; Daniel 1959; Futcher and Phillips 1986; King 1988; Leahy 1974). They emphasise that commercial practices may not directly translate into appropriate systems for churches, and that accounting must serve the spiritual goals of these organizations, but still espouse the benefits of 'better', but 'appropriate', accounting practices for churches.

The general tendency, therefore, has been to prescribe 'better' accounting practices based on those developed for commercial organizations, which have come to be espoused as the norm for all organizations by the accounting profession. There has also been partial recognition that the different belief systems of churches may be a basis of resistance to the use of 'good' accounting practices. As one paper graphically put it, churches are the "...last bastion of resistance to modern financial management techniques" (Futcher and Phillips 1986, p.28).

[5]   As for the accounting literature, it should be noted that the scope of the organization studies literature has been mainly restricted to Western, Christian organizations.

[6]   For more general discussions of the importance of beliefs in the study of organizations see Beyer (1981) and Sproull (1981).

[7]   Hinings and Foster noted that the declining membership of many mainstream churches in the later half of this century has led to problems with and changes to their organizational structures. Similar effects within the Church of England were noted by Laughlin (1984).

Chapter 3
Research Method

I. INTRODUCTION

There have been increasing calls for more case study[1] research within the accounting literature in the last decade (for example, Cooper 1981; Hopwood 1983; Kaplan 1984). Part of the justification for such a research strategy has been its suitability for increasing the understanding of accounting in practice (for example, Kaplan 1986; Laughlin 1990b; Scapens 1990). As Scapens states:

> "Case studies offer us the possibility of understanding the nature of management accounting in practice; both in terms of the techniques, procedures, systems, etc. which are used and the way in which they are used" (1990, p.264).

This advantage is particularly relevant for the problematic of this study, with its requirement to understand how and why accounting can be purposeful within an organizational and social context. A case study design was adopted, therefore, because it was a highly appropriate method for the research questions addressed.

However, the recent increase in the use of case studies in accounting research[2] has had two major streams, a European approach and a North American one (Scapens 1990). Both are concerned with trying to increase the understanding of accounting practice but give a different emphasis to the role of case studies. The North American approach, represented principally by the work of Robert Kaplan and Robin Cooper (see Spicer 1990 for a review), tends to view case studies as either illustrative of 'good' accounting practices or exploratory in that they provide a more grounded basis for future model building and hypothesis formation. This view flows from the unquestioning acceptance of neoclassical economics based assumptions about the role of accounting in organizations (Scapens 1990).

73

74   *Management Control in a Voluntary Organization*

From the point of view of the problematic of this study, this is a major weakness as the purposefulness of accounting can only be considered from a technical perspective. The consideration of the socially constructed nature of the purposefulness of accounting, as argued for in the previous chapters, is defined away. In contrast, the European approach starts from the premise that the purposefulness of accounting is socially constructed (for example, Burchell et al. 1985; Nahapiet 1988). In this approach, case studies are seen as an important means of developing, elaborating or testing explanations of the role of accounting in organizations (Scapens 1990). It is within this latter approach that this study is located and that forms the primary basis on which the adoption of case study method is justified.

Some major attributes of this style of case study method derived from the useful discussions provided by Mitchell (1983) and Yin (1989) illustrate the suitability of a case study approach for the concerns of this study. First, a case study usually investigates a *contemporary phenomenon*. While it is possible to talk of historical case studies, a significant attribute of case study research is the examination of a social situation as it unfolds. Second, however, a simple narrative account of any contemporary phenomenon is not case study research. The phenomenon examined should be of *theoretical significance*. It should be noted that this does not mean that a case study must always be based on a prior theory, only that it should be concerned with a subject of research interest. Third, case study method involves the *detailed examination* of the phenomenon *within its real-life context*. The aim is to provide depth of analysis, which includes not only the phenomenon itself but also the context within which it is located. This often involves a trade-off against breadth of analysis. Fourth, this recognition of context involves more than just the specification of antecedent and moderating variables, but the recognition that any phenomenon is *embedded in its context*. Thus, case study method gives attention to the intertwining of phenomenon and context. However, such detailed examination can be applied only within the specified boundaries of the case. As Mitchell (1983) quite rightly emphasizes, all cases are themselves situated in some wider social context that cannot be directly taken into account. "These contexts constitute some panoply of *ceteris paribus* conditions which the analyst will need to allow for..." (Mitchell 1983, p.192) by either controlling for them in case selection or by incorporating critical

Research Method 75

factors in the theoretical framework brought to bear on the case. Fifth, the detailed examination of the phenomenon and its context usually involves a *longitudinal analysis*. The concern with the unfolding of a social situation leads to an emphasis on the phenomenon in process, and thus the explicit attention to the time dimension in case study method. This can be manifested both in the continuing collection and analysis of data over the study time period, and in attention to history as part of the understanding of current context. Finally, case study research usually makes use of *multiple sources* of data. There is no prior fixed commitment to any particular form of data collection or analysis. Depending on the researcher's theoretical and disciplinary commitment, the phenomenon, access and resources, data collection can involve some combination of qualitative and/or quantitative techniques applied to direct observations, archival material, artefacts, and/or interviews in an attempt to capture the complexity of the phenomenon and its context. However, the commitment to depth of analysis usually means that qualitative methods dominate. These six major attributes of case study method as a research strategy are particularly relevant to the research questions and theoretical concerns developed in the preceding chapters.

In the last decade an extensive evaluation of case study and associated qualitative research methods has appeared in the accounting literature (Abdel-Khalik and Ajinkya 1983; Birnberg et al 1990; Brownell and Trotman 1988; Bruns 1989; Chua 1986b; Covaleski and Dirsmith 1990; Hagg and Hedlund 1979; Kaplan 1986; Laughlin 1990b; Morgan 1983; Scapens 1990; Tomkins and Groves 1983a, 1983b; Willmott 1983). While it would be rash to claim that this literature has addressed or presented solutions to all the issues and problems associated with this approach to research, a fairly useful overview of the major concerns has been provided. Accordingly, this chapter will not review case study and qualitative research methods. Instead, in the first section the subject organization is briefly described and its selection justified. Then the focus in the next section will be predominantly upon the specifics of the case study design and data selection and collection techniques used in this study. However, the chapter summary will conclude with a summary highlighting the major strengths and limitations of the research method adopted, and in particular will comment upon two more general case study method

76 *Management Control in a Voluntary Organization*

issues pertinent to the single case study design used in this study, the problems of data triangulation and the ability to generalize findings.

II.   THE SUBJECT ORGANIZATION

The Northern Division of Mainstream Church

The case study organization was one division of a national Australian church. At the request of the organization, its identity and that of its specific operating units and personnel have been disguised. The church is referred to as Mainstream Church, while the specific division that was the subject of study is referred to as Northern Division. While doing so does not effect the quality of the analysis able to be presented in the following chapters, it does restrict the depth of basic descriptive material that can be provided in this chapter. In particular, no discussion of the recent history of the organization is presented as this would identify the organization for any semi-knowledgeable reader. Within these restrictions, the following provide a brief introduction to the subject organization.

Mainstream Church is a major Protestant church. In the last couple of decades the church has experienced relatively stable levels of membership, with national 'confirmed members' being 228,196 in 1978 and 217,998 in 1985. This stability has been evident also in the church's Northern Division, which experienced only a small growth in membership over the period 1981 to 1987 (30,498 to 31,303). However, this growth rate was lower than that of the population of the northern region within which it operates for the same period (2,265,935 to 2,587,315). Despite an expanding Australian population, this lack of growth in Mainstream Church, reflects, in part, a decline in the support for all major churches in Australia in the second half of this century[3]. About 44% of the Australian population attended church at least monthly in 1960, with this percentage steadily declining over the next two decades until it finally stabilised at about 25% during the early 1980s. Within this pattern, the relative decline was greater for Mainstream Church (8% in 1960 to 3% in 1984).

Mainstream Church is organized as a decentralized federated structure. The key organizational units are the seven divisions, each responsible for the church's activities in different regional areas of Australia. The divisions employ the majority of full and part-time

Research Method

management and administrative staff, and are responsible for oversight of worship, witness and the management of the church within their regions. As part of these duties, divisions are responsible for overall financial and property management, and for the oversight of a wide range of church institutions and agencies (for example, schools and welfare agencies). The coordination of division level activities is achieved by the National Council of the church (equivalent in concept to a corporate 'head-office'). The National Council has final decision-making powers in all matters of general church policy on doctrine, worship, government and discipline, theological education, etc., but is required to consult widely through the division structure in doing so.

The Northern Division is the third largest in Mainstream Church, accounting for about 18% of total church membership. In financial terms the Northern Division is a major organization in its own right. In the mid 1980s the total income of its Parishes was around $9 million per year; and the budget for the division's 'head office' activities was approximately $2 million dollars per year (about 8 times this would be expended at the Parish level on direct support of ministers and other activities). Few reliable figures are available on total asset values for the division. However, like most established churches it had significant land and buildings holdings throughout its region. On average during the mid 1980s yearly property sales were about $2 million, purchases were about $1.5 million and there were building works of about $12 million. More liquid assets such as cash and endowments were much smaller than property holdings. These figures apply only to the core activities of the division. If the division's associated church schools, hospitals and welfare agencies were included the annual funds flows would be in the $100s of millions.

The Mainstream Church organizational structure allows considerable freedom in how divisions organise their own internal administrative processes, as long as these do not conflict with the broader aims and features of its constitution and other founding documents. The organizational structure of the Northern Division (see Figure 3.1) consists of a central administrative 'head office', 9 Presbyteries and 141 Parishes. The 'head office' has four departments covering the major functional areas of division administration. This structure is relatively new, having been formally adopted by the division in October 1983, implemented during 1984 and forming the basis of operations from January 1985.

Management Control in a Voluntary Organization

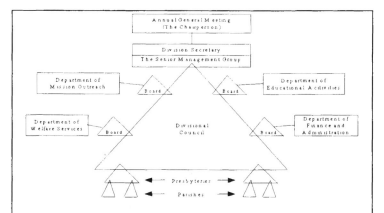

Key:

The **Chairperson**, the head of the Division, is responsible for spiritual and pastoral leadership. The Chairperson exercises control over the policy forums of the Division by chairing the Annual General Meeting and the Divisional Council. The Chairperson has the power to rule on interpretations of policy, take disciplinary action against members of the Division, and represent the Division in public and inter-church councils. A new incumbent is elected annually by the Annual General Meeting to the position of Chairperson-Elect, holding this position for one year before assuming the position of Chairperson at the next Annual General Meeting. After the year in office, the incumbent continues to serve as Past-Chairperson for a further year. To give a breadth and continuity of leadership experience to the Division, all three Chairperson positions are represented on the Annual General Meeting, the Divisional Council and the Senior Management Group.

The **Division Secretary**, the chief executive officer of the Division, is elected by the Annual General Meeting for a term of five years. The Division Secretary's duties are; to maintain appropriate records, ensure the legal responsibilities of the Division are met, ensure the proper functioning of the Division, oversight of ministerial settlements and discipline, oversight of Division personnel, Convener of the Senior Management Group, policy oversight of Directors and departments, liaison with Presbyteries and the wider church, and managing the processes of organizational integration of the Division.

Presbyteries are regional councils within a Division concerned with the co-ordination and pastoral oversight of the Parishes within their boundaries. Specific responsibilities are the stimulation, encouragement, and the provision of assistance and council to their Parishes and congregations. Presbyteries have only minor administrative and financial functions.

Parishes are the most local level of the church and the focus for the pursuit of its mission in the world. A single or multiple congregations in a region form a Parish. They are responsible for the local life and mission of the Church, and other responsibilities that may be specified from time to time by other councils of the Church.

Figure 3.1: Organizational Structure of the Northern Division

Research Method 79

The adoption of a new organizational structure arose from concerns about the inefficiency, overlaps of responsibilities and lack of clear lines of control in the previous structure of fourteen separate Boards and departments. The new organizational structure was seen as resolving these concerns, particularly by placing more emphasis on the professional management of the division through the centralisation and formalisation of management practices and the greater use of professional managers (particularly the new Department Director positions).

The constitution of Mainstream Church requires extensive consultation on all policy development and a strong commitment to high levels of 'grass-roots' involvement by the laity at all levels of decision-making. However, this commitment in the church to extensive 'grass-roots' involvement does not mean that organizational structures are meant to operate as representative democracies that determine and implement the will of church members. Various church documents make it quite clear that the role of the representatives is to "seek the will of God" in the fulfilment of the mission of the church, which may not necessarily be the same as the opinions of the membership. The organizational structure is thus a framework within which the religious mission of the church is seen as dominant, even though high levels of grass-roots participation are sought.

These aims are achieved in the Northern Division structure by using a 'link-pin' format with overlapping membership of representative Boards and councils. The Annual General Meeting, with a membership of about 500 which is relatively evenly divided between clergy and lay church members, is the peak council and has overall policy development responsibility. However, as it only meets annually, its Standing Committee, the Divisional Council, is the key body through which more regular policy development, implementation and oversight of the operations of the division are achieved. The Divisional Council meets quarterly and is composed of the Division Secretary, the Chairpersons of the division, Department Directors, Board Chairpersons, and elected Presbytery representatives. The Senior Management Group, which is chaired by the Division Secretary and composed of the Chairpersons of the division and the Department Directors, meets fortnightly to coordinate the implementation and development of division and church policy, thereby providing a further more direct means of regular oversight of division operations.

80 *Management Control in a Voluntary Organization*

Department of Mission Outreach
Responsible for the provision of services to and leadership of the Parishes and Presbyteries for the spiritual aspects of church life; for example, evangelism, discipleship, types of ministries, missionary activities, social responsibility activities and ecumenical relations. It is composed of 17 sections, the majority of which are engaged in direct Parish support activities. One major section that did not provide direct Parish services was the Conference Centres (CCs). CCs provided 'budget priced' conference centre and camp facilities in a number of locations throughout the northern region. They were run as profit centres through rental to Parishes, other church groups and other customers. CCs were the only independent income earning source of the department, except for some minor service charges in other sections that only recovered part of the cost of operations. The Director, who commenced duties in January 1985, was a minister with an extensive background in mission outreach activities and church administration. The large majority of the staff were either ministers, lay pastors or specialists in the various areas of mission covered by the sections.

Department of Educational Activities
Responsible for the oversight and co-ordination of the Division's theological and other educational activities and the co-ordination and implementation of the communication activities of the Division; for example, ministerial and lay training, oversight of church schools and colleges, media liaison, and publication of Division journals and resource materials. The major sections are theological and lay education, communication services and a student hostel. The hostel was the only major source of independent income in the department. It provided accommodation and meals mainly to theological or university students, or to young people from the country working in the capital city of the northern region. During university holidays it also rented facilities to short-term holiday makers and conferences. Apart from this the only income sources were from journal subscriptions in the communication services unit and from 'continuing education' type courses run by the theological college. The Director had a background in tertiary education and was a lay preacher with a long involvement in the Church. He commenced duties in September 1984. The staff were a mixture of ministers and specialists in communication and the other areas of the department. All had a strong Church background.

Department of Welfare Activities
Responsible for all aspects of the Division's involvement in providing services to the community, and the encouragement of Parish and Presbytery involvement in this area. Also, responsible for oversight of the many community service agencies under the control of the Division. There are four major sections; Caring Services (residential care, sheltered workshops, prison chaplaincy), Hospitals (7 church hospitals across the region), Aged Care (home nursing services, nursing homes and retirement villages, home care), and Family Welfare (emergency accommodation, youth centres, welfare centres). All sections were self-funding through either government grants, charges for services and/or independent fund raising. The Director was a specialist in organizational sociology and industrial democracy. He commenced duties in January 1985. All other staff were at agency level and were either ministers or had qualifications appropriate for their area of service.

Table 3.1: Functions of the Northern Division Departments

Research Method 81

Department of Finance and Administration
Responsible for carrying out all administrative, financial, budget, legal and property management functions of the Division, and the oversight of the activities of the rest of the Division in these areas. In particular, the Director is responsible for the budgetary oversight of all four departments. There are five major sections; computer services, financial services, Church Investment Service (CIS), Accounting and Office Services (AOS), and property. AOS provided all Division accounting services on a cost recovery basis to both the other departments and other sections of Finance and Administration. CIS acted as a 'bank' for the Division, taking interest bearing deposits from individual laity, Parishes, Church agencies (e.g. nursing homes, schools) and departments, and reinvesting these funds in real estate and various money markets. It was run as an internal commercial operation, except that it dealt only in 'ethical investments'. Also, it paid interest rates at slightly lower than commercial rates to depositors, which was promoted as a contribution by depositors to the Church. The department also controlled the Northern Book shop (NBS), a major northern region book retailer founded and 100% owned by the Division. NBS was originally founded to make Christian literature more available within the northern region, but had developed into a major commercial operation as a general bookseller that paid 'dividends' to the Division from its profits. During the 1980s its Christian book sales were relatively small and significant ties to the Division were essentially only at Board level. During the early 1980s it experienced severe competition from discount booksellers, and was unprofitable from 1985 until its sale by the Division in late 1987. The Director, who commenced duties in July 1984, is a qualified accountant with a strong Church background. All the senior staff were also accountants or had accounting backgrounds, many within the commercial or public sectors.

Table 3.1: Functions of the Northern Division Departments - Continued

The four departments are responsible for implementing the policies of the division and supporting the Presbyteries and Parishes in their pursuit of the mission of Mainstream Church (see Table 3.1 for a summary of functions and activities). The Board of each department provides a linkage with Presbyteries and Parishes through members with expertise and experience relevant to the activities of each department being appointed by the Annual General Meeting from among the membership of the church . The Boards act as the policy bodies of the departments, provide guidance to the Directors and as accountability mechanisms for the activities of the full-time staff. The Directors are responsible for advising Boards on policy development, overseeing policy implementation and the day-to-day management of their departments. They are required to have both extensive professional qualifications and experience in the specialist fields related to their department's functions and to be active and committed members of Mainstream Church.

82   *Management Control in a Voluntary Organization*

Selection Justification

The Northern Division of Mainstream Church was selected as the organization that would act as the extreme case for this study. The primary reasons for selection were issues of access, the significance of the organization and theoretical appropriateness. Each of these areas is discussed further below.

Access

It is generally agreed that one of the major issues in case or field study research is organizing access (Burgess 1982; Yin 1989). At the time that it became necessary to select the focal church for this study, one of my co-supervisors had just completed a period of lengthy involvement with the Northern Division of Mainstream Church as an honorary consultant on changes to the division's management structure. He was able to act as a sponsor for the study with the Northern Division and provide access to potential internal sponsors among the senior division staff. They were contacted and the general nature of the project explained. These staff were enthusiastic about the project, agreed to support the access required, and had it officially approved by the division's executive body. Therefore, one major reason for selecting the Northern Division of Mainstream Church was that sponsorship for access was available and there was a strong positive reaction to the project from the subject organization.

A second access issue was the selection of only the Northern Division for study. During the period in which the field work was to take place, I was based in the city were the head office of the Northern Division was located. The Northern Division, therefore, provided the ease of physical access necessary for a case study approach. However, focusing on the Northern Division was also justifiable from an organizational perspective. As described above, Mainstream Church has a federation type structure in which the major units are the divisions, of which there are seven. In most matters divisions are self-governing within the parameters of the constitution of the church. Much of the regional policy formation and development, and the major administrative, institutional and agency structures to accomplish and implement this are based at the division level. This includes most of the formal accounting activity and the major budget focus. Also, the division level was the location of the greatest concentration of full-time managers and specialist accounting staff. The Northern Division,

Research Method 83

therefore, was basically a discrete organizational subunit of Mainstream Church that could validly be studied as an organization in its own right.

The Significance of Mainstream Church

Mainstream Church is also worthy of study because of its significance as one of the major churches in Australia. While exact figures cannot be shown due to the need to hide the identity of the organization, it is one of the three largest religious groups in Australia. In terms of regular monthly church attendance figures, about 24% of the population are actively involved in these three large churches. Beyond this, these three major churches support a wide array of medical, educational and social welfare organizations that have an even more significant impact on a broader cross-section of the Australian population. In social terms, therefore, Mainstream Church is a significant organization.

The Northern Division is the third largest division in the Mainstream Church. It accounts for about 18% of total church membership. Its relative significance would be slightly higher if adjustment was made for the fact that nominal affiliation to Mainstream Church in its region of about 10% is slightly lower than that Australia wide. Also, as briefly described in the previous subsection, the Northern Division is a major organization in terms of its financial profile.

In terms of being an organization affecting the lives of a significant number of Australians, the Mainstream Church and its Northern Division then are significant organizations.

Theoretical Appropriateness

There were three major reasons why the Northern Division was an appropriate case study given the theoretical arguments advanced in the previous chapters.

First, the division had recently implemented a divisional management structure for its central head office administration. The rationale for this change included a perceived need to have 'modern management techniques' and professional managers for the organization to be more efficient and effective. This indicated that the Northern Division was experiencing at least some level of rationalization. Therefore, it was a potentially fruitful site for the concerns of this study.

84 *Management Control in a Voluntary Organization*

Second, the Northern Division was known to have been experiencing a financial crisis in recent years. This crisis was part of the motivation behind the management structure changes. Financial stringency has been shown to be associated with increased concerns with money-based means-ends relations and an increased focus on accounting and financial control in a variety of organizations (Ezzamel and Bourn 1990; Hertenstein 1985; Olofsson and Svalander 1975). Therefore, this contingency also increased the potential fruitfulness of the site.

Third, it is obvious that churches differ in their religious beliefs, however, Hinings and Foster (1973) argue that the type of theology affects the way a church is organized. "The beliefs of the Roman Catholic Church have clear and direct implications for the amount and type of decentralization. Likewise, the beliefs of the Congregationalists directly limit the extent to which liturgical functions can be specialized and routinized" (Hinings and Foster 1973, p.102). This implies that the theologies of churches vary in their extent of commitment to the values of free association, co-operation and consensus. From the arguments developed in chapter 2, it would be expected that churches with theologies more committed to the values of free association, co-operation and consensus would be more extreme cases for analysing the limits of the processes of rationalization.

Mainstream Church possesses such a theology. Briefly, it favours a conciliar form of governance where management is entrusted to a set of interrelated councils at local, state and national levels. This forms a representative democracy where the aim is not to seek the collective opinion of the membership but, as noted above, "...to seek the will of God, and give expression to the mind of Christ" (Communication Services Unit 1984, p.9). Thus, the Church:

> "...recognises that the responsibility for government in the Church belongs to the people of God by virtue of the gifts and tasks which God has laid upon them. ...[Mainstream Church]... therefore so organises her life that locally, regionally and nationally government will be entrusted to representatives, men and women, bearing the gifts and graces with which God has endowed them for the building up of his Church" (Mainstream Church 1984c, p.12).

Mainstream Church thus has a theology that is strongly committed to values of free association, co-operation and consensus. It is, therefore, theoretically a very appropriate church for understanding the limits of rationalization and the purposefulness of accounting.

Research Method 85

This section has presented the reasons for the selection of the Northern Division of Mainstream Church as the focal organization for this study. It has argued that this is a suitable organization because; i) adequate access was obtainable, ii) it was a significant church in terms of membership and financial resources, and iii) it was theoretically significant because it was experiencing some rationalization, was under financial stress and its theology had a strong commitment to the voluntary organization values of community and democracy.

III. CASE STUDY DESIGN

This section describes the major features of the case study design of this study. The description of the methods used in any case study is difficult. While some issues can be addressed before the study commences, others evolve or can only be addressed as the research progresses. This flexibility is one of the strengths of case study method, but it also makes it difficult to detail the dynamics of the research methods employed. To simplify the discussion in this section the case study design is described sequentially under three main steps; basic design, the boundaries of the case and the sources of data. Where necessary the development of the methods during the research process is detailed.

Basic Design Type

The basic form of the case study design used in this study was a single case study with embedded multiple units of analysis (Yin 1989), using primarily qualitative data collection and analysis techniques. The use of qualitative data, as noted in the introduction, was appropriate given the theoretical orientation of this study. Attention here is directed to the two other major features of the design, a single case and embedded multiple units of analysis.

The first research choice was between a single and multiple case design. Basically, this choice involved a trade-off of depth of analysis against greater generality of the findings through the use of comparative analysis. Depth of analysis via a single case design was chosen for two reasons. First, as there is a paucity of prior research on accounting practices in churches (Booth 1993), it was felt that attention should be given to increasing depth of knowledge via a

86   *Management Control in a Voluntary Organization*

reasonable length longitudinal study. Second, as this research was undertaken on a part-time basis with limited resources and it needed to be completed within a reasonable time span, it was felt that it would not be possible to do more than one organization in the required depth. Also, additional justification for a single case design was felt to exist in the domination of this approach in the previous case study based accounting research. Therefore, it was decided to focus effort on a minimum one year study of one organization, the Northern Division of the Mainstream Church.

The second aspect of this design was the use of embedded multiple units of analysis. This involves the use of either vertical or horizontal or both subunits of the focal organization as a means of internal comparative analysis (Yin 1989). The prior work by Laughlin (1984) of the Church of England (see Booth 1993 for a review) is an example of such a design with his comparison of Parish, Diocese and Central units. Early in the fieldwork for this study it became apparent that comparison could be made of the use of accounting across the head office department structure of the Northern Division. This was particularly relevant as the departments also represented variation in terms of sacred and secular units, and accountant and clergy managers, which were of theoretical interest in this study. Therefore, it was decided to structure data collection around the departmental units of the Division to increase the strength of the research design.

Boundaries of the Case

An important design issue in case study method is the establishment of the boundaries of the case in both time and space. This enables both the specification of the specific empirical context to be analyzed (that within the case boundaries) and the wider context (that outside the case boundaries) which forms the set of *ceteris paribus* conditions which have to be allowed for (Mitchell 1983). The general parameters of these boundaries have already been set and justified in the selection of Northern Division as the subject organization. More specific details are given below.

Figure 3.2 shows the contemporary time boundaries of the case study. The Northern Division was selected as the subject organization in March 1986 and permission obtained in May to conduct the study. Fieldwork commenced in June that year and continued until July 1988,

Research Method

involving the three distinct stages shown above. The critical issue was the selection of the period to commence and complete primary data collection. It was decided to study the organization through one complete operating and budget cycle. This commenced in October each year with the acceptance of the next year's budget by the Annual General Meeting of the division and continued through the financial and budget year from January to December. However, the 1988 budget was not approved in full detail in October 1987 and primary data collection had to be extended to February 1988 to complete the observation of the budget approval process. It was felt that this time period would expose the researcher and the subjects to a range of regular accounting and other activities, and should have been long enough to ensure that the researcher became highly familiar with and accepted within the organization. It also represented an organization based time cycle, rather than a researcher imposed period. These choices should help to minimize researcher bias.

Stage 1 Familiarisation		Stage 2 Primary Data Collection		Stage 3 Debriefing
June	October	October	February	July
1986	1986	1987	1988	1988

Figure 3.2: Time Periods of Involvement with the Subject Organization

In addition to these time periods of contemporary involvement with the organization, there was also a time boundary on the collection of historical material. A significant reorganization of Mainstream Church had occurred in 1977, which changed many of its historical roots. This reorganization date was set as a historical time boundary on the collection of data.

As well as these time boundaries, space boundaries internal to the Northern Division had to be set on data collection. The division is a large and complex organization. The structure of the Northern Division was briefly described in the previous section. With the resources and time available, it became apparent during the familiarisation period that it would not be possible to study accounting practices in a full cross-section of the division across Parishes, Presbyteries and head office operations. As for the overall design choice in the previous subsection, it was decided to opt for depth rather

88 *Management Control in a Voluntary Organization*

than breadth of analysis by concentrating analysis at one level of the organization, the division head office operations.

This focus was chosen as preliminary fieldwork had indicated that most accounting and management activity were located at this level. It administered the central accounting systems of the division and had the major budgetary responsibility. Also, the head office operations were the site of the largest concentration of occupational groups working in management positions, particularly clergy and accountants. Finally, pragmatically this level made regular access to the organization easier as I was also located in the same city. It was felt, therefore, that the head office operations of the Northern Division would provide a suitable site to investigate the significance of accounting practices.

It is recognized that this boundary choice could lead to a biased view of the significance of accounting practices in the Northern Division. Following Laughlin's (1984) findings for the Church of England, organization members at other levels may have totally different views of the uses and importance of accounting practices. Such potential bias may be partly mitigated in the case of Mainstream Church because its democratic governance structure ensured high levels of involvement of Parish members in head office management. Also, as the key management level of the organization, activities at head office level could have significant effects on activities throughout the division. In an attempt to gauge the extent of any bias in the findings, it was decided to conduct some limited data collection at Parish and Presbytery level during Stage 3 of the study. A city Presbytery and a country Presbytery were selected for this purpose based on discussions with senior staff that indicated that country Presbyteries had more conservative views on management issues than city Presbyteries. This extension to the case study boundaries was minor, but should provide some indication of the generality of the head office findings.

In summary, the key time boundaries for this case study can be specified as a period of ten years of historical data collection and just over two years contemporary involvement, with a 17 month period of this being the most intense data collection phase. The space boundaries were the head office structure of the Northern Division. This meant that both some sections of the organization and the wider social

Research Method   *89*

context became part of the *ceteris paribus* conditions (Mitchell 1983) that must be taken into account in the analysis.

Sources of Data

The general mix of data sources used is summarized in Table 3.2. The primary data sources were observation, interviews and official organization documents. Secondary sources, such as unofficial histories, were also used. The mix of data sources varied both across the various stages of the study and the major aspects investigated. In both cases, at least two major sources (shown in bold) were used. The vertical order of the sources indicates their relative importance in each cell. This pattern of data sources demonstrates that this study attempted to ensure that advantage was taken of one of the primary strengths of case study method, the triangulation of multiple data sources.

Aspect under study	Time Periods			
	History	**Stage 1**	**Stage 2**	**Stage 3**
Accounting Systems	**Documents** **Interviews**	**Interviews** Documents	**Observation** **Interviews** **Documents**	**Interviews** Observation **Documents**
Uses of Accounting	**Documents** **Interviews**	**Documents** **Interviews**	**Observation** **Documents** **Interviews**	**Interviews** **Observation** Documents
Organization and Social Context	**Documents** **Secondary** Interviews	**Interviews** **Documents** Secondary	**Observation** **Documents** **Interviews** Secondary	**Interviews** **Observation**

Table 3.2: Overall Pattern of Multiple Data Sources Used

The following subsections detail the data collection methods, including any differences across stages of the study, for the three primary sources - observation, interviews and documents. Due to their variety and number, secondary sources are not detailed. Many secondary sources of data were used to obtain general information about the history and functioning of Mainstream Church. These sources were important in that they provided an independent assessment of data obtained from official documents. They varied from studies of membership trends in Australian churches (Kaldor 1987) through academic analyses of churches (references cannot be given as they would reveal the organizations identity) to an independent history

90   *Management Control in a Voluntary Organization*

of the first ten years of the Mainstream Church[4]. These are referred to where necessary in the following chapters.

Observation

Observation data varied from casual watching during other activities, for example attending interviews, to much more formal regular attendance at meetings. This discussion concentrates on the latter. Regular formal observation of the Northern Division head office activities was complicated by the complexity of the organization. As described in the previous section, there were 7 main elements of the administrative structure; the Annual General Meeting, the Divisional Council, the Senior Management Group and the four division departments, with the latter having a wide array of internal sections and associated organizations. In addition, access to this diversity of activities was further complicated by the four departments being in three different locations within the city where the head office was located. Finally, regular observation had to fit in with my limited time resources due to my other academic commitments. The formal observation strategy was to give as wide a coverage as possible given these constraints.

To achieve this strategy, permission was obtained to observe meetings of the boards of the four departments during 1987 (commencing in February as there were no January meetings). The board was the body directly responsible for the operational oversight and policy development of a department. Also, two of the departments had formal committees whose role it was to exercise an operational and financial control and review role; the Finance Committee of the Department of Mission Outreach and the Directorate of the Department of Educational Activities[5]. These were also observed. In addition, the meetings of the Divisional Council (regular plus a yearly special meeting to consider longer term strategy) and Senior Management Group[6], and the annual budget preparation meeting - the Budget Conference - were observed. The details of the meeting cycles of each body and extent of observation actually carried out is shown in Table 3.3. Finally, the 1986 and 1987 Annual General Meetings were attended.

A good coverage of all these forums was obtained, but total coverage could not be achieved due to either clashes with my employment commitments, timetable clashes between meetings or, in a few cases, communication breakdowns (for example, when times were

Research Method 91

changed or for more irregular meetings such as the Directorate). Employment commitments clashed with the meetings of the Mission Outreach and Welfare Services Boards for all of 1987, except for one meeting in each case. Such clashes also caused half of the sessions of the 1986 Annual General Meeting to be missed. In addition, a commitment during the second half of the year clashed with three meetings of Mission Outreach's Finance Committee. The most significant timetable clash was between the meetings of the Education Activities' Board and Mission Outreach's Finance Committee. The board meetings were attended as it was felt that more theoretically interesting activities were developing there at that time. However, this did mean that more of the Finance Committee meetings were missed than may have been necessary because of an unanticipated employment commitment that occurred later in the year. To attempt to mitigate as much as possible the unavoidable gaps in this observation pattern, copies were obtained of all meeting documentation (agendas, minutes, etc.) and interviews held with relevant staff.

Arena	Meeting Cycle	Period Observed	Number Observed	Tot. No. Meetings
Department of Finance and Administration				
- Board	Monthly	Feb. to Dec.	9	10
Department of Educational Activities				
- Board	Monthly	Feb. to Aug.	6	10
- Directorate	Irregular	May to Sep.	4	NA
Department of Mission Outreach				
- Board	Bimonthly	Sep. only	1	6
- Finance Committee	Monthly	Feb. to Nov.	5	10
Department of Welfare Activities				
- Board	Bimonthly	March only	1	6
Central Committees				
- Senior Management Group	Fortnightly	June to Nov.	8	NA
- Divisional Council (regular)	Quarterly	Feb. to Dec.	4	4
- Divisional Council (special)	Yearly	Feb. only	1	1
- Budget Conference	Yearly	Aug. only	1	1
Where total number of meetings is less than the theoretical maximum given the cycle and full time period, this was due to meetings being cancelled. NA = not available.				

Table 3.3: Observation Pattern of Division Head Office from February to December 1987

92   *Management Control in a Voluntary Organization*

In addition, some limited observation of Presbytery activities were undertaken during Stage 3 of the study. The March 1988 Presbytery meeting for one country Presbytery and the May 1988 for one city Presbytery meeting and its preceding Financial Committee meeting were attended.

Field notes were recorded on one side of the page only in spiral bound note books with consecutively numbered pages. In all, ten consecutively numbered and dated books were used, containing 571 pages of field notes. All sessions observed were recorded in as full detail as possible (including noting of no discussion of items) with appropriate references to date, time, place and attendees, and entries were cross referenced to meetings' agenda item numbers and supporting documentation. Also, clear distinctions were made between description and theoretical notes on explanations or new lines of inquiry. In addition, to give a basis of simple quantification (Silverman 1985a) of observed patterns, the time of the commencement and end of discussion for each agenda item or other issues arising from the meeting were recorded, with internal breakdowns for long items or sub-issues.

Finally, the observer role adopted should be noted. I consciously adopted an 'Observer as Participant' role (Junker 1960). That is, my role as a researcher was made public from the start and was based on direct involvement in the organization, but not active participation. Higher involvement roles such as a complete participant were rejected on ethical, as they often require secrecy, and practical, as a part-time researcher, grounds. At the commencement of the study, I had an announcement placed in the monthly Northern Division magazine explaining the project, and throughout the study I made every effort to inform members of the situations I was observing of my background, intentions and aims for the project. I feel that the acceptance of my role was extremely high. The division members with whom I came into contact were highly co-operative, open, supportive and seemed genuinely interested in the study. It is my belief that any researcher bias from lack of acceptance by subjects or deliberate withholding of information was extremely minimal.

Interviews

The primary interview method used was semi-structured. Interviews were focused on a particular topic or issue, and a general range of questions to be answered were prepared before the interview

Research Method 93

session. However, the interview itself was conducted as a free ranging conversation. The questions were not followed up in a fixed order, and issues raised by subjects were pursued. In general, interviews conducted during the study were not tape recorded as access to verbatim conversations was not considered necessary. Interviews were recorded in the field notes during the interview session, and checked and added to after the completion of the session.

The exact method of collection of interview data varied with the stage of the project. Early in the fieldwork, interviews were used to gather initial data about the structure of the Northern Division, the nature of the Division Departments and the operation of the accounting systems. Interviews at this point were more structured and subjects were selected by the key informant technique (Tremblay 1982), that is senior personnel were interviewed first and asked to suggest other members of their Departments or the organization who could supply or expand upon the needed information. To provide within concept triangulation (Denzin 1978), the interviews were alternated between the four Departments and other senior staff as much as possible given the practical constraints of organizing appointments.

Later in the study, interviews were used in a much less structured manner to follow-up issues arising from observation and document analysis. Such interviews usually had only one or two focus questions, and were conducted as free ranging conversations around these questions and any other matters that were raised. Interviews at this stage were used as a flexible back-up to the observation programme.

The most extensive formal use of interviews was in the final debriefing stage of the study. These interviews were used to discuss the general administration and functioning of the organizational structure of the Division and the use and importance of accounting systems within the Church. All questions were put in only very general terms and subjects were encouraged to define their own meanings for the questions, and raise any additional issues that they saw as relevant. As these conversations were very free ranging in scope but also attempted to discuss issues relevant to the analysis in some depth, these interviews were tape recorded. In addition, a less detailed written log of the conversation was kept. The subjects for these interviews were the senior managers of the Division, including board chairpersons, and

94   *Management Control in a Voluntary Organization*

all senior accounting personnel for each Department, including voluntary as well as paid staff. This selection policy was not followed for the Department of Welfare Activities due to the large number of quasi-autonomous health and welfare organizations under its oversight. On the advice of the director, two such organizations were selected as suitable representatives of these diverse components. The full interview schedule is shown in Table 3.4. As much as possible, these interviews were triangulated by interspersing their order across the groups shown in the right-hand column and levels of seniority.

Organization Position	Interviewees
Chairperson	- Chairperson-Elect
	- Chairperson
	- Past- Chairperson
Division Secretary	- Current Secretary
	- Previous Secretary
Department of Finance and Administration	- Board Chairperson
	- Director
	- Assistant Director: Investments
	- Assistant Director: Property
Department of Educational Activities	- Board Chairperson
	- Director
	- Business Manager
	- Co-ordinator of Communication Unit
	- Theological College Principal
Department of Mission Outreach	- Board Chairman
	- Director
	- Deputy Director
	- Deputy Director and Administrator
	- Youth and Conference Centres Officer
	- Finance Manager
	- Finance Committee Chairperson
	- Treasurer (Honorary)
Department of Welfare Activities	- Board Chairperson
	- Director
	- Directors of two units

Table 3.4: Interview Schedule of Senior Division Staff

Research Method 95

Finally, interviews were the primary data source used for the Parish and Presbytery extension to the case design. The Chairperson, Treasurer and Chairperson of the Finance Committee of one city and one country Presbytery were interviewed. In addition, three Parish Treasurers were interviewed from Parishes within the city Presbytery. A similar sample could not be obtained for country Presbytery due to the travel time and costs involved. The city sample was selected by asking the Presbytery Treasurer to identify Parishes representing a diversity of size and financial strength. He selected a large middle class Parish with an aging membership that was of medium financial strength, a small poorer Parish, and a large inner-city Parish that had a strong financial base. The interviews with all subjects concentrated on obtaining data about the operation of the Presbytery/Parish, its financial and accounting systems and attitudes to their use. In particular, treasurers were asked about the type of accounting records used, the forms of regular financial reporting, the preparation of budgets and whether they are used for control or other purposes.

Documents

A large number of official organizational documents were collected during the study. The most voluminous of these were full sets of meeting agendas, supporting documents, and minutes for all the meetings of the Division covered by the observation schedule. In addition, a complete set of agendas, reports and minutes of all the eleven Annual General Meetings held by the Northern Division to the end of the study period were obtained. These were collected as prime sources of the historical development of major policy issues in the church. They also included the financial reports of the Division. As well, copies of standard accounting reports, and various descriptive materials on the operations of various sections of the Northern Division were obtained.

Other information on the Northern Division was obtained from its publications. From June 1977 to December 1985 the Division had its own official fortnightly newspaper, Life and Times. This was replaced with a monthly magazine, Journey, from February 1986. All issues of both publications were reviewed for material on; (i) the development of the Northern Division, (ii) its management, (iii) reports on Annual General Meetings, (iv) the implementation of major

96 *Management Control in a Voluntary Organization*

policies, (v) the operations of commercial sections of the Northern Division, and (vi) its financial affairs.

Finally, more general information on the church was obtained from the official documents outlining the basis on which Mainstream Church was founded and other documents detailing the nature and formation of the church, the Government Act setting up the church, and its current rules and regulations.

IV. CHAPTER SUMMARY

This chapter has described the case design and data collection methods used. It is worth emphasizing that a predominantly qualitative case study approach was adopted because it enabled detailed examination of the research phenomenon in context. Further strengths of the design were the use of multiple data sources in a longitudinal research design. These features of case study method were particularly suitable for the theoretical concerns and problematic of this study. The major limitation of the design was its use of a single case. This was necessary because of resource and time constraints and the decision to opt for depth of analysis over breadth given the current limited state of knowledge on accounting in voluntary organizations. Still, the limitation such a design places on the potential to generalize from the findings should be acknowledged.

Two potentially problematic issues in research method are relevant to the case study design used here; the validity of the triangulation of multiple sources of data and the ability to generalize from the study of a single organization. In closing this chapter, some brief comments on the position taken in this study on these two issues are offered.

A common internal validity problem argued to apply to case study method is difficulties in establishing the extent of support for inferences (Birnberg et al. 1990). A major data collection method often recommended to mitigate this problem is triangulation; that is, the use of multiple data sources to obtain convergent validation of findings. Denzin (1978), one of the greatest advocates of triangulation, suggests it has two forms, within method and between method. Within method triangulation is where multiple sources or measures are used within one data collection method to strengthen the internal reliability of the results. This approach is commonly adopted in survey research where

Research Method 97

multiple scales are used to measure one construct. Between method triangulation involves the use of multiple data collection methods to analyse a common dimension of a phenomenon. If the data from two or more independent methods converge, then it is argued that greater reliance can be placed on the findings.

In general, the use of within method triangulation should be encouraged as it can be used to increase researcher confidence in the picture being constructed. For example, cross checking of the reports of subjects within the one site, cross checking across sites or different types of subjects and iterative interviewing of different types of subjects (for further discussion of potential uses see Glasser and Strauss 1967; Miles and Huberman 1984). While convergence of data from triangulated sources within one collection method cannot be interpreted as definite proof of internal validity, it is one powerful tool that can aid the researcher in assessing such validity, and in reducing researcher bias.

However, the use of between method triangulation cannot be given the same general support. At dispute is not the usefulness of multiple sources of data, as this is one of the important characteristics of case study method, but how they can be interpreted. If between method triangulation is meant simply to remind us of the partiality of any one method of data collection, then it serves a useful purpose. However, its advocates (Denzin 1978; Smith 1975; Webb et al. 1966) argue that rigour is increased by the convergence of data from multiple methods, leading to a more certain and complete picture of the phenomenon. This has three major problems. First, there are many practical difficulties in determining convergence. How many methods must converge? How similar do the results need to be? Should all methods be weighted equally? Second, it is assumed that all the methods used do not have the same weakness (see Jick 1979 for a fuller discussion of these two issues). Finally, and more importantly, this type of triangulation violates an underlying premise of a qualitative approach, that data must be understood in context (Silverman 1985a, 1985b, 1989). Each different type of data may capture a different picture of reality. To insist that they must converge is to insist that there is only one reality rather than different realities depending on the interpretations of different subjects or the existence of different situations[7]. Between method triangulation inappropriately wants to adjudicate between different data, calling some true and some

98 *Management Control in a Voluntary Organization*

false. Instead it should be asked; what does each type of data tell us about the phenomenon (see also, Halfpenny 1979; Hammersley and Atkinson 1983)[8]?

Triangulation, therefore, can be used to mitigate internal validity problems in case studies, but care and judgment must be exercised by the researcher, particularly where inferences are being drawn from data of different forms and from different settings. Such comparison can take place, but it must pay attention to treating differences as validly as similarities.

Finally, the problem of generalizing the findings of case studies has probably been the most common and most telling criticism of case study method. In part, this criticism is reasonable in that many early social science case studies, perhaps as an over reaction to natural science based research (Laughlin 1990b), focused almost exclusively on the deep description of situations with little attempt to provide theoretical explanations. There was little ability to generalize such specific findings. However, where more general explanation is attempted, does this criticism still apply? The simple answer to this is no, as the criticism is based on the premises of a statistical sampling logic that is inappropriate to case studies (Mitchell 1983; Scapens 1990; Yin 1989).

Why can't you generalize from a single case? The common answer given is that the case may not be representative of the population, or even if representative that the results are unique to this one instance. As Yin (1989) and Scapens (1990) point out, most experiments could be criticised on similar grounds, yet generalizing from experiments is more widely accepted. Scapens (1990) argued that the reason for this is that experiments are based on replication, not sampling, logic. The results of an experiment are evaluated against theory and accepted if they are consistent. The more the results are replicated in other one-off cases, the more the theory is accepted as an explanation of the phenomenon. The emphasis here, which should also be applicable to single case studies, is on *theoretical* generalization, not *statistical* generalization.

Mitchell (1983) provides an extended discussion of a similar point. He also argues that the reason that people often criticise the specificity of case studies is that they fail to recognize that case studies have different criteria of generality than traditional quantitative research methods. Traditional methods use a combination of statistical

Research Method   99

and causal or theoretical inference to argue generalizable results. First, statistical theory is used to design a representative sample of the population or situation. The findings from this sample or situation then can be extrapolated to the whole population. This is statistical inference. However, these results are only correlations between variables and all that can be generalized is that the same pattern of findings should exist for the population. To generalize about the nature of the relationships between variables, that is about causal or logical relationships, the researcher must use theoretical inference. By showing how the findings and research design relate to a body of theory, why the variables may be important, how and why they may be related, etc., the researcher can also generalize about the logical or causal relationships exhibited by the findings. However, case studies rely only on theoretical inference for the generality of their findings. The criteria for generalizable findings from both single and multiple case studies should be, do they "...relate theoretically relevant characteristics reflected in the case to one another in a logically coherent way" (Mitchell 1983, p.200). The generality of case study findings then depends on the use of analytic induction, that is the process of generalizing by abstracting from the specific, rather than the deductive logic of more traditional methods (see also Hammersley and Atkinson 1983; Silverman 1985a).

These two related arguments demonstrate that a strong case exists for the ability to generalize findings from even a single case design. There is no doubt that greater support for the generality of the explanation can be provided by comparative analysis through either multiple case study designs or replication of cases. However, the strength gained here is not from having a bigger or more representative sample, but from the demonstration of the theoretical relevance of the explanation. This is the primary criteria of the ability to generalize from case study method.

Notes

[1] No distinction is made in this study between case studies, field studies or fieldwork. They are all taken as applying to the same general research strategy (see Birnberg et al 1990; Scapens 1990).

[2] It should be noted that this increase could be referred to as a resurgence. Some of the most significant contributions to the early work on behavioural research in management accounting were case studies (for example, Argyris 1952; Hofstede 1967; Simon et al

1954). However, the literature then started to draw primarily on various branches of psychology, with consequent demands for, so called, more 'rigorous' research methods (Birnberg and Shields 1989; Hopwood 1989; Lord 1989), and case studies fell out of vogue.

[3] A related effect was that some of the growth in the Australian population during this period was from migration from generally non-Protestant European countries and non-Christian Asian countries.

[4] This reference cannot be given as it would reveal the identity of the subject church.

[5] The latter was formed during the first half of 1987, after the observation programme had commenced.

[6] Permission was not sort to attend Senior Management Group meetings until June. It was felt that as this forum was used by senior managers to argue policy, raise interdepartmental conflicts, etc., I needed to be especially sensitive to the issue of observer intrusion bias. By June it was felt that I was well known to most participants, that they were used to my attendance at various meetings, and that therefore attendance could commence with minimal risk of intrusion bias.

[7] For example, a factory labourer and a factory manager may have totally different interpretations of the role of monthly performance reports, or the manager may give different accounts depending on whether she is using the report in the context of a meeting with her foremen or in a quarterly review meeting with her peers and superiors.

[8] It should be noted that similar concerns can also apply to within method triangulation, but not to the same degree.

Chapter 4
Accounting Systems I: Formal Features and Financial Dynamics

I. INTRODUCTION

This chapter commences the analysis of the significance of accounting in the Northern Division of Mainstream church. It does this by considering two interrelated areas. First, the official, formal features of the accounting systems of the head office structure of the Division are considered. This enables an evaluation of the technical sophistication, emphasis and origins of these systems. As well, a comparative analysis of the formal features of the accounting systems across the four Division departments is presented. Second, the potential effects of the financial dynamics of the Division upon the use of the accounting systems are considered. This analysis enables a consideration of the existence within the Division of financial crises, their causes and their impacts upon various operational units. As argued in chapter 2, such secular crises are potentially important in understanding the significance of accounting within churches. Together, these two areas of analysis provide an initial view of the significance of accounting within the Northern Division.

This chapter is organized as follows. The first section considers the formal features of the major accounting systems of the Division. The second section analyses the financial dynamics of the Division. The chapter concludes with a summary of the major implications of the discussions.

II. FORMAL ACCOUNTING SYSTEMS

In chapter 1, an organizational accounting system was defined as a "...formal system which expresses in fundamentally numerical terms past, present and future financial actions of such an enterprise" (Laughlin 1984, p.8). This broad definition allows an accounting system to be any organization based system which expresses the financial aspects of actions in a formal or orderly manner (Laughlin 1984). There are two major systems which fit this description in the Northern Division, a budgetary control system and a budget formulation system. Naturally, these two accounting systems are interdependent but they have sufficiently different foci and operational cycles to be analysed as separate systems. In the remainder of this study, these two systems will be referred to as the Management Accounting Control System (MACS) and the Budgeting System respectively. The Division has no separate financial accounting system as there is no major external reporting function. Annual audited financial reports are prepared and tabled at the Annual General Meeting. These reports are derived through some additional consolidation and accrual adjustments made at year end to MACS data. This financial reporting function is integrated with the MACS discussion. The focus of the analysis in this section is on the formal features of the two Division accounting systems[1].

Providing a parsimonious description of any accounting system for a complex organization is difficult as no commonly accepted parameters of analysis have been established in the accounting literature. However, reproducing the full details of the MACS and the Budgeting System would be a tedious alternative. Instead, it is proposed to summarize the distinctive features of each system using part of the framework proposed by Amigoni (1978). This framework has recently been adapted and empirically applied by Jones (1986) in a study of the changes in accounting systems following mergers. Amigoni (1978) set out to develop a contingency model of accounting control systems that linked three levels of analysis; environment variables, distinctive features of accounting systems and the control tools used. It is only the second level, the distinctive features of accounting systems, that is relevant for this section. The rest of Amigoni's framework is rejected as it is based on normative assertions

Accounting Systems I   *103*

about links between the three levels of analysis rather than actual analysis of accounting in action.

Orientation	The extent to which the accounting system favours certain activities, objectives, or time periods in its information flows, e.g. marketing - production; financial information - qualitative information; past - future.
Formal Responsibility	The extent to which financial sub-goals are specified for responsibility centres. The more developed the financial targets the higher the formal responsibility that the system supports.
Quickness	The timing of the reporting cycle of the accounting system, e.g. daily; monthly; quarterly.
Detail	Accounting systems vary in the degree of aggregation of information into specific sub-classifications. The detail of the system increases with the extent by which data are collected for sub-classifications, e.g. by products and functional units.
Accuracy[+]	The extent to which information supplied is based upon actual as opposed to estimated inputs (estimates may be used to expedite the provision of information). This is related also to the extent and calculation basis of accruals in the system.
Consultation[+]	Consultation measures the extent to which users are involved in the input process for sections of the accounting system that are related to their responsibilities for outcomes.
Availability as a Data Base[+]	The extent to which users have access to raw data to generate their own system outputs in addition to regular system outputs.
Procedural Rigidity	The frequency with which regular system outputs are varied in favour of ad hoc formats. This is related to 'availability as data base', but concerns variations in the standard system outputs.
Technology[+]	The types of methods used to operate the accounting system, e.g. manual - computerized; internal staff - external staff.

+ Added by Jones (1986).

Table 4.1: Distinctive Descriptive Features of an Accounting System

Amigoni (1978) proposed eight features of accounting systems - detail, relevance, selectivity, formal responsibility, procedural rigidity, style of control, quickness and orientation - which he argued could vary in degree across different systems and thus be used to differentiate between them. Some of these features are mainly descriptive items, for example, quickness requires a statement on the timing of the reporting cycle. However, others require assessments of the actual use of the systems, for example, style of control requires an analytical assessment of the use of accounting information, similar to Hopwood's (1972) notion of leadership style. These features, which comprise style of control, relevance and selectivity, will not be used here as the analytical assessment of features of the actual use of

104   *Managment Control in a Voluntary Organization*

accounting information goes beyond the focus on the description of the formal features of accounting system. Such issues are dealt with later in this and the following chapters. Jones (1986) also added four other descriptive items in his application of Amigoni's framework; accuracy, consultation, availability as a data base and technology. Combining these with the remaining Amigoni items gives nine basic distinctive features for describing an accounting system, as set out in Table 4.1. These nine descriptive features still require judgmental assessments by the researcher, but this is unavoidable in any attempt to analyse the formal or informal features of accounting systems. It is proposed that the utility of such an approach is that it systematizes such judgments, thereby laying them more open to independent assessment (Silverman 1985a, 1989).

This section is divided into four subsections. The first two subsections describe the features of the MACS and Budgeting System respectively. The third subsection presents a comparative analysis of these two systems across the four Division departments. The final subsection summarizes the three analyses and presents some major implications for the concerns of this study.

The Management Accounting Control System

This subsection analyses the structural features of the MACS of the Northern Division. This is the main accounting reporting system for the administrative infrastructure. Table 4.2 describes the MACS in terms of the nine distinctive features derived from Amigoni (1978) and Jones (1986). The discussion concentrates on the outputs of the system and their official usage rather than the recording process to avoid unnecessary technical accounting detail.

The MACS is a partial accrual system running on a centralized, computerized general ledger system administered by the Accounting and Office Services (AOS) section of the department of Finance and Administration. The majority of transactions recorded in the system are on a cash basis with monthly accrual adjustments for accounts payable, accounts receivable, nominal internal interest charges and other inter-departmental service charges. Adjustments for depreciation and other accruals are only entered at year end for the preparation of final annual reports. In particular, the existence of nominal interest

Accounting Systems I 105

charges for cash usage by departments and inter-departmental charges for services represent fairly modern management accounting practices.

Orientation	Immediate past (current year) and future events. Focus on financial information for departments and cost centres within departments. Highly integrated with Division budget system.
Formal Responsibility	High. System reports on financial performance to budget for expense and income categories by both cost centres and departments overall. Cost centre and department managers are responsible for meeting budget. Capital and cash flow implications also covered by reports by department.
Quickness	Basic reporting cycle is monthly, with reports also showing year-to-date aggregations. Quarterly reports also produced. Reports available five days after month end. Draft annual reports available one month after year end, audited three months after year end. Calendar annual financial year is used.
Detail	High for monthly transaction reports which detail all transactions by cost centre. Moderate for monthly cost centre and department reports which summarize transactions by expense and income categories. Highly summarized for annual reports.
Accuracy	High in terms of being based on monthly transaction data only. Estimate based accruals mainly only entered at year end. Comparison to budget sometimes difficult as 'actual' entries do not always follow same timing assumptions as budget, e.g. yearly grant received in advance shown in one month when budget spreads it over twelve.
Consultation	Moderate to High. Departments are responsible for preparing most inputs for processing by Accounting and Office Services (AOS). Finance and Administration retains control over inter-departmental charges for funds usage and several other areas. Draft annual report checked by departments for accuracy.
Availability as a Data Base	Restricted access. Only AOS can operate system to generate special reports, but facility is available for departments on request. Transaction report provides basis for access to disaggregated information but in manual only mode.
Procedural Rigidity	High. Basic reporting system standardized across departments and cost centres. No variation during period of study.
Technology	Computerized general ledger system run by AOS. No online access for other departments.

Table 4.2: Distinctive Features of the Management Accounting Control System

Data preparation is primarily a department responsibility, with data entry and reports generation by AOS. All accruals and functions such as pay-roll and fringe benefits tax are done centrally by AOS. The official turn around time for report generation is 5 days after month end. However, during the period of study this semi-regularly overran by about 3 or 4 days. The system is not fully integrated, with the highest level of consolidation being a department. This results

106   *Managment Control in a Voluntary Organization*

from the accounting system being structured around autonomous funding units which could only be consolidated to the department level. In recent years there has been some discussion of producing one set of fully consolidated annual reports, but no moves had been made in this direction. In summary, the MACS is a partial accrual system orientated around departmental units with a monthly reporting cycle and with primary control over the system residing within Finance and Administration.

Three types of report are regularly generated for the departments; the General Ledger Transaction Report, monthly income statement and balance sheet by cost centre[2] (approximately 150 cost centres), and the monthly department reports containing an income statement summary and surplus/deficit summary for each cost centre. The first report acts as a quality check on the data entry and processing functions of the system. The latter two are the main summary reports. They are also produced as quarterly summaries with copies going to the Divisional Council as well as to the departments. Examples of all reports except the General Ledger Transaction Report are provided in the appendix.

The structure of these reports is the primary interest in this subsection. Horizontally, the income statement and surplus/deficit reports have three major columns, 'this month', 'year to date', and 'total year'. Within the first two, the 'actual', 'budget' and 'variance' are given. The total column shows the 'yearly budget' and a 'forecast' column to enable revision of budget expectations during the year. This latter facility was not in use at the start of the field work, but was implemented by Finance and Administration during the period of the study. Vertically, the reports show functional classifications of income and expenditure for the cost centre reports and cost centre totals for the department summaries. The horizontal structure of the balance sheets is account balances for the 'start of year', 'current month', 'changes in balances' and 'annual budget'. The changes in balances column is further divided into the 'actual' and 'budget' for the current month and the 'actual', 'budget' and 'variance' for the year to date. Vertically, they have fairly common asset and liability classifications. The net asset figure is made up of trust accounts and accumulated funds and reserves. These structural features indicate that the MACS reports formally emphasize a strong budgetary control focus. This is supported by formal responsibility allocation within the Division.

Accounting Systems 1 107

Departments are responsible for meeting their budgets. They are expected to analyse their own reports and identify any needed control actions. However, as pointed out in chapter 3, Finance and Administration also has formal financial responsibility for the Division as a whole, which includes budgetary oversight of the other departments.

The basic structural design of the MACS had been in place from early in the life of the Division. In December 1978 the major accounting firm of Arthur Young and Company was retained to provide a report on the design of an appropriate accounting system for the Division. Their final report was delivered in April 1979. The only restriction laid down by the Division was that the accounting system should not infringe on the decentralized decision-making structure of the church. The approach proposed by Arthur Young was to implement a full accrual, fully integrated accounting system with a fairly standard responsibility accounting format suitable for a firm with a divisional structure, and to increase uniformity of accounting practices within the Division. It was also strongly recommended that the new accounting system be computerized. In other words, the consulting report recommended the adoption of a single entity accrual accounting system instead of the cash based fund accounting system that had been used by the Division to that time.

The recommendations on the new accounting design were adopted almost in their entirety and implemented as soon as possible after 1979. A couple of minor recommendations that would have required some alterations to the management structure at that time were not adopted. Also, the movement to a single entity structure has not been achieved due to a continuing commitment to some level of fund accounting structure. The system was finally computerized in 1981. The Finance and Administration Assistant Director - Finance stated that since then the system has undergone a slow evolution, but was still basically the system envisioned in the Arthur Young report.

There is no clear indication in Division documents as to reasons for the report into and changes to the accounting systems. However, as will be considered further in the next section, around the time of the report there were grave concerns about the cost of running the administrative structures of the Division and the financial ability of the Parishes to give the needed support. Several enquires were held into these issues, with some recommending centralization and

108   *Managment Control in a Voluntary Organization*

standardization of accounting procedures as part of the solution (see Northern Division 1977, 1978, 1979a,b). It seems likely that the moves to 'modernize' the accounting systems of the Division were part of this felt need for greater financial control and rationalization.

From the distinctive features summary and the additional details above it can be seen that the MACS is a fairly sophisticated and detailed system. It produces very detailed reports on a timely basis to a highly disaggregated level of the head office structure. In all respects, except its partial accrual basis and department fund structure, it is the type of accounting system one would expect to find in a modern reasonably sized business organization. From a rationalization perspective, the detailed cost centre structure potentially enables a fairly standardized financial gaze into these very detailed levels of the Division's operations. This also potentially enables a significant level of comparison of performance and actions on a financial basis across all operational units of the Division. The only technical hindrance to this comparison process is the remaining fund accounting structure which does not allow a full standardized financial picture of operations to be derived. Rationalization processes are also evident in the use of a major accounting firm to design the accounting system. Such mimetic processes (DiMaggio and Powell 1983) are part of the process of cultural rationalization of voluntary organizations discussed in chapter 2. There has been some indication that voluntary organizations have been increasingly under pressure to 'modernize' their management practices, structures and managers' skills through the adoption of commercial approaches and experience (for example, Griffiths 1988; Woodfield et al 1987). The use of professional accounting consultants offering fairly standardized occupational solutions is one of the major ways this diffusion process may occur. In terms of the technical features of the MACS, this would seem to have occurred in the Northern Division, although the remnants of the fund accounting structure indicate that it may not have been a totally unquestioning acceptance of outside ideas.

The Budgeting System

In this subsection the formal processes of the Budgeting System, which covers the budget formulation processes within the Northern Division, are analysed. The emphasis in the discussion is upon the

Accounting Systems I   109

general nature and formal structure of the Budgeting System rather than the more technical detail of the numerical aggregating process.

Orientation	Forward for twelve month period, split into monthly forecasts. Focus on department and overall resource contributions and allocations. Detail on cost centre planning dealt with by departments. Balanced budget is sought. Highly integrated with MACS.
Formal Responsibility	Annual General Meeting approves budget, but preparation is the operational responsibility of the Director of Finance and Administration. Other department Directors and Assistant Director - Finance for Finance and Administration responsible for preparing department submissions. Divisional Council also involved during formulation process.
Quickness	Formulation process quite lengthy, taking approximately nine months with fairly intensive effort for half of these. Budget normally approved two months before becomes operational.
Detail	Moderate. Total income and expenditure for cost centres or major operating areas within departments. Some sections shown only as net surplus/deficit effect. Detailed department budgets based on disaggregations of approved total budget.
Accuracy	Moderate. Aim is to provide a realistic estimate of all income and expenditure, but existence of unavoidable errors and department optimism recognized.
Consultation	High. Bottom-up development process with high levels of involvement by departments and moderate by Presbytery and other elected representatives of membership. Initial key parameters (e.g. income growth) developed by Finance and Administration. The Finance and Administration Director and Board may arbitrate on changes to achieve balanced budget.
Availability as a Data Base	Moderate. Approved budget and department disaggregations entered into MACS.
Procedural Rigidity	Moderate. Fairly standardized format modelled on management structure and development procedure used. Some variations in both did occur during period of study. Departments have total virement over allocations between cost centres unless specific Annual General Meeting direction given for particular programs. Virement between departments not possible after budget approved.
Technology	Manual and computerized. Preparation at department level depends on their resources. Some use spreadsheet models. Final integration on simple spreadsheet model.

Table 4.3: Distinctive Features of the Budgeting System

The distinctive features of the Budgeting System are summarized in Table 4.3. As for the MACS above, the Budgeting System is highly developed. It follows a form of detailed financial and related resources planning and allocation that would normally be expected in a business organization of this size. The budget formulation approach used can be described as a fairly participatory

110   *Managment Control in a Voluntary Organization*

bottom-up process. For the last 10 years, the primary Division budget policy guiding this process has been a balanced budget, although this has not always been achieved (discussed further later in the chapter). A typical budget formulation timetable, that has been in use since 1984, is shown in Table 4.4. As this indicates, the Division departments play the most central participatory role in budget formulation. This reflects their position as the main focus of the budget, as discussed further below. Also, as would be expected given the governance structures of the church, the Parishes and Presbyteries also formally participate through elected representatives at two key stages. The Budget Conference is the main means used to allow Presbytery representatives to provide guidance on budget strategy and the programmes of the departments before finalization of the budget. Also, final budget approval is the responsibility of Presbytery representatives at the Annual General Meeting. However, it must be acknowledged that the practical ability to significantly modify the budget at this stage is limited, although the formal authority exists. Other less formal opportunity is given through the discussions that occur with Presbytery Finance and Administration Committees, where possible, on their level of notional contribution to the budget. The distinctive features show a fairly sophisticated, flexible and participatory Budgeting System aimed at allocating the financial resources of the Division between the departments (These issues are discussed at greater length in chapter 6).

January	Request for information on Parish income for the previous year (e.g. for 1988 budget request 1986 income details).
March	Consultation of the Divisional Council on broad strategy issues for the Division. Finance and Administration examines Parish income returns and determines notional Presbytery allocations for contributions to budget. Also request information from departments on income and expenditure forecasts.
April/May	Consideration of budget estimates by Senior Management Group and Finance and Administration Board.
May/June	Budget discussions with as many Presbytery Finance and Administration Committees as possible to discuss notional allocations.
July	Budget Conference of expanded Divisional Council to consider draft budget.
August/ September	Consideration by Finance and Administration Board and Senior Management Group of final budget adjustments.
October	Budget presented to Annual General Meeting for approval.

Table 4.4: Typical Budget Formulation Timetable

Accounting Systems I 111

However, one point that tends to reduce budget flexibility is the high percentage of fixed costs. Most of the recurrent expenditure of the departments and Presbyteries is on staff positions, closely followed by related support costs. Once programmes are approved, it is difficult to vary these costs within the budget period, particularly as the Division is reluctant to terminate staff after making a commitment to a programme (this is related to the different nature of wage relations in voluntary organizations, as discussed in chapter 2). Much of the budget expenditure, therefore, tends to be locked in and can only be reduced or reallocated by making significant changes in the programme profile. The Director of Finance and Administration saw this low level of discretionary expenditure as a major problem in budget formulation. Laughlin (1984) reported a similar problem for the budgeting process in the Church of England. It may be that this problem of high committed expenditures is a common problem in voluntary organizations as they tend to be labour intensive.

In terms of extent, the budget covers principally the funding of the activities of the Division departments, both recurrent and capital. Also, covered are the Presbyteries' budgets and a contribution to central church finances. However, both the latter are very minor compared to the funding of the Division department activities. In an attempt to reflect the focus of the budget on services of the head office departments, the budget is officially called the "Mission and Service Fund". Structurally, the budget reflects the department fund structure discussed under the MACS. Only general indications are given of the income and expenditure areas for each department, which have total virement rights over internal allocations unless a specific Division policy directs the use of funds. What is critical from each department's perspective is its net total position with respect to allocations of Parish contributions via the Presbyteries. In this respect, the departments for Welfare Services and Finance and Administration are net contributors to the budget, with the latter playing the major role in this regard. Welfare Services basically is financially totally independent of the budget (see next section). The other two departments are net drawers on the budget and, therefore, the main competitors for the allocation of discretionary resources.

A principal function of the Budgeting System, therefore, is to allocate contributions from the Parishes among the Division departments, mainly the departments for Mission Outreach, and

112 *Managment Control in a Voluntary Organization*

Educational Activities. Parishes budget independently of the Mission and Service Fund, their only formal linkage to the budget being this provision of funds. As indicated in the budget timetable in Table 4.4, Finance and Administration allocate budget contributions to a Presbytery based on the income of Parishes under its oversight in the previous year. On average in recent years this has been about 20% of total Parish income. Presbyteries then allocate this contribution to their Parishes, often in the proportions determined by Finance and Administration but they can alter these as they see fit, determine if they are attainable given current expectations and advise Finance and Administration of the anticipated level of contributions. This process is one reason for the participation of Presbyteries in the Budget Conference as they are able to both confirm the level of available Parish income support and have an input into the priorities for the use of this funding. The Budgeting System, therefore, is the accounting system through which Parish and Presbytery views are linked to the activities of the Division departments.

The Budgeting System, therefore, follows an often recommended modern business budgeting practice with its bottom-up participative process. The main function of the system is the allocation of funding from the Parishes between the activities of the Division departments and Presbyteries. In practice, this comes down to allocations between the departments for Mission Outreach and Educational Activities as Finance and Administration is a major net contributor of funds and Welfare Services is financially independent of the budget. This process is potentially made more difficult by the high level of committed expenditure and the official goal of a balanced budget. Further insight into these funding dynamics are given later in the chapter. The other principal feature of the structure of the Budgeting System that should be noted is the power given to Finance and Administration to present a budget to the Annual General Meeting for final approval.

Accounting Systems Across the Departments

The previous two subsections have described the formal structural features of the MACS and Budgeting System of the Division. In this subsection, a comparative analysis of any differences in these systems across the four Division departments is presented. In

Accounting Systems I   113

chapter 2 the sacred and secular orientation and type of occupational group were identified as two possible theoretical dimensions of comparison within and across churches. These two dimensions are used here as a basis for the comparative assessment of accounting system differences across the four departments of the Northern Division.

The formal responsibilities of the four Departments show a split between sacred and secular activities. Finance and Administration is responsible for all major secular support functions. The other Departments deal with different areas of sacred concern. Mission Outreach has a strong sacred focus on core mission issues concerning Parishes and Presbyteries, as well as national and international mission activities. Educational Activities also has a strong sacred activity in theological education; mixed with sacred support functions in the areas of communication, and secondary and tertiary education. Welfare Services deals with mission outreach in the community, health and welfare areas. While the staff regarded these activities as having a strong sacred function, there was an indication that some members of the church did not see a strong connection between community service and the work of the church (Northern Division, 1987a, p.88). There seems to be some indecisiveness, therefore, about the relation of the activities of Welfare Services to the mission of the church. Therefore, the four Division Departments exhibit some diversity in their sacred and secular orientation. Finance and Administration may be considered the most secular. Mission Outreach may be considered the 'most sacred' and Welfare Services is probably the 'least sacred'. Educational Activities may be considered to have a fairly sacred position, but probably somewhere between that of the other two sacred departments.

In addition, there is a variety of occupational groups employed across the four Departments. The ministers and religious specialists found in Mission Outreach would be expected to be strong on sacred support. The same may be expected for the ministers and religious educationalists in Educational Activities. The religious orientated specialists in Welfare Services should also support a sacred orientation, but their position may be more ambiguous, in line with the more ambiguous position of their department. The accountants in Finance and Administration would be expected to be much stronger on support of secular ideas.

114   *Managment Control in a Voluntary Organization*

The four Division departments, therefore, appear to offer some potential as internal units of analysis because of their variation on two dimensions, sacred and secular orientation, and dominant types of occupational groups. However, the effects of sacred and secular orientation of a department, and those of accountants and sacred occupational groups, cannot be separately identified. This would require, at a minimum, another secular department managed by a 'non-accountant' occupational group to act as a comparator to Finance and Administration, which does not exist in the case of the Northern Division. Therefore, while it is possible to talk about differences across sacred and secular departments in descriptive terms, analytically any differences in the attributes of the accounting systems across the departments may be due to both their orientation within the management structure of the Division, and the occupational group that dominate their management. In this comparative analysis distinctions are made only between the three sacred departments (dominated by sacred occupational groups) and Finance and Administration, as the sole secular department (dominated by accountants).

This classification suggests three main potential areas of difference across the four departments. First, the coverage of the two accounting systems might differ, being less in the sacred departments than the secular departments. This may occur because there is less perceived need in sacred departments for accounting systems. However, different coverage across the departments is considered unlikely given the overall central design of the Division's systems. Second, another way in which such a difference could occur is in the use of independent, department based accounting systems. It may be expected that these are more likely to exist in Finance and Administration than in the sacred departments, for the same reason as above. Third, the level of accounting and financial management expertise may vary; being higher in Finance and Administration than the sacred departments. These three areas are considered in turn below.

Coverage of the Accounting Systems

The MACS covered all the core activities of Finance and Administration, Educational Activities, and Mission Outreach. The only exceptions to this were the semi-autonomous commercial operation under the oversight of Finance and Administration, the

Accounting Systems I 115

Northern Book Shop, and the similar relation of church schools and colleges under the oversight of Educational Activities. The same pattern was evident for the Budgeting System for these three departments.

The exception for both the MACS and the Budgeting System was the coverage of Welfare Services. No part of the operations of Welfare Services were on the MACS. Also, as indicated previously, this department had only a minor relation to the budget. The running costs of the department were covered by a levy on its agencies. This was shown as offsetting income and expenditure flows in the budget. Also, the department made a contribution towards the hospital chaplaincy activities of Mission Outreach, resulting in it being a small net contributor to the budget. The net effect of these arrangements was that Welfare Services could effectively be regarded as not linked to the Division accounting systems. However, this uncoupling appeared to have nothing to do with its sacred orientation or dominant occupational groups. One reason was the independent financial status of its agencies. These were either funded by government grants or their own fund raising programmes. As these funds were tied to these programmes, and were very much larger in total than the Division's financial activities, the Division was felt that it was not possible, or necessary, to consolidate these within its accounting systems. Another reason appeared to be that historically the agencies had developed fairly independently of the Division. There was some feeling of tensions between the agencies and the church, and a major role for the new Director was to integrate community and welfare agencies back into the church. However, the Welfare Services Director stated that he saw this happening on a liaison and policy level, not a financial level. Welfare Services, therefore, had a unique position relative to the other three departments. It was an equal in terms of the governance structures of the Division, but outside the ambit of its accounting systems.

Therefore, no significant pattern of variation was evident for the coverage of the MACS and Budgeting System across the departments. As suggested above, this was to be expected given the formal central design of the accounting systems. The exception was Welfare Services, which fell outside the coverage of the systems because of its independent finances, and the fact that its agencies had developed independently of head office activities. Two other departments also

116   *Managment Control in a Voluntary Organization*

had their own internal income sources. Finance and Administration earned a large surplus from the Mainstream Church Investment Service, and Mission Outreach had surpluses from its Conference Centre activities. However, both these activities had developed within the ambit of the Division head office operations, and they were not significant enough to give these departments independent financial status. For example, while Finance and Administration was a net contributor to the budget, the only other major income source it had was charges for its services to the other departments and the church agencies. Therefore, the very loose coupling of Welfare Services to the accounting systems seemed to be a special case.

Independent Department Accounting Systems

Independent accounting systems in departments could potentially take two major forms, either the use of the Division systems to generate non-standard outputs, or separate recording and processing systems[3]. The former are independent in the sense that they indicate use of the existing systems by the departments to meet their own specific perceived needs for information not provided under the standard MACS report design. The latter are often used either to make up for perceived problems with the standard systems (for example, Preston 1986), or to provide more detailed, accessible systems for particular functions. In both cases, the existence of such systems is considered to be less likely in sacred departments.

Very little use of non-standard reports was disclosed by senior staff in any of the departments. Only two types of interrogation of the MACS seemed to take place, either checks on the accuracy of the recording system or detailed analyses of the causes of budget variances. Both these uses simply involved disaggregation of the existing reports when exceptional variances or amounts were noted. Such uses were reported by all three of the departments on the MACS.

All three departments also had some minor separate recording and processing systems. These were systems designed to handle the detail, or particular processing requirements, of a specific operational area, with the aggregated information from these systems still being processed through the MACS. For example, the operations of the Church Investment Service in Finance and Administration required special banking type investment and deposit accounts, which could not be handled under the MACS. Similarly, the Communication Unit of

Accounting Systems I 117

Educational Activities had a separate system to deal with subscriptions to the Division's monthly magazine. Finally, Mission Outreach had simple cash accounting systems at its Conference Centres. These were geographically disperse and their managers needed day-to-day access to receipts and payments, which could not be provided under the MACS. Therefore, some minor independent accounting systems existed in all three departments covered by the MACS, and the reasons for these appeared to be specific operational differences unable to be accommodated by this accounting system.

An exception to this pattern was the use by Mission Outreach of a Personal Computer spreadsheet based long-term budget known as the Seven Year Plan, which was a detailed operational and capital budget for the period 1987-93. It included income and expenditure plans, capital works schedules, asset sales schedules, monthly cash flow forecasts, and schedules of loan interest and repayments. Development of this system was commenced by the department in 1986, and it was being used within the department during the period of the field work in 1987. However, it was still not fully developed, and was not finally approved until near the end of 1987. The Seven Year Plan was meant to act as a working strategy for the financial management and the future development of the department.

The existence of the Seven Year Plan within a sacred department, Mission Outreach, is against expectations. This accounting system appears to be formally orientated at the management of the finances and operations of the department, and was independently developed and implemented by the department. This seems to run counter to the argument presented in chapter 2 that sacred units would be major sources of resistance to the use of accounting within churches. Anticipating future discussions later in this chapter and in chapter 5, it will be argued that this finding is a special case related to the significant debt position of this sacred unit, and that there were limits placed on the intrusion of the Plan into sacred operations. However, at this point it should be acknowledged that the existence, and formal nature, of this independent accounting system appears to contradict the theoretical expectations flowing from the sacred and secular divide argued in chapter 2.

In summary, the existence of independent accounting systems did not support expectations based on the sacred and secular department classification in two ways. First, all departments covered

118 *Managment Control in a Voluntary Organization*

by the MACS had independent systems. These appeared to exist to meet the particular information requirements of specific activities of the departments that could not be accommodated within the MACS. Second, the Seven Year Plan in Mission Outreach showed the use of an independent accounting system formally orientated at the management of activities in a sacred, not a secular, department. This finding contradicted the expectations for sacred church units.

Accounting Expertise

There was significant variation in accounting expertise across the four departments.

At one extreme was Welfare Services. No accounting expertise existed at the directorate level of the department. The Director and the Board Chairperson stated that they did not see financial management of their department as one of their responsibilities, and neither had any accounting expertise. Financial management was considered to be a responsibility of the agencies, and all accounting expertise was at that level. The only financial policy that the Director saw as relevant for his oversight of the agencies was their breadth funding sources. He felt that they depended too much on government grants. In its linkage with the Division structure then, Welfare Services had no accounting expertise and felt that there was no need for such knowledge.

As expected, at the other extreme was Finance and Administration. As mentioned in chapter 3, all the senior staff of the department were accountants, many with significant experience in the public and business sectors. Other experienced accounting staff were employed in the Accounting and Office Services unit of the department in the operation of the MACS. The Director also expressed the opinion that more, and better, qualified accounting staff were needed to improve the service the Department offered. Finance and Administration, therefore, was high on accounting expertise.

Educational Activities and Mission Outreach were closer to the Welfare Services position, but had some levels of accounting expertise. Educational Activities had a Business Manager who had commercial management experience, including a reasonable level of financial management knowledge and the practical use of accounting systems, but he was not a qualified accountant. He had originally been hired to oversee the building of the department's hostel accommodation, but had since taken on broader management responsibilities. No other

Accounting Systems I 119

staff had any level of accounting expertise except that gained through using the Division systems. Mission Outreach employed one accountant to manage its use of the MACS, assist in budget preparation and handle the technical issues of the Seven Year Plan. Two other staff members engaged in running operational units of the department also had some practical commercial financial management experience. By far the majority of the large number of staff had no accounting expertise, being employed for their expertise in the mission service areas of the department. Both Educational Activities and Mission Outreach, therefore, were low on accounting expertise.

Again, however, Mission Outreach was a partial exception to this tendency in one respect. In 1985, Mission Outreach had established a Finance Committee to overview its financial management. This committee was composed of senior staff, including the Director, and two volunteer members of the church (one with accounting and the other with management expertise). It was responsible for the monthly review of the financial performance (as indicated by the MACS reports), identifying remedial action, and financial management strategies, including implementation of the Seven Year Plan. The Finance Committee represented the only formal structural means in any of the departments for dealing with accounting and financial management matters. The Director stated that it was set-up to overcome a perception of the department's low accounting expertise. Anticipating discussions in a later section and chapter 5, it will be argued that this is another example of the effects of the debt position of the department. Also, the creation of a separate Committee to deal with accounting and financial issues can interpreted as consistent with the sacred orientation, and dominance by sacred occupational groups, position of this department, as it is a structural way of separating off such secular concerns from sacred activities. Laughlin (1984) reported similar arrangements within sacred units of the Church of England. However, at this stage the existence of the Finance Committee in Mission Outreach should be recognized as an apparent contradiction to its sacred classification.

The variation in accounting expertise, therefore, does tend to support the expectations of the orientation and occupational group differences of the four departments. The secular financially orientated and accountants dominated Finance and Administration has significantly higher levels of accounting expertise, as would be

120   *Managment Control in a Voluntary Organization*

expected. The sacred orientated and sacred occupational groups dominated Educational Activities and Mission Outreach have fairly low levels of accounting expertise. Welfare Services supports this pattern, but also should be seen as a special case due to its lack of linkages to the Division accounting systems. This department seems to present a view of a total negation of the relevance of accounting to its operations. Finally, the apparent contradiction of the existence of the Finance Committee within Mission Outreach to its sacred classification needs to be explained.

Implications of the Comparative Analysis

Overall, this comparison of the formal use of accounting systems across the four Division departments has raised some interesting issues.

First, in general the sacred or secular orientation and occupational groups differences of the departments does not seem to explain the coverage of the MACS and Budgeting System, or the existence of department based accounting systems. Variation in the former does not exist due to the overall encompassing design of the Division head office accounting structures, except for the absence of any significant coverage for Welfare Services. This was explained by its independent financial status and the uniqueness of its development in relation to the activities of the Division. The independent accounting systems also were in general explained by responses to the operational characteristics of specific units within departments. These may be interpreted as diffusion effects on these units in a need to articulate with the dominate official accounting systems, and/or as responses to particular information needs of these units which are not meet by the dominant systems. The sacred or secular classification of the departments, therefore, does not appear to effect the formal features of the Division accounting systems.

Second, not unexpectedly, variation in sacred or secular classification does appear to be correlated with variation in accounting expertise across the departments, although again Welfare Services may need to be treated as a special case. It does appear as if the alignment of occupational views about accounting is related to the sacred orientation of the sacred departments and the particular financial secular orientation of Finance and Administration, as proposed in chapter 2.

Accounting Systems I *121*

Finally, two aspects of operations in Mission Outreach appear to contradict the expectations of the sacred and secular divide proposed in chapter 2. The existence of the Seven Year Plan and its management by the Finance Committee in this most sacred of the Division departments seems to indicate independent moves towards greater use of accounting, rather than resistance to it. These findings need to be explained in later analysis.

Summary of Formal Accounting Systems

This section has described and analysed the formal features of the two main accounting systems of the head office structure of the Northern Division; the Management Accounting Control System and the Budgeting System. It has also considered the applicability of these systems across the four Division departments and any variation apparently related to their sacred or secular orientation and dominance by accountants or sacred occupational groups. Several important theoretical issues have been identified during the discussion. These are commented on below.

First, the Management Accounting Control System and Budgeting System were stated to be highly developed systems. The former structurally had a strong budgetary control focus which potentially enabled a financial gaze into and of the cost centres of the Division. Thus giving a financial visibility of very detailed levels of the head office operations of the Division. Similarly, the Budgeting System structurally integrated the activities of the departments along a financial dimension, except for Welfare Services, and potentially focused attention on the competition for the allocation of financial resources between them. This was particularly so for Educational Activities and Mission Outreach, which were net drawers on the Parish contributions to the budget. Also, the coverage of these systems, or the use of adjunct systems, did not appear to be related to their use in sacred or secular departments. This may be interpreted as indicating a strong structural penetration of the systems within the Division. In sum, the formal features of these two systems indicate that the accounting systems of the Division were fairly sophisticated.

One implication of this finding, discussed for the Management Accounting Control System, was that the sophistication of its design may be evidence of the effects of the processes of rationalization upon

122   *Managment Control in a Voluntary Organization*

the Division. This seemed to have occurred through professional accountants acting as consultants on 'appropriate' system design, and thus acting to diffuse business practices to the voluntary sector. It was also possible that the changes to this accounting system were in response to, at least perceived, financial pressures experienced by the Division early in its existence. This may be consistent with the effects of secular crises argued in chapter 2. This issue will be considered further in a later section. The fairly sophisticated nature of the Division accounting systems, therefore, may indicate that some level of rationalization has already affected management control in the Division.

Another implication that follows from this is that the technical sophistication of the accounting systems design may represent a crude measure of the level of significance of accounting within the Division. That is, the more technically sophisticated the design of the accounting systems of an organization, the greater the potential significance of accounting within the organization. The stress must be placed on potential, as it is theoretically possible that even 'state of the art' systems may not be used, and thus have no significance at all. This crude measure is consistent with the treatment of accounting systems in most accounting textbooks (for example, Horngren and Foster 1987). It is also consistent with arguments about the historical development of accounting systems by Johnson (1978, 1983) and Chandler and Deams (1979), and with Kaplan's (1984) arguments about the problems with modern management accounting practice. In addition, a similar inference is implied by part of Laughlin's (1984, Ch. 5) arguments about the level of significance of accounting systems in the Church of England. While it is recognized that contingency theory arguments would indicate that there can be no simple linear relation between sophistication of design and significance (for example, Otley 1980), it is proposed that a crude indication of the potential significance of accounting can be gauged from the technical sophistication of the accounting system design in an organization. On this basis it can be concluded at this point that there is high potential for accounting to be significant in the Northern Division. Whether this potential is realized is a question the remainder of this study will consider.

Second, a significant independent accounting system and formal financial management committee was found to exist in the

Accounting Systems I 123

most scared department, Mission Outreach. This was the opposite to the expectation arising from the department's sacred orientation and the dominance of its management by sacred occupational groups. Thus, this finding appears to contradict the theoretical arguments developed in chapter 2. This issue will be considered further in the remainder of this study.

Finally, as well as the above broader theoretical concerns, several findings seemed to be due to the specific context of this organization. For example, the relation of Welfare Services to the accounting systems and the use of some department accounting systems. The possibility of such specific organizational effects always needs to be recognized in any case study.

III. FINANCIAL DYNAMICS AND ACCOUNTING

In chapter 2 it was proposed that secular crises may prioritize secular control problems within churches, and thereby the deployment of rational management control practices. In the particular case of accounting practices, financial crises were indicated to be potentially the most relevant form of secular crisis. Above, it was suggested that one reason for the adoption of the MACS was concern over the limited financial resources of the Division. During the early stages of the field work the tight financial position of the Division was identified as a current concern. It seemed to be associated with heightened tension between the accountants and the sacred occupational groups over the use of the accounting systems. In this section, the existence of financial crises in the Northern Division is considered. The period analysed is from the start of the historical boundaries of the case study in 1977 (see chapter 3) up to the time of the fieldwork. This analysis will provide an insight into the relevance of the financial dynamics of the Division on the use of accounting.

The first subsection analyses the formulation of the budget from 1977 until the 1988 budget (the budget formulated during the period of fieldwork). This identifies key perceptions of the existence of financial crises within the Division. The following subsection considers the basis of these crises in the income and expenditure patterns of the Division. The section concludes with a summary of the major implications for the use of accounting systems within the Division.

Financial Crises and Budget Formulation

In 1987, the 10th anniversary year of Mainstream Church, the Department of Finance and Administration initiated, with the co-operation of the other Division departments, a programme called 'Before the Next Step' to promote the achievements of the budget (the Mission and Service Fund) to the Parishes. Part of this programme was the distribution of a four page pamphlet with a one page insert on the areas of contribution of the Mission and Service Fund to the 'life of the church'. The insert, inter alia, raised and answered the following question.

> **"Is the Mission & Service Fund adequate to meet all requirements?**
>
> The church, like each one of us, must live within its means. Activities dependent upon the Fund are still feeling the effect of drastic cutbacks in recent years. Without a significant increase in revenue, new initiatives in mission and new ventures in developing areas cannot be contemplated unless other existing programmes are to be curtailed" (Northern Division 1987c, insert).

The raising of this question and the form of the answer given indicates that 'in recent years' a state of financial restrictions has been a major feature of the Division budget. An analysis of the annual budget formulation reports[4] presented each year to the Annual General Meeting with the budget when it is approved show that such a perception has existed since 1977. A summary of the major budget formulation issues in these reports is given in Table 4.5.

Several patterns of concerns in Table 4.5 indicate that, at least during budget formulation, there has been a long history of a perception of limited financial resources. These patterns are:

i) The consistent pattern of initial budget submissions with sizable deficits indicates that the desires of Presbyteries and departments for financial resources to carry out their mission and other activities has always outstripped available funds. Further this 'expectations gap' of the Presbyteries and departments has been sizable in terms of percentage of projected income. There seemed to be, therefore, a constant feeling of limited resources.

ii) In all these cases, there was mention of Presbyteries and departments being asked to cut their plans. There was some searching for additional income, and church agencies were sometimes able to contribute more, but eliminating the deficits always seemed to mean cutting expenditure submissions. Therefore, Presbyteries and

Accounting Systems I   *125*

departments could be assumed to have had a fairly constant perception that their activities have been limited by the financial resources available.

Budget	Events and Issues
1978	An initial budgeted deficit of $339,149 (44% of projected income) was submitted to the Budget Conference. It was commented that it was difficult for departments to plan given the newness of Division. Many cuts that were felt to be 'emergency measures' for 1978 only were initiated. The final deficit approved was $21,342. However, the means for a balanced budget for this and future years was to be investigated. The report concluded with the statement that "We could have wished that the Mainstream Church was spared the trauma of the budget crisis. The way ahead in our church and community is not one of economic ease".
1979	The initial deficit considered by the Budget Conference was $180,595 (23% of income). Departments were asked for a severe revision of askings and it was acknowledged that a balanced budget meant elimination of new work and "in many instances even the current levels of work would have to be reduced". Extra income pledged from church agencies and reductions by departments and Presbyteries led to a balanced budget being recommended.
1980	For the first time a priority system was used at the Budget Conference to judge between competing claims. An initial deficit of $148,389 (18% of income) was considered. Adjustments by reductions in department expenditures, increases in agency contributions, appropriations of net Presbytery surpluses from previous years and challenges to Presbyteries to increase contributions resulted in a final deficit of $2,172.
1981	The Budget Conference considered an initial deficit of $271,038 (21% of income). $94,000 of expenditure was referred to committee for review. Further consultations resulted in reductions in askings of $168,150 and some increase in Presbyteries contributions. A final deficit of $82,733 was recommended.
1982	After evaluation of priorities and elimination of some askings, expenditure of around $1.6m was proposed to the Budget Conference. Even with the indications of an expected significant increase in income to be received from Operation Breakthrough this gave a deficit of $100,000 (7% of income). This was after elimination of almost all new work from askings. Due to the uncertainty of Operation Breakthrough a 'balanced budget' was recommended which included a 'faith component' of an extra $100,000 from Presbyteries' contributions.
1983	Initial askings considered by the Budget Conference exceeded income by $719,511 (42% of income). Major reductions in programmes were recommended but some were seen as unrealistic due to contractual and moral commitments. Investigations led to income being increased by $25,000 and final projected askings allowing for commitments as still $142,349 in excess of this. Scrutineers were appointed to review askings and a deficit of $130,723 was approved. Some of this was to be recovered by special grants from the Church Investment Service and Northern Book Shop. In addition, reports on how departments planned to reduce 1984 askings were called for.

Table 4.5: A Chronology of Major Budget Formulation Issues

126   *Managment Control in a Voluntary Organization*

Budget	Events and Issues
1984	Initial budget submissions were requested to be made on the basis of 1983 cost levels. This was to provide a constant basis of comparison as significant changes to reduce budget askings, as requested the previous year, were expected. These indicated a deficit of $106,636 (6% of income) before expected inflation increases of 8%. Additional contributions were sought from agencies, and departments were requested to reduce askings after allowing for expected inflation. A final deficit of $46,573 was approved.
1985	Departments and Presbyteries had been asked to limit askings to an 8% increase over the previous year. Initial submissions represented a 43% increase, some of this was due to the additional costs of the new management structure. This represented a deficit of $535,127 (33% of income), "an unacceptably high figure". Finance and Administration advised of extra income becoming available and of its intention to find a way to replace the loss Northern Book Shop contribution. In addition, cuts of $100,000 were requested. This left a final deficit of $135,127 to be recommended and approved.
1986	After discussions at the Budget Conference a deficit of $62,000 (2% of income) remained. How to reduce this further could not be decided, so the matter was referred to the Senior Management Group to consider how to present a balanced budget. After this process a final budget with a small surplus of $6,661 was recommended and approved.
1987	It was reported that the "process of preparing the [budget] has not been easy". There had been conflict between the needs and desires to expand and continue programmes and fit within the limitation of the available funds. The aim had been to have a budget where expenditures did not exceed forecast income, and a minimal surplus of $756 was consequently recommended and approved.
1988	Budget report stated that since 1983, "the preparation of the annual budget ... has been surrounded by tension and uncertainty as the difficult task of allocating limited income resources to a larger list of expenditure proposals was undertaken". To balance the budget (with a small surplus) it was necessary to reduce programmes in some departments, thereby increasing these tensions this year.

Table 4.5: A Chronology of Major Budget Formulation Issues - Continued

iii) In many cases, the attempts to eliminate deficits gave rise to comments about cutting new work from the budget, or cutting or restricting existing programmes. While not mentioned in Table 4.5, there were also many instances where the reports stated that there was a new activity that should be supported, but that sufficient funds were not available. This pattern indicates that not all of the 'expectations gap' was 'wish lists', and that the limited funds did restrict the actual activities of Presbyteries and departments.

iv) Despite the stated policy that the budget should be balanced (Northern Division 1977), there were many budgets where deficits were approved. This would seem to indicate that there was a

Accounting Systems I 127

perception that certain activities had to be conducted and balancing the budget was not morally or practically possible. However, the balanced budget policy recognized that the Division had limited resources and approval of these deficits was always accompanied with comments on how they could be financed and the difficulties involved in doing so.

v) The pressure on budget submissions increased after 1982. There were considerable attempts to limit expenditure and significant anticipated programme cuts were listed in the 1983 budget report (Northern Division 1982a,b). From this time onwards, budgets were generally limited to increasing in terms of inflation only. The total emphasis of the budget process appears to have been on expenditure containment within increasingly limited funding resources. This seems to have come to a minor crisis in 1985, with a major deficit approved. Since then the emphasis has been on strictly balancing the budget. To do so has necessitated significant expenditure reductions in the 1987 and 1988 budgets, with the latter being the first instance since the introduction of the new management structure where programmes and staff positions have been cut. In recent years, then, the perceptions of funding restrictions seem to have become a central focus of the budget formulation process, as the opening discussion in this subsection emphasized.

In summary, the budget formulation process in the Northern Division has continually been operating under a perception of limited financial resources. There is a long history of 'budget crises', even from the first budget of the Division. This perception seems to have increased in recent years to one of much tighter financial stringency. The 1988 budget report commented that there was significant tension between needs and desires for programmes and the level of available funds:

> "When the growth in income is less than the increase in expenditure needed to continue the existing programs there are going to be budgetary problems. These problems are increased when we want to expand existing programs or introduce new programs without reducing or eliminating existing operations" (Northern Division 1987b, p.74).

The history of the budget formulation process in the Northern Division, therefore, supports the existence of at least the perception of a series of financial crises surrounding the budget. Crises which have worsen since the 1983 budget. Thus, there appears to be a good basis for the view of senior staff expressed during the early stages of the

128   *Managment Control in a Voluntary Organization*

field work that a tight financial position has heightened the tension over the use of accounting. In particular, it would seem that the sacred occupational groups working in the sacred departments have a reasonable foundation for a view that financial resources, and their management through accounting systems, have acted as constraints on their activities. The sources of these constraints and how they have impacted on the departments is considered further in the next subsection.

Financial Trends and Impacts

This subsection analyses the income and expenditure trends in the Division budget over the period 1978 to 1986 and their impact on the Division departments[5]. It is difficult to get a clear overall picture of these financial trends for several reasons. First, the use of fund accounting, the lack of any consolidated statements of the funds beyond department level, and a matching lack of clear indications of all transfers between funds, makes the calculation of the overall financial position of the budget difficult from published or internal sources. Second, comparison of accounting reports over time was made difficult by changes in nomenclature, management structures and reporting formats. Third, not all of the financial information was published consistently for all of the time period, especially in the earlier years of the analysis period. Despite these limitations, it is felt that the data does give a useful general indication of the major income and expenditure trends for the budget.

The overall pattern in the total income and expenditure of the budget for 1978 to 1986 is shown in Figure 4.1 in 1978 dollar equivalents[6]. Total income performance appears quite reasonable for 1978 to 1984 as it was increasing faster than inflation, particularly in 1983. The sharp rise in that year was due to an extensive one-off budget promotion campaign called 'Operation Breakthrough'. However, since then there has been a sharp drop in total income in real terms back to around 1979 levels. As was indicated by the budget formulation discussion in the previous subsection, expenditure growth often exceeded income growth up to 1982, with deficits of 5.5% of income on average when income was increasing at about 3% per year. Since then, a much closer match between the two has existed, except for the reasonable surplus in 1984, indicating the much tighter

Accounting Systems I 129

attention to the official balanced budget policy. It should also be noted that the major deficit approved for the 1985 budget was avoided in practice. The major patterns for total income and expenditure in the budget, therefore, seem to be over expenditure up to 1982 and a sharp decline in income in real terms after 1984.

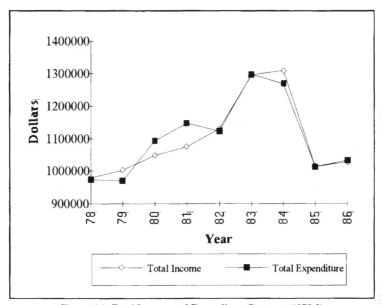

Figure 4.1: Total Income and Expenditure Patterns (1978 $)

The perceptions of budget related financial crises, therefore, appear to have two different causes within the overall financial dynamics of the Division. In the early years of the Division, they seem to have been related to the expansion of programmes faster than income growth, which itself was quite steady for many years. Crisis in this period then may have been more one of having growth reduced rather than really financially constrained. However, since 1984 the crisis has been one of a significant decrease in the available level of financial resources following from the sharp income decline. It is not surprising, therefore, that there were perceptions of a tightening financial situation for the Division and that this was associated with a focus on 'cutbacks in recent years' and consequently as a constraint on department activities.

What has been the cause of the decline in total income? Two sources generally accounted for over 90% of total income from 1978 to 1986; contributions from Parishes and from church agencies, with the former being dominant by a ratio 2.5 to 1 on average. Figure 4.2 displays the trends in Parish and agency income contributions to the budget in 1978 dollar equivalents. The trend for Parish contributions is relatively stable in real terms. It declined slightly to 1981, then recovered and has basically remained at around 1978 levels since, although there may be a slight downward trend after 1984. This general stability in Parish contributions is related to a similar general stability in the membership levels of the Northern Division. Table 4.6 shows the percentage of Parish income derived from pew and other offerings, which demonstrates that giving by members is the dominant source of funds for Parishes. With a stable membership, it would be expected that Parish contributions would change significantly only if average giving per member increased or decreased significantly, which does not seem to have occurred. Parish contributions, therefore, do not appear to be the cause of the fluctuations in total income.

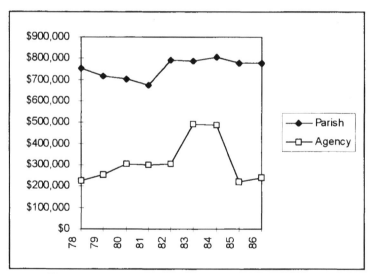

Figure 4.2: Trends in Parish and Agency Contributions (1978 $)

In contrast, the pattern for contributions from church agencies is more volatile and shows a sharp decline after 1984. Two agencies

Accounting Systems I 131

provided almost all of these contributions over the period, the Church Investment Service (CIS) and the Northern Book Shop (NBS). As mentioned in chapter 3, CIS acts as a 'banking' service for the Division departments, agencies, Parishes and members. Financially, it has performed strongly since 1977 and has experienced significant growth. While it experienced some minor financial difficulties in the early 80s, since 1983 it has continued to make sizable direct financial contributions to the total income of the budget. The same pattern does not exist for NBS. In the 1970s and the early 1980s, NBS was a major northern region bookseller and contributed significant funds to the Division. However, it suffered a loss of profitability in 1984 and made no financial contributions to the Division from 1985 onwards, resulting in lost income contributions of about \$200,000 per year. The continuation of this poor financial performance with little prospect of a turn around in the foreseeable future, and the need for the injection of capital to achieve any trading improvement, led to NBS's sale in late 1987. To offset the loss of the NBS contribution after 1985, CIS would have had to increase its level of contribution by 57%. A figure that had not been achieved by 1987. In fact, in real terms the contribution of CIS decreased slightly in 1986. It appears, therefore, that the trading failure of NBS after 1984 led to the loss of a significant 'commercial' funding source for the Division. This appears to have been a major cause of the drop in the Division's income after 1984.

Presbytery	1978	1981	1983	1985	1987
Region 1	77.6	80.2	78.8	79.2	82.0
Region 2	81.7	85.8	88.5	91.1	88.5
Region 3	84.6	87.6	88.4	88.8	88.7
Region 4	83.4	82.2	84.1	88.8	82.5
Region 5	82.1	85.2	84.1	87.0	83.9
Region 6	82.0	82.3	84.6	85.0	85.3
Region 7	87.0	88.4	83.6	87.6	86.0
Region 8	86.7	85.5	83.1	87.3	88.2
Average	83.1	84.7	84.4	86.8	85.6
Source: Department of Finance and Administration presentation to the 1987 Annual General Meeting					

Table 4.6: Percentage of Total Parish Income Derived from Offerings

A major cause of the increased financial crisis in the Division since 1984, therefore, has been a loss of a significant commercial funding source and the apparent inability of other agencies or Parish contributions to make up the decline in total income. At the time of

132 *Managment Control in a Voluntary Organization*

this study, the perception that the total income available for the budget would be declining or static seemed reasonable, unless either new funding sources could be found, church membership significantly increased or giving per member increased.

How did this decline in income affect the expenditure patterns of the budget, particularly the share going to the departments? Two categories account for over 90% of the distributions of budget income, grants to the departments and to the Presbyteries, with the former being by far the major category. Grants to departments remained fairly stable in real terms (1978 dollar equivalents) up to 1982. They then increased significantly until they declined sharply to below 1978 levels from 1985 onwards. In contrast, although the absolute level has been minor, grants to Presbyteries have increased fairly steadily over the period, except for a small decline in 1983. There appears to be, therefore, a trend for funds to be diverted away from the departments to Presbyteries in relative terms, although departments still get by far the bulk of funds (a ratio of about 8 to 1 in 1986).

The implication of this trend is that the Division departments have experienced a larger proportional fall in distributions than the rate of income decline since 1984. In fact, grants to Presbyteries increased about 25% in real terms in 1985, although they were basically static in 1986. Some of this recent increase in Presbytery funding is related to the establishment of full-time Presbytery Officers in several Presbyteries. A policy decision was taken at the 1986 Annual General Meeting that, in principle, all Presbyteries should have a full-time Presbytery Officer (Northern Division 1986b, minute 86.74). This policy was to be phased in over three to four years for those Presbyteries not already having such a position, commencing with at least one additional officer in 1988. This policy should eventually lead to about four additional appointments. The Annual General Meeting minute recognized that this decision would have an impact on the budget of about $40,000 per appointment per year and directed Finance and Administration to make provision for these appointments in the 1988 and future Budgets. This policy could be expected to continue the relative movement of funds away from the departments. It seems, therefore, that the brunt of the financial crisis problems after 1984 fell directly on the departments and could be expected to continue to do so.

Accounting Systems I   *133*

Year	1983	1984	1985[*]	1986[*]
Division Secretary	NR	NR	$58,993 4.3%	$56,155 4.8%
Finance and Administration	$443,230 26.1%	$481,190 29.3%	----- 0.0%	$(55,884) (4.8)%
Mission Outreach	$873,708 51.5%	$797,872 48.6%	$857,812 62.8%	$746,670 64.1%
Educational Activities	$352,738 20.8%	$336,791 20.5%	$449,453 32.9%	$417,436 35.9%
Welfare Services	$26,787 1.6%	$25,680 1.6%	----- 0.0%	----- 0.0%
Total	**$1,696,463 100.0%**	**$1,641,533 100.0%**	**$1,366,258 100.0%**	**$1,164,377 100.0%**
NR = Not reported for that year. * Reporting change to show only net budget for Finance and Administration and Welfare Services.				

Table 4.7: Budget Allocations to Departments: 1983 to 1986 (1983 $)

Further insight into the impact of the financial crisis on the Division departments can be gained from their relative shares of budget allocations. Due to the change in the management structure in 1984, it is not possible to reconstruct these for the total period, however, comparable figures for 1983 to 1986 are available[7] (see Northern Division 1984a, 1985a, 1986a). These are shown in Table 4.7 in 1983 dollars. As indicated previously, Mission Outreach and Educational Activities are the major users of funds. Some changes in the relative shares of the departments can be seen over the period. The most significant is the gain in the size of Educational Activities compared to Mission Outreach, which had an 33% increase in 1985 while Mission Outreach had a 7% increase. Over the period, Educational Activities increased from about 40% of the size of Mission Outreach in 1983 to 56% in 1986. Also, these two sacred departments experienced a budget reduction in real terms[8] in 1986, Mission Outreach (13%) and Educational Activities (7%). The financial crisis impact on the departments, therefore, has mainly affected the two sacred departments most dependent on it for funds, Mission Outreach and Educational Activities. However, it would seem that most of this strain has affected Mission Outreach which has lost a significant budget share relative to its main competitor for funds, Educational Activities.

In summary, this subsection has analysed the income and expenditure trends in the Division budget over the period 1978 to 1986 and their impact on the Division departments. The aim has been to

134   *Managment Control in a Voluntary Organization*

identify the sources of the perception of crises that has surrounded the Division budget. Total income and expenditure trends revealed that there were two distinct types of crises. First, up to 1982 the budget crises appear to have been caused by expenditure demands exceeding the growth in available income. Second, after 1984 the crises were caused by a sharp decline in total income in real terms. The major source of this drop in income seemed to be loss of contributions from commercial orientated church agencies and the inability of contributions from Parishes to fill this gap. It appears reasonable to assume that this trend would continue for the immediate future. This latter trend seems to be the source of the perception by senior staff of the 'tight financial position' of the Division identified during initial field work. It was concluded, therefore, that there was a strong financial basis to the perceptions of budget crises since 1984.

Such drops in income in real terms must obviously have an impact on those Division units dependent on the budget. Expenditure trends revealed that the main brunt of these impacts have been borne by the departments. While they still take the bulk of funds, they have steadily lost share to the Presbyteries, a trend which is likely to continue in the immediate future under the Division policy to create more full-time staff positions in Presbyteries. Another factor increasing this effect is hidden within the trends. The introduction of the new management structure after 1984 added a new layer of cost for the departments in the form of the salaries of the Directors[9]. This was equivalent in size to the decline in agency contributions. Thus greater pressure was placed on department budgets. However, this pressure has not evenly impacted on all the departments. The two sacred departments most dependent on the budget have taken most of the impact of declining funds, with Mission Outreach faring worse than Educational Activities.

Summary and Implications

This section has considered the existence of financial crises in the Northern Division for the period 1977 to 1988. An examination of the budget formulation process revealed that there is a long history of perceptions of budget crises and that this concern has increased since 1983. This has been reflected in greater adherence to the official balanced budget policy of the Division. The early perceptions of crisis

Accounting Systems I 135

were seen to be related to expenditure exceeding income, but the increasing concern since 1983 has been associated with sharp declines in income. These declines have resulted in parallel sharp decreases in budget expenditure in real terms. The majority of the impact of these expenditure reductions have been borne by the Division departments, with the two sacred departments of Mission Outreach and then Educational Activities experiencing most of the impact. The Northern Division, therefore, has experienced a worsening financial crisis since 1983 that has impacted most on the activities of the sacred departments.

The aim of this analysis was to consider the potential impact of such a secular crisis on the Division. In chapter 2, the theoretical implications of such crises was argued to be an increase in the relevance of rational management control practices and those occupational groups promoting such solutions. In particular, financial crises may be expected to increase the relevance of accounting and accountants within the organization. However, such increased relevance would be resisted by sacred occupational groups who would prefer to interpret the secular crisis in sacred terms and apply their own occupational solutions. Indications of such effects were observed in the initial period of field work. There appeared to be a significant tension between accountants and sacred occupational groups over the use of the accounting systems and the interpretation of how to respond to the financial crisis. Given the picture of the financial dynamics of the Division developed in this section, the potential implications of these tensions can be identified in more detail.

First, the continuance of the financial crisis into the time period of this study will continue the apparent heightened relevance of accounting and accountants to its solution. There were indications that church accountants seem to see this crisis as a financial reality that must be adapted to, which has been matched by a continued programme of expenditure cuts to match declining income.

Second, the addressing of the financial crisis through expenditure cuts will make it be perceived as a sacred crisis in the sacred departments as it will involve cuts to their mission programmes. This will increase resistance to the use of accounting and accountants' solutions to the crisis. Most of this resistance should come from Mission Outreach and Educational Activities as the two sacred departments affected in this way, with Mission Outreach potentially being the greater source.

Third, the key arena through which these tensions should be played out is the Budgeting System. This is the mechanism through which the financial dynamics of the Division are brought to bear on the activities of the sacred departments and in which alternative solutions to the crisis will compete. Thus, it should be the main arena of conflict between the accountants and sacred occupational groups of the Division. Also, such tensions are likely to spill over into the budgetary control element of the Management Accounting Control System.

IV. CHAPTER SUMMARY

This chapter has analysed the formal features of the accounting systems of the head office structure of the Northern Division and their potential linkages to the financial dynamics of the Division. Detailed summaries of the findings of each stage of the analysis have been provided within the chapter. These findings have indicated both the potential for accounting to be significant within the Division and some of the factors that may affect the achievement of this potential. The major implications of these findings are summarized below.

It was proposed that the high technical sophistication of the accounting systems of the Division indicated a high potential for accounting to be significant within it. The potential for a significant impact of accounting was also indicated by the substantial structural penetration of the accounting systems within the Division departments. These are admittedly crude measures, but they provide one basis against which the uses of the accounting system in practice can be gauged in chapters 5 and 6.

In addition, the creation of this potential appeared to be related to the penetration of rational management control technologies into the Division through the importation of the occupational ideas of professional accounting consultants. Therefore, the technical sophistication of the accounting systems evidenced previous impacts of the processes of rationalization upon the Division. Also, there was some indication that the perceived need for such modernization was related to financial pressures within the Division.

Accounting Systems I 137

Such financial pressures were found to be related to a long history of a perception of budget crises within the Division. Since 1977 there has been strong pressure to contain the expenditure of the Division head office activities funded through the budget. Since 1983, this pressure has increased, with a sharp decline in budget income in real terms leading to increasing needs for expenditure cuts to balance the budget. The Northern Division, therefore, has experienced a worsening financial crisis in recent years.

The extent and long history of the Division's financial crisis suggests that the basic environmental uncertainty for the Division has shifted from sacred membership issues to secular financial ones. In chapter 2, membership issues were argued to be one of the dominant control problems with which voluntary organizations, including churches, are concerned. Since the early 1980s the membership levels of the Mainstream Church and the Division have been basically static. As a tentative inference, therefore, it is proposed that financial uncertainties have replaced membership uncertainties as the major environmental issue facing the Division. Following the arguments in chapter 2, such circumstances would mean that the competitive advantage in providing solutions to the major uncertainties facing the organization have shifted from the clergy and other sacred occupational groups to accountants. That this may have occurred was indicated by the importance placed on the need to solve the financial crisis by senior Division staff.

Anticipating the analysis in the following chapters, the potential effects of such a change in the major control problems of the Division may have been related to the apparent tensions between accountants and sacred occupational groups within the Division observed during the initial period of field work. During interviews the accountants argued that the accounting systems were necessary to rationally manage the Division, and to discipline the activities of the sacred occupational groups, particularly in view of the pressures of the financial crisis. This seemed to indicate a preference by accountants to substitute management control technologies for trust as the basis of managerial relations within the Division. In contrast to this position, in their interviews the sacred occupational groups evidenced some areas of resentment of the accounting systems, and appeared to resist the view that accounting could assist them in rationally adapting to the financial crisis. Their preference was to solve the financial crisis in a

138　　　　*Managment Control in a Voluntary Organization*

way that did not constrain their sacred activities. Such resistance may be expected to be heightened by the increasing negative impacts of the financial crisis on the ability to support sacred activities. Accountants and sacred occupational groups, therefore, appeared to have different occupational views on how and whether the potential significance of the accounting systems of the Division should be achieved. However, one possible exception to this tendency which needs to be explained was the apparent efforts directed at financial control (the Seven Year Plan and the Finance Committee) in the most sacred department, Mission Outreach.

The indications of the analysis so far, therefore, are that the achievement of the potential high significance of the accounting systems of the Northern Division is related to their prioritization by the increased emphasis on secular financial control problems arising from the financial crisis, the promotion of such accounting control solutions by the accountants within Finance and Administration, and the opposition to such solutions by sacred occupational groups in the sacred departments. The effects of the financial crisis and the actions of occupational groups on the use of accounting within the Division is considered further in chapter 5.

Notes

[1] This analysis is based on interviews with key head office accounting staff, the four department Directors and examinations of official documents and accounting system output. The discussion represents an 'official view' of the accounting systems and how they should operate.

[2] The accounting system documents refer to both profit and cost centres as cost centres. Both types existed in the system but the large majority were cost centres.

[3] Excluded from the discussion are the independent accounting systems of semi-autonomous church agencies discussed under the coverage of the Division systems above.

[4] These reports cover the 1978 to 1988 budgets (formulated in 1977 to 1987 respectively). See Northern Division, 1977, 1978, 1979a, 1980a, 1981a, 1982a, 1983a, 1984a, 1985a, 1986b, 1987b. No budget recommendation was available for the six months of operations during 1977 as the first Annual General Meeting of the Division was not held until October of that year. All these reports, except that of 1985 which only had two brief paragraphs, contained several pages of comments on budget outcomes, the process of budget formulation and changes to department activities. They

Accounting Systems I

139

provide an historical account of the perceptions of those preparing the budget on the planning issues and the financial situation faced by the Division .

[5] The analysis is based on the annual audited financial statements of the Northern Division and the annual reports of the Department of Finance and Administration, and its predecessor, the Budget and Finance Board, to the Annual General Meeting. No figures are given for 1977 as that year only had a six month financial period. It would not, therefore, provide a valid basis for comparison to the other years. The figures also exclude the internal income sources of the departments. It was not possible to reconstruct these contributions in a manner consistent with the other figures analysed in this subsection due to a lack of detail in the financial reports. This does not represent a major problem, however, as generally all such income is retained by each department and in total it is smaller than that going through the budget. Therefore, the income figures in this subsection represent the discretionary income that is available for distribution through the budget.

[6] To provide a better basis for examination of trends over this nine year period the figures have been adjusted for inflation using the Consumer Price Index: All Groups Index prepared by the Australian Bureau of Statistics.

[7] Note that 1983 preceded the new management structure but reconstructed figures for that year were provided as a comparison to the 1984 figures in the report for that year.

[8] In actual terms the budget of Educational Activities increased slightly in 1986 and that of Mission Outreach decreased.

[9] According to the structure design these salaries would be made up by efficiency savings within two to three years. It was the view of all senior staff that this had not occurred and that the new positions were an additional drain on the budget.

Chapter 5
Accounting Systems II: How is
Accounting Used in Practice?

I.   INTRODUCTION

It was concluded in chapter 4 that the technical sophistication of the accounting systems of the Northern Division indicated the potential for a significant impact by accounting. However, the possibilities of achieving this potential appeared to be related to the efforts by accountants to promote the greater relevance of accounting to the management of the Division, and the resistance to such use by the sacred occupational groups. Also, the efforts of accountants may have been aided by the financial crisis of the Division prioritizing financial secular control problems to which accounting solutions seemed most relevant. In this chapter, the extent to which, and the ways, that accounting was actually used within the head office operations of the Division is analysed. The aim of this analysis is to examine the level(s) of significance of accounting within the Division, and to present explanations for the ways in which it was used drawing on the theoretical and empirical arguments presented in the previous chapters.

The analysis of the levels of significance of accounting within the Division is based on three types of data. First, process measures of the level and types of uses of accounting are employed to provide quantitative evidence on the extent to which accounting is used within the Division. As such measures have limitations, the judgment on significance also relies upon a qualitative assessment of the extent and ways that accounting was used, based on detailed non-participation observation in a range of settings. Also, key issue cases are analysed to

141

142   *Managment Control in a Voluntary Organization*

support and amplify the qualitative judgments from the observation data. Together, these three analyses provide a strong basis on which to gauge the levels of significance of accounting within the Division, and the reasons for the levels observed.

In conducting the analysis, distinctions are made between the uses of accounting by sacred occupational groups and by accountants. This enables the arguments presented in chapter 4 of the potential importance of these two occupational groups to the significance of accounting to be assessed. Such a segmentation of the analysis is also pragmatic, as the sacred occupational groups and accountants were generally located in different sections of the Division. The accountants, particularly all those with senior management responsibilities, were located primarily in Finance and Administration, the secular support department of the management structure. The ministers and other religious specialists comprising the sacred occupational groups were located in the three sacred departments, and also dominated the Divisional Council. As argued in chapter 4, this structural differentiation of sacred and secular orientations, and types of occupational groups, would provide the potential to assess the relevance of both these dimensions to the significance of accounting if another secular, non-accounting comparator was available for Finance and Administration. However, it was the only secular unit of the management structure, and it had a particular focus upon the financial management control responsibilities of the Division. Therefore, due to the absence of any comparators to assess the effects of secular orientation on the significance of accounting separate from the actions of accountants, the analysis in this chapter will concentrate upon the occupational group level of analysis.

The chapter is organized into three main sections. The first section examines the significance and uses of accounting by sacred occupational groups within the sacred departments. The next section examines the same issues for accountants in Finance and Administration. The third section extends the discussions in the first two sections to consider tensions between accountants and sacred occupational groups, including a discussion of the issue of trust. The chapter concludes with a summary of the results and implications for chapter 6.

Accounting Systems II 143

II. USES OF ACCOUNTING BY SACRED OCCUPATIONAL GROUPS

This section analyses the uses of accounting by sacred occupational groups. The aim of this analysis is to understand to what extent, how and why accounting practices are used by these occupational groups. As explained above, sacred occupational groups are primarily located in the three sacred departments. Chapter 3 detailed the orientation of data collection around the activities of these departments. However, due to access problems, it was not possible to evaluate the activities of staff in Welfare Services in the same depth as Educational Activities and Mission Outreach. Therefore, analysis here is restricted mainly to these two sacred departments. In addition, the sacred occupational groups of all departments were prominent in the operations of the Divisional Council, a key policy and operational forum of the Division (see chapter 3). The uses of accounting within this forum are also discussed in this section[1]. Together, the analysis of these forums provides an assessment of the extent of, and reasons for, various uses of accounting by sacred occupational groups.

This section is divided into four subsections. The significance of accounting is assessed by a mixture of quantitative and qualitative evidence. The first subsection provides the quantitative assessment of the level of significance of accounting across the sacred departments and the Divisional Council. The next three subsections then provide a qualitative assessment of significance in Educational Activities, Mission Outreach and the Divisional Council, and propose explanations for the observed patterns.

Variations in the Extent of Use of Accounting by Sacred Occupational Groups

This subsection considers the relative uses of accounting across observed meetings within Educational Activities, Mission Outreach, and the Divisional Council. In chapter 4, the technical sophistication of the accounting systems was proposed as one measure of the significance of accounting, but only in terms of its potential to be used. One way of assessing the achievement of such potential is to quantify how frequently various types of accounting practices and ideas were used during interactions by sacred occupational groups in meetings;

144   *Managment Control in a Voluntary Organization*

the broad implication being the higher the level of usage, the more significant accounting was within the meetings. Such an analysis provides simple measures to meet Silverman's (1985a, 1985b) call to support qualitative analysis with quantitative analysis that gives "..a sense of the flavour of the data as a whole" (Silverman 1985a, p.140). The aim of the analysis in this subsection, therefore, is to provide a process measure of the significance of accounting.

The specific forums covered by the analysis are the Board and Directorate of Educational Activities, the Finance Committee of Mission Outreach, and the Divisional Council. The observation patterns for these forums were detailed in chapter 3. All meetings of the Divisional Council were observed, and 50% or more of the meetings of the Educational Activities' Board and the Mission Outreach Finance Committee, which can be considered a semi-random selection as circumstances determined which meetings were not observed. The typicality of the Directorate meetings observed was harder to determine as it had an irregular meeting pattern. Again, those observed may be considered a semi-random selection as circumstances determined the observation pattern. It is felt, therefore, that the analysis is indicative of the typical pattern of the extent of use of accounting within these forums during this time period.

To conduct the analysis it was necessary to code the field notes on observations of meetings by use and non-use of accounting, the type of interaction involved, and the type of accounting practice (if an accounting interaction). The final coding scheme[2] used is given in Table 5.1. All interactions during meetings were classified using these codes, except for procedural items (for example, confirmation of minutes and welcomes to new members). The codes were treated as mutually exclusive, with interactions being broken down into sub-units based on one code category being dominant. It is recognized that some of the coding categories may overlap in practice (which suggests an alternative coding procedure of multiple codes for any segment of an interaction), but the process of breaking down interactions into sub-units significantly mitigated such instances. Also, the simpler coding procedure was felt adequate as this analysis is used only as a general indicator of the significance of accounting. Once coded, the frequency of each type of code was counted for each meeting observed. Also, data on the time duration of interactions was available (see chapter 3). This enabled the calculation of the discussion time devoted to each code[3].

Accounting Systems II   *145*

The frequency and time interval (in minutes) results were calculated separately for each forum by each meeting observed. The overall patterns of the frequency and time results are summarized in Table 5.2. Only the detailed results for the 'type of accounting practice' codes for accounting interactions are shown as these are the main focus of the analysis. The non-accounting interactions were coded by the 'context of use' codes, but only the gross total of these codes are shown in Table 5.2. The accounting interactions were also coded by the 'context of use' codes, but these are not reported here.

GENERAL TYPE OF USE	
NA	**Non-Accounting** - Interaction did not use any accounting reports, numbers or concepts.
A	**Accounting** - Interaction did use accounting reports, numbers or concepts.
CONTEXT OF USE	
O	**Operational Decision** - Interaction was discussion of decision or policy that dealt with the past, current or immediate future management of the church or department.
S	**Strategic Decision** - Interaction was discussion of decision or policy that dealt with the future direction and aims of the church or department.
D	**Department Performance** - Interaction dealt with a discussion of the current or past performance of the department. Performance being broadly defined as efficiency and effectiveness of its activities.
U	**Unit Performance** - Interaction dealt with a discussion of the current or past performance of the an operational unit of a department. Performance being defined as above.
TYPE OF ACCOUNTING PRACTICE	
Y	**Accounting System** - Accounting usage referred to technical aspects of the operations of the MACS of the Division, particularly impacts upon sections of the Division.
R	**System Reports** - Accounting usage involved referring to regular reports generated by the MACS of the Division.
N	**Accounting Numbers** - Accounting usage involved application of numbers of an accounting nature to discussion, but no direct reference to MACS reports.
B	**Budget** - Accounting usage referred to an aspect of a past, current or future budget of the Division. This includes budget formulation issues and more general discussions of budget impacts.
C	**Accounting Concepts** - Accounting usage involved application of accounting concepts, e.g. cost, profits, to discussion but not numbers.

Table 5.1: Coding System Used to Classify Interactions During Meetings

However, a limitation of this analysis should be noted. To make reliable judgments about what level of accounting usage in the

146   *Managment Control in a Voluntary Organization*

Division is significant or insignificant requires comparative data of this type for other churches, voluntary organizations, or other organizational types. No comparable attempts to quantify the extent of usage of accounting in meetings in any type of organization was found in the literature. This makes it difficult to interpret the numbers generated by this analysis. Therefore, some simple judgment rules were applied. When either the total frequency or time duration usage of accounting codes (shown in bold in Table 5.2) was greater than 50% of interactions and the other was greater than 40%, then usage was judged to be of high significance. If either frequency or time duration usage of accounting codes was less than 30% and the other was less than 40%, then usage was judged to be of low significance. If both measures were in the intermediate position between these two rules, then significance was regarded as indeterminate. While ad hoc, these rules are felt to provide some common sense distinctions about the level of significance in terms of extent of usage, and, at a minimum, to provide a relative indication of the significance of accounting across the forums. It should be stressed that it is felt that some attempt at quantification, even with arbitrary elements, is better than no attempt (Silverman 1985a 1985b). Also, this measurement procedure provides a base on which future research may usefully build.

The results in Table 5.2 provide a picture of the relative usage of accounting across the forums. It should be noted that the pattern for both frequency and time duration within each forum are very consistent, which implies that basing the judgment rules on both may provide reasonable assessments of significance patterns. The implications of these patterns, given the judgment rules, are:

i) In both the Educational Activities Board and the Divisional Council, accounting appears to be of low significance. In the Divisional Council, both the frequency and time duration of use of accounting are less than 20%. The time duration for the Educational Activities Board is less than 30%, with frequency just slightly greater. Also, such a pattern was found to be consistent across almost all meetings of these forums. Reinforcing the point of the low significance of accounting in these two forums is the fact that budget related discussions comprise a large majority of accounting interactions (over 50%). Without the budget discussions, accounting would be of minimal significance in these forums. Accounting, therefore, is of low significance in the Educational Activities Board and the Divisional

Accounting Systems II 147

Council, with the discussion of the budget being the most used accounting practice.

MEASURE	NON-ACC. CODES TOT	ACCOUNTING CODES					
		Y	R	N	B	C	TOT
EDUCATIONAL ACTIVITIES BOARD							
Frequency	60	3	3		15	6	27
Code %	*69*	*3.5*	*3.5*		*17.2*	*6.8*	*31*
Time	516	15.5	14.5		123	44	197
Code %	*72.4*	*2.2*	*2.0*		*17.2*	*6.2*	*27.6*
DIRECTORATE							
Frequency	33		1	3	33	4	41
Code %	*44.6*		*1.4*	*4.0*	*44.6*	*5.4*	*55.4*
Time	209		2.5	15.5	153	16	187
Code %	*52.8*		*0.6*	*3.9*	*38.6*	*4.1*	*47.2*
FINANCE COMMITTEE							
Frequency	53	1	24		33	35	93
Code %	*36.3*	*0.7*	*16.4*		*22.6*	*24.0*	*63.7*
Time	106	6	58		65	77	206
Code %	*34.0*	*1.9*	*18.6*		*20.8*	*24.7*	*66.0*
DIVISIONAL COUNCIL							
Frequency	167		3	3	25	7	38
Code %	*81.5*		*1.5*	*1.5*	*12.2*	*3.3*	*18.5*
Time	891		11	14	54	28	107
Code %	*89.3*		*1.1*	*1.4*	*5.4*	*2.8*	*10.7*

Table 5.2: Significance of Accounting in Forums Dominated by Sacred Occupational Groups

ii) Overall, accounting is of high significance in the Directorate, with frequency of use greater than 50% and time duration only slightly below 50%. Also, the budget is by far the dominant accounting practice (approximately 80% of all accounting interactions). However, this pattern is not consistent across all meetings. In two of the meetings around the time of the Budget Conference, budget discussions dominated. If these meetings were not included, the remaining meetings would satisfy the judgment rules for low significance (frequency 33% and time duration 19%). Accounting, therefore, appears to be of cyclical significance in the Directorate, being high when the budget is being discussed, and low at other times.

iii) The Finance Committee easily satisfies the rule for high significance, with both frequency and time duration being over 60%. Unlike the Directorate, this pattern of high usage was consistent across all meetings. Also, while the budget was a major accounting practice,

148 *Managment Control in a Voluntary Organization*

there was much more use of other accounting practices in this forum. The high extent and broad usage of accounting within the Finance Committee is consistent with its formal role to oversee the financial management of Mission Outreach and help overcome its lack of accounting expertise, as noted in chapter 4.

iv) Within the accounting related interactions across all forums, there is a fairly consistent pattern of the relative significance of different types of accounting practices. As indicated above, the budget is the dominant area of usage of accounting. In most cases the budget is three or more times as significant than any other accounting practice. The only other accounting practice to have any consistent impact is that of accounting concepts. A notable pattern is the very low levels of significance of the MACS and use of its reports, except within the Finance Committee. This may be consistent with its formal responsibilities. However, the Educational Activities Board and the Divisional Council also have formal responsibilities to review financial performance, but dealing with accounting reports is very insignificant in these forums.

In summary, the aim of the analysis in this subsection has been to provide quantitative process measures of the relative levels of significance of accounting during meetings in forums dominated by sacred occupational groups. The advantage of such measures is that they provide more concrete comparisons of the extent of usage of accounting across different arenas. However, their interpretation in this case was difficult because of the lack of previous use of such measures by accounting researchers. Acknowledging this limitation, there appears to be a variable significance of accounting among sacred occupational groups. In two forums, the sacred occupational groups appeared to treat accounting as of low significance. In the Directorate, this was also the case for some circumstances, but not others. When the budget was being discussed accounting seemed to be a significant concern, but when it was not, accounting appeared to be of low significance. Against this pattern was the apparent broadly based high significance given to accounting by the sacred occupational groups in the Finance Committee. This may be associated with the formal financial management function and responsibilities of this Committee. However, this does not appear to be a total explanation as all the other forums also had such responsibilities (although not to the same degree), but with much lower levels of accounting usage. Possible

Accounting Systems II   *149*

reasons for the high usage of accounting by sacred occupational groups in this forum will be addressed in the remainder of the chapter.

These findings provide one indication of the level of significance of accounting when it is used by sacred occupational groups within the Division. However, it should be stressed that process measures indicate nothing about the relative impact of accounting on outcomes within sacred forums. Thus, a use of accounting which appears to have little significance in terms of length of time of discussion may be much more or less significant in terms of the effects that it has on the actions of sacred occupational groups. To assess such matters, the quantitative evidence on the significance of accounting for sacred occupational groups provided in this subsection must be considered against other qualitative measures. In the following subsections, overall qualitative observational assessments and key issue cases are presented to clarify the impacts of accounting when it is used by sacred occupational groups.

Department of Educational Activities

This subsection considers the use of accounting by the sacred occupational groups within the Department of Educational Activities. As indicated in the previous subsection, two forums within this sacred department are considered, its Board and Directorate. The discussion is based on a qualitative analysis of non-participant observation data on the interactions during meetings of these two forums. Each forum is considered separately below.

Board

The analysis in the previous subsection indicated that accounting was of low significance in the Educational Activities Board, with budget related discussions being the most prominent use of accounting. This inference of low significance is supported by the low importance attached to accounting matters by the sacred occupational groups in this forum during these interactions.

First, when MACS reports were presented to the Board, little interest was evidenced in them. No reports, or any other indications of the financial performance of the department, were presented until the June meeting[4], nor had any questions been asked about such matters. From the June meeting, the reports were not circulated prior to the

150 *Managment Control in a Voluntary Organization*

meeting and the limited number of copies made available at meetings were not actively reviewed by members. Also, there was usually little discussion of the Business Manager's verbal report to the meetings. The MACS reports, therefore, were not actively used to discuss the financial performance of the department, or as inputs to its other discussions.

Second, in the limited number of cases where accounting, other than the budget, was used in discussions, there was usually minimal or no supporting numbers or analysis given. The level of impact tended to be a vague, general use of accounting concepts, which were treated as secondary and tangential to the main issue being discussed. For example, the fees for lay preacher education courses run by the theological college were reduced from $50 to $20. The recommendation supporting this reduction indicated that this would not cover the full cost. However, no details of the budgetary implications of this shortfall were given, and the decision was made without opposition, or any apparent concern over the indefinite accounting implications, because of the mission needs for lay preacher education. In general, accounting matters appeared to be considered as very secondary to the mission priorities of the department.

Third, even though there were a number of budget related discussions in this forum, these did not involve the active use of budgeting as a 'rational' financial planning device, or even as a political device. Instead, these discussions indicated that the sacred occupational groups perceived a tension to exist between the use of the budget to direct their priorities and the dominant role of sacred ends. Two of the major budget discussions illustrate these tendencies.

The first major budget discussion (see Case 1) involved the initial discussion of the department's submission for the 1988 budget. It illustrates that the sacred occupational groups were not interested in the details of the budget documents, they were interested only in the budget's aims. Also, the ignoring of the Finance and Administration's budget parameter of a reduction in real terms, in favour of a large gambit claim denotes the rejection of a financial planning role for the budget. However, the use of the 'gambit budget' terminology and idea does seem to indicate the adoption of a more political approach to the budget (for example, Covaleski et al 1985). When the 'gambit budget' was challenged on such grounds as being a dishonest secular approach, it was pointed out that the aim was not political manoeuvring, but the

Accounting Systems II 151

expressing of the mission priorities of the department. The gambit claim was not padded, but was a signal of the development directions the department wanted to pursue. Given the prospect of cuts, this was not a very viable, or likely, political budget strategy. Instead, the role selected for the budget was as a promotion device for the sacred ends of the department. The financial or political 'realities' that a budget could be used to address were not seen as relevant. Of prime, and only, concern were the sacred functions of the department.

Case 1 - The Gambit Budget Submission

The Business Manager (BM) presented the draft 1988 budget submission to the April meeting of the Board. There were limited copies available at the meeting and few members made any attempt to look at those available. The BM outlined that Finance and Administration had advised that the overall parameters that should be assumed in preparing the budget were costs growth of 8.5% and income growth of 3.5%. Therefore, with limited independent income sources, the department would be facing a reduction in activities. Despite this the senior staff had decided to submit a gambit budget which included desired areas of programme expansion. The budget represented about a 33% increase over the 1987 budget. The head of the theological college commented that this strategy may be risky as, knowing that cuts would be needed, others outside the department may decide them. Several other staff of the department argued that it was 'preference expressing', and that defined fall-back positions could be built into the submission. The theological college head responded that a gambit budget represented a hidden agenda. This was not an honest approach to the budget, it was not a church approach but a secular approach. There was some expressed support for this argument, but it was also pointed out that the budget was not padded, it represented new programmes which the department wanted to pursue. The meeting decided to proceed with the draft and work on fall-back positions.

The second major budget discussion involved the reviewing of the outcomes from the Budget Conference (see Case 2). In this case, the financial crisis appeared to have a significant potential impact on the department through the draft 1988 budget. Sizeable cuts were proposed for the department (further details given in next subsection), but despite the potential created by these cuts for the budget to be used as a financial planning device or political tool, no interest was evident in using accounting actively in either of these ways at this point in time. There was obvious shock and disquiet shown at the level of the cuts, and the sacred occupational groups felt that something had to be done about them, but neither the budget or other accounting ideas were actively used to address these problems.

Overall, therefore, the indications for the Educational Activities Board were that accounting was regarded as of little significance by its sacred occupational groups. They made little use of accounting in their

152   *Managment Control in a Voluntary Organization*

decision-making and evidenced minimal interest in accounting reports. The formulation of the budget was the only area of any significant level of accounting discussion. Even here, however, accounting was seen as secondary, in either a rational or political sense, to the main focus of the department, the achievement and development of its sacred activities. In this regard, a limited role for the budget was seen as the promotion of the sacred ends of the department. However, this was merely as a convenient signalling device within the management structure, not any significant use of accounting practices.

Case 2 - Outcomes from the Budget Conference

The Business Manager (BM) commenced by outlining the means by which cuts for the total Division budget had been assessed during the Budget Conference. The BM outlined the significant expenditure cuts proposed and commented that he felt the department had been relatively hard done by in its share of cuts. He then stated that closer examination of the proposals since the Conference had led to him to the belief that the department could not make the savings and retain its current programme profile. The Director then commented further on some of the proposed cuts and why he agreed that they may not be viable avenues of savings. There were no significant questions about this scenario from members. Some questions were asked about what options were being looked at, but these were just items of clarification. There was no discussion at all over the justifications or effects of the cuts.

These findings illustrate the operation of the sacred and secular divide, as argued in chapter 2. The sacred concerns of the sacred occupational groups act to marginalize accounting to the department's theological education and other sacred ends. Also, the potential importance of the impact of the financial crisis through the budget is indicated. In this setting, however, the impact of this secular crisis does not appear strong enough to override the sacred concerns and prioritize greater relevance for accounting. Both these effects can be seen more clearly in the use of accounting in the Educational Activities Directorate.

Directorate

The Directorate had a cyclical quantitative significance pattern of accounting, being high when the budget was being considered and low when it was not. In the low significance situations, which principally involved the use of accounting reports, numbers and concepts, accounting was seen by the sacred occupational groups as only an adjunct to much broader discussions of the issues surrounding decisions. Accounting was not a major influence on these decisions,

Accounting Systems II 153

rather it was treated as one of a set of secondary constraints to their main, generally operational, focus. It was perceived as a minor boundary condition on decisions that should be addressed, but should not determine the outcome.

The more 'rational', although still marginalized, role given to accounting in these situations is still consistent with the sacred and secular divide. The generally operational nature of the decisions (buying a computerized library system, assessing the interest cost of a delayed land sale, the minute detail of the financial management of the publication of the church's magazine) did not directly bring the sacred activities of the department into question; that is, choices were not being made about sacred ends. The decisions were about the means used to attain such ends, but they did not in themselves have obvious immediate sacred impact. Accounting (and the financial implications of decisions) was seen as a clearly segregated secular support function that did not challenge the primacy of the sacred ends of the department. Whether this form of usage was because accounting did have some utility in making such decisions, or because people were drawing upon socially accepted understandings of how such decisions should be made, or both, does not matter. The primary factor that appeared to affect the extent of the use of accounting by sacred occupational groups was that it did not challenge the sacred ends of the church.

Case 3 - 'Initial Optimism'

The Director reported to the meeting that the budget submission reviewed at the previous Board meeting had been submitted to Finance and Administration. He stated that Finance and Administration had decided not to ask departments to redo their submissions even though there was a sizeable planned deficit. The Finance and Administration Director was looking at ways of reducing the deficit by himself. The Director stated that he and the Mission Outreach Director favoured putting more pressure on the Presbyteries to increase income. He felt that there would be a positive response to such an approach. He finished by stating that he would be having a meeting with the Finance and Administration Director to discuss options and that he felt there was a very positive approach to the budget process this year.

When accounting appeared to be of high significance in this forum during budget related discussions, the tension between accounting and sacred concerns was more overt. Three key issue cases (3 to 5) indicate the development of this tendency within this forum. In Case 3, the initial optimism within the department to the final outcome of their gambit budget submission is expressed. Cuts in the gambit

154   *Managment Control in a Voluntary Organization*

budget were to be expected, and there was nothing to signal at this stage that their core sacred activities would be threatened. Such a position was supported by the interpretation of the 'positive approach' being taken by the accountants in Finance and Administration, and the feeling that the financial crisis could be solved by increasing income from the Presbyteries. The budget at this point was perceived to be a fairly benign control technology with respect to the sacred activities of the department.

Case 4 - 'Feeling the Pinch'

The meeting started with the Business Manager outlining the cuts of $118,000 that had been made by Finance and Administration to the department's gambit budget submission. He stated that most of these were reductions of 'desires' to 'realistic', but still felt that Educational Activities had lost more than the other departments. Now, on top of these cuts, the three cuts scenarios had to be considered. He continued by stating that the level of cuts were of such magnitude that they meant people, staff or theological students, had to be cut. He did not see any potential for big boosts in department income, so $50,000 meant two staff had to be cut.

The Head of the Theological College then asked about the cut Finance and Administration had made in allowances for new students from 10 to 5. He stated that this meant the church was accepting a de facto cut in the size of the College (The Division had a policy authorising allowances for up to 10 new theological students per year. Allowances for 10 had always been put in the department's budget but, in the last few years, 2 or 3 students had been the normal College intake). The Director pointed out that this was probably not a problem as there were no known names of potential students at this time.

There was then extended discussion of the options for cuts and the existing financial pressure on the budget. During this the feeling was expressed that the pressure to balance the budget was leading to unrealistic figures that could not be met. The staff saw no way in which staff could be rationalized or by which ministerial education could be reorganized in the short-run. It was suggested that one option was to move financial responsibility for students back to their nominating Presbyteries. The meeting did not succeed in moving beyond the discussion of the problems with any options for cuts. None of the three requested scenarios were outlined. The discussion concluded with the decision to conduct an evaluation of ministerial education to identify long-term options.

About two months later, as described in Case 4, this attitude started to change, with the department being requested by the accountants in Finance and Administration to prepare cut scenarios of $50,000, $75,000 and $100,000 for discussion at the Budget Conference. The positive feeling about the budget process disappears in this discussion, as it is seen as impinging upon the sacred activities of the department. In particular, the potential for conflict with sacred ends is indicated in the concerns over the nominal cut in the intake of

Accounting Systems II 155

Case 5 - 'The Cuts Bite Home'

The Budget Conference had decided on substantial cuts to both the Educational Activities and Mission Outreach budgets. This meeting considered how achievable their cuts were and what other options may exist for operating within the same level of Division funding. The Director commenced by outlining the cuts. The first discussed were the further cut made to student allowances, which was perceived as a significant problem. It was suggested that a means for moving student allowances off the Division budget should be investigated. This would keep them out of the hands of the Budget Conference. It was also suggested that other proposed changes to student training may be outside the authority of the Division to impose on the College.

The discussion then moved to the Business Manager outlining the options he had reviewed to achieve the cuts. He felt there was some scope to increase the Hostel's income by increasing utilization during student vacations. Also, some cuts could be achieved by exercising very tight control over expenditure. Next, greater funds may be available through putting greater effort into continuing education training for ministers. This could possibly raise enough to cover the proposed $20,000 cut in the lay training budget.

These options were then discussed. The Head of the Theological College felt that prospective students already knew about allowances and may be put off by changes. The idea of moving allowances off budget, maybe through a separate capital fund, was raised again. Other options for increasing income were then discussed. The decision was then made to take the student allowances issue to the Annual General Meeting and to try to get it to change the budget. However, it was recognised that this would lead to conflict with Mission Outreach (It was perceived Mission Outreach would have to bear the additional burden if Educational Activities was successful). Prior consultation was felt necessary to avoid such conflict. Also, the need for a careful strategy of how to present the issue to the Annual General Meeting was recognised.

Next the discussion moved to the proposed $35,000 staff cut. It was felt that there was no way this could be coped with and the department may be already contractually committed for the next year. Again, the discussion moved to alternative fund raising options within the department, perhaps even more could be extracted from continuing education activities. The discussion was winding down at this point as it was felt enough details were not available to evaluate these options. It was agreed that these suggested options needed to be worked on and more detailed planning done to see how realistic they were.

theological students, even though recent experience would indicate no real restriction was being applied (or in actuality was intended by the accountants). The tension over the use of the budget to 'rationally' consider cuts to sacred activities surfaces in the perception of a lack of ability to make any cuts and the feeling of dealing with 'unrealistic figures'. Sacred occupational groups perceived that using the budget in this way would mean bringing it into direct confrontation with sacred ends. Instead, discussion focused on why the budget could (should) not be used in this way. At this time, therefore, the sacred and secular

156   *Managment Control in a Voluntary Organization*

divide came into play to generate resistance by the sacred occupational groups to the threat to sacred ends from the use of accounting.

The threatening nature of the budget was made even more obvious less than a month later when the Directorate had to discuss the cuts that had been requested of the department during the Budget Conference (see Case 5). In this case, the sacred occupational groups had to acknowledge that the budget may impinge on sacred activities. However, this did not mean that the logic of the budget was accepted. Again, discussion focused on ways of resisting this intrusion on sacred activities. Sacred ends were still the prime criteria of action.

An interesting approach adopted in this resistance was the use of budgeting ideas to help specify the boundaries of the problem, and how it might be addressed. For example, the budget was seen as a framework that specified sets of financial relations, both with other departments and for what programmes came under its discipline. Thus, the discussion could consider potential conflict areas, and strategies for moving programmes outside the budget's gaze. Also, the problem was reinterpreted as one of increasing income sources to avoid the need for the proposed cuts in sacred activities. Thus, accounting ideas were actively drawn upon as one way of resisting the conflict with the budget over sacred ends.

The sacred and secular divide, therefore, still determined the significance of accounting within the discussions of sacred occupational groups about the budget in the Directorate. Such secular concerns were always seen as secondary to the pursuit of sacred ends. However, the impact of the financial crisis of the Division did affect this process. When the crisis led to cuts being proposed to the sacred activities of the department, the use of a financial rationality to generate a greater conception of the ranges of action open to the department was evident. This represents the intrusion of accounting into the actions of sacred occupational groups, potentially constraining their views of appropriate managerial actions. However, the potential for such a rationality to also enable the construction of new avenues of resistance to the threat of the budget was also evident. Thus, while the financial crisis prioritized, through the impact of budget cuts, an accounting rationality, which seemed to weaken the dominant position of sacred ends within this department, it also paradoxically created the potential for new forms of accounting based resistance to emerge.

Accounting Systems II 157

In summary, in the vast majority of cases accounting played a very limited role in the actions of sacred occupational groups within the Directorate. Generally, when it was used, it was seen as a minor secondary constraint that may be addressed in the pursuit of sacred ends. The sacred and secular divide appeared to influence this marginalization of accounting even within the much higher levels of concern devoted to discussions of the budget. This resulted in conflict between the secular financial concerns of the budget and the sacred ends of the sacred occupational groups, especially when the financial crisis led to proposed budget cuts. The commitment of the sacred occupational groups in Educational Activities to their sacred ends meant that they actively sought ways to resist the financial logic of the budget. However, the conception of the conflict in such terms also tended to constrain their conception of their range of actions within a financial rationality. Paradoxically, this weakening of the sacred and secular divide also enabled accounting rationalities to be used to conceive of new forms of resistance. Despite these developments, the overall tendency still seemed to be for the dominance of the sacred over the secular.

Department of Mission Outreach

The process measures analysis indicated that accounting was of high significance to the sacred occupational groups of Mission Outreach during discussions in the Finance Committee. While there were still high levels of non-accounting interactions, this section of this sacred department seemed to make much more use of accounting than the other forums considered in this section.

It was suggested previously, that this high significance may have reflected the functional orientation of this Committee on the co-ordination of the financial management of the department (as explained in chapter 4). This suggests an alternative explanation for the resistance of sacred occupational groups to accounting argued in the previous subsection. It is possible that this was due, in part, to the setting in which they were involved, which had broader management responsibilities for the Department of Educational Activities. Some support for the effect of the more functional orientation to financial management issues of the Finance Committee on the significance of accounting was found in the common structure of meetings. There

158   *Managment Control in a Voluntary Organization*

were three major sections; General Business, where mainly building and development work on the department's Conference Centres (CCs) was discussed; the Financial Situation, where the latest MACS monthly reports were reviewed; and the Capital Development Fund, where loans to CC projects were considered[5]. The first two sections usually took most of the time in any meeting, with General Business dominating. Accounting was used in different ways in each of these sections.

Capital Development Fund discussions were usually brief. They were accompanied by a one page outline of outstanding loans, the month's repayments and advances, and new loans to be considered. Most loans were for minor amounts, usually less than $5,000 (the total fund was less than $100,000). There was typically little discussion of the situation, except to check that the programme of loans was within budget. Only on one observed occasion did a member challenge the loan programme as he was worried that things were becoming tight within the parameters of the Seven Year Plan (see chapter 4), although this did not generate much discussion. These interactions, therefore, appeared to be financially focused, with accounting concepts and budgetary implications being referred to when making decisions. However, this did not result in any detailed discussion of the financial dimensions of decisions by the sacred occupational groups.

General Business discussions dominated the meetings and usually involved significant references to accounting concepts and ideas by the sacred occupational groups. Questions were often raised about the costs of projects, how they could be fitted within the budget, and whether the financial performance of particular CCs warranted the programme or capital development being discussed. However, no observed use of the MACS reports to support these discussions was observed. Questions were generally answered from memory by a staff member, or the information was to be sought and presented to a later meeting. There was also significant discussion of the non-financial aspects of projects and decisions, but still it appeared as if financial control was a prime concern of the Finance Committee members.

This concern was expressed most strongly through the use of the Seven Year Plan as the primary focus for evaluating the financial dimensions of decisions. The sacred occupational groups regularly referred to the 'effects on the Seven Year Plan' during discussions. The Seven Year Plan was a programme of department operational

Accounting Systems II 159

income and expenditure, and the restructuring of CCs by a programme of sales and capital development, aimed at reducing the department's sizeable debt over the next 7 years. It was seen by members as a means by which they could solve the financial problems of the department. The strength of this view was expressed in the Chairman of the Committee referring to it as our 'Scheme of Arrangement'[6] during a meeting when the approval of the plan was being discussed with the Finance and Administration Director. The use of such terminology evidences a high concern within this Committee with the debt position of the department. The Seven Year Plan, and financial control issues in general, therefore, were prominent during General Business interactions, particularly in how to 'trade their way' out of their debt problems.

The Financial Situation section was the only part of the meetings where the MACS reports were used. Here a similar concern with financial control was evidenced. Members attempted to review the monthly performance relative to budget of the department as a whole and its cost centres. The causes of variances were discussed and any needed actions were explored. There seemed to be genuine interest in understanding how the department was performing financially, and why. Early in the year some difficulties in doing this were experienced because of problems in understanding the detail of the MACS reports. After several meetings, a summary variance report was produced, which identified only total income and expenditure for each cost centre, the favourable or unfavourable variance relative to budget for each, and brief comments on the causes of variances, if known. This summary report enabled more members to take part in the discussion and to focus more actively on identifying problems and actions. During this section of the Finance Committee meetings, then, significant use of accounting reports for financial control discussions was observed.

These varied uses of accounting by sacred occupational groups within the Finance Committee suggest a highly significant 'rational' use of accounting for financial control and decision-making within Mission Outreach. Part of the explanation for this focus on accounting seemed to be the specific responsibility of the Committee for oversight of the financial management of Mission Outreach. However, this secular support role orientation was, in turn, a reflection of the high debt burden of the department, which was stated as having arisen from the previous poor financial management. The sacred occupational

160   *Managment Control in a Voluntary Organization*

groups perceived that this problem had to be solved by 'better financial management' and 'trading their way' out of debt. The Seven Year Plan was a concrete expression of this concern. In addition, the emphasis on poor financial performance was reflected in financial control discussions often focusing more on unfavourable than favourable variances. This tendency was so strong that when it was reported in the May meeting that the department was ahead overall on the budget, there were shocked expressions and jokes made about the department being ahead of budget. No-one appeared to know how to deal with positive financial performance. Therefore, it was a specific financial crisis within this department (which was exacerbated by the more general financial crisis, as there was a perception of little likelihood of extra budget allocations to solve the debt problem), and a perception that this was related to previous 'poor' financial control, and had to be solved by 'better' financial control, which appeared to be associated with the high significance of accounting in this Committee.

However, does this high concern with financial control and a significant use of accounting mean that accounting was considered as more important than sacred ends by the sacred occupational groups? A consideration of how accounting interacted with sacred ends when sacred occupational groups attempted to achieve 'better' financial control suggests that this was not so.

First, the majority of the decisions considered within the Finance Committee did not seem to challenge any of the sacred ends of the department. They were about activities that were part of the established programmes of the department, and it was how these would be implemented that was decided, not whether they should be conducted. Accounting was used, therefore, as an implementation constraint on how sacred ends could be fulfilled, but not whether they should be fulfilled. Also, even in these situations, it did not appear as if the decision depended on the accounting constraints. Often, decisions were made before the full cost or budget implications had been worked out. The critical concern was their contribution to the mission goals of the department. In these situations, therefore, accounting was secondary to mission. Financial dimensions were recognised as implementation constraints, but not something that should conflict with sacred ends.

Second, the subordinate position of accounting was more overtly evident in those decisions where conflict between 'better' financial

Accounting Systems II   *161*

control and the sacred ends of the department surfaced. Case 6 demonstrates this in terms of a discussion of financial versus mission return on capital. The CC redevelopment project was recognised as pivotal for the ability of the Seven Year Plan to solve the financial problems of the department. Yet, despite the centrality of this decision to these critical financial issues, the primacy of mission over an accounting rationality was still asserted. The financial problems prioritized the need for some recognition of a minimum accounting return as one variable in the decision, but the dominant criteria was the achievement of the sacred ends of the department.

Case 6 - Financial versus Mission Return on Capital

A pivotal project in the Seven Year Plan was the redevelopment of one major CC. This involved the sale of some land to a shopping centre developer to raise funds to build a modern conference facility on the remaining land. This was by far the biggest single project in the Plan and the conference facility was seen as a key future income source for the department. During the March meeting the members were considering a full project budget on the proposed conference facility. The department's accountant led the meeting through the budget. The calculations he presented included a financial return on capital invested. At this point he commented that the projected financial return was very low for the large amount of funds involved and that he did not think the investment was worthwhile. This drew immediate comment from the Director that financial return was not the only return, CCs were a significant part of the mission outreach of the department. There was then several minutes discussion of the trade-off between financial and mission return. The outcome of this was that members agreed that these could appear to be in conflict but that financial return should not be considered the prime criterion. Programmes should always be assessed on their contribution to mission.

This issue of a trade-off between mission and financial return was also raised during discussions later in the year with the Finance and Administration Director on the approval of the parameters of the Seven Year Plan (see Case 7). Here again the secondary position of accounting to sacred ends was asserted. Interestingly, this position also seemed to be accepted by the Finance and Administration Director, the senior accountant in the Division. However, he appeared to have a different interpretation of this trade-off than the sacred occupational groups. To this accountant, the acceptable level of financial return was a more critical decision variable, and such accounting criteria were promoted as being much more relevant to the rationalization of Mission Outreach programmes than the sacred occupational groups seemed prepared to accept. They argued strongly against such views, with the financial rationalizations necessary to solve the department's financial problems expressed in the Seven Year Plan being seen as the

162   *Managment Control in a Voluntary Organization*

maximum acceptable intrusions on their mission programmes. Beyond this, sacred occupational groups felt that accounting criteria did not have a role to play in assessing mission programmes. Therefore, while the dominance of sacred ends over the use of accounting was accepted, there were also different occupational views on the extent of this dominance.

Case 7 - Seven Year Plan Approval

The Finance and Administration Director was present at the meeting to discuss the deliberations of the Finance and Administration Board on the parameters of the Seven Year Plan. The Board agreed with the policy objectives, had asked for updated income and expenditure projections given current knowledge, and the addition of a clear statement of recurrent programme plans. The latter point led to comments being made on the desirability of the current Mission Outreach programme structure, particularly CCs. The Finance and Administration Director commented on the low level of financial return for some CCs. He particularly commented that the planned major redevelopment (see Case 6) had a low projected return. He wanted Mission Outreach to examine its programme structure to ensure that further rationalizations could not be made. These comments prompted a discussion of 'what is an appropriate level of monetary return'. In response, the Finance and Administration Director said he recognised that there were other returns and that these had to be counted in determining what was an 'adequate' financial return. However, he urged Mission Outreach to consider if the level of return was adequate. The meeting agreed that there must be an adequate financial return but felt that the structure in the Seven Year Plan, combined with better management, would solve the financial problems.

In summary, the analysis in this subsection has indicated that there is significant use of accounting by sacred occupational groups in the Finance Committee of Mission Outreach. Accounting reports, concepts and the budget were used in reviewing the financial performance of the department, and its cost centres, and in making a range of operational and capital decisions on its programmes. In doing so, accounting appeared to be utilized as an input to 'rational' financial decision-making. The major reason for this significant use of accounting by these sacred occupational groups was the existence of a 'high debt burden' financial crisis within Mission Outreach, and a perception that this had resulted from previous poor financial control and had to be solved by improving financial control. Accounting, therefore, appeared to be significant in the actions of sacred occupational groups within this forum, but only because there was a perception of both a need to address a particular secular financial control problem and the relevance of accounting to its solution.

However, this significance given to accounting for this specific purpose did not mean that it was dominant in this setting. In the

Accounting Systems II 163

majority of instances where accounting was used, the sacred ends of the department were not challenged. Accounting was seen as one implementation constraint for activities whose existence had already been determined on sacred grounds. This secondary position of accounting within the Finance Committee was most strongly evident whenever financial dimensions of decisions came into conflict with sacred dimensions. In these cases, the dominance of sacred ends was explicitly stated and enforced. The sacred and secular divide, therefore, still acted to marginalize accounting within this forum. These findings suggest that the setting of use of accounting does have some effect on its significance, and therefore may be part of the explanation of its low significance observed in Educational Activities, but that the dominant factor across settings is the primacy given to sacred ends by sacred occupational groups.

Also, this secondary position of accounting seemed to be accepted by the most senior accountant in the Division. However, he appeared to have a different interpretation of the extent of the marginalization of accounting than the sacred occupational groups, favouring a much more active role for accounting in the determination of the sacred programmes of the department. Active resistance to such an increased role for accounting was evident in the preference of sacred occupational groups for a much more limited role for accounting. While the sacred and secular divide, therefore, acts to marginalize accounting, there is sufficient indeterminacy to this tendency for debate, conflict and resistance around different occupational interpretations to take place.

Finally, accounting played a part in the defining some of the parameters of this debate. The development of the Seven Year Plan by the sacred occupational groups in Mission Outreach as an accounting tool for addressing the department's financial problems provided a financial visibility into its activities that was not previously available. This enabled the accountants in Finance and Administration to conceive of how Mission Outreach programmes may be further rationalized, and to engage the sacred occupational groups in a debate on financial versus mission return that would not have been as concrete without this detailed financial expression of the mission programmes of the department. The playing out of debate, conflict and resistance over the sacred and secular divide between different occupational groups, therefore, is related also to how accounting

164 *Managment Control in a Voluntary Organization*

practices enable aspects of this relationship to be visible in the first place.

Divisional Council

The process measures for the Divisional Council indicated that the sacred occupational groups that dominated it (over 90% of the membership) gave very little significance to accounting in their deliberations. This is emphasized even more strongly if the qualitative nature of the limited accounting interactions is considered. In general, a large majority of the interactions involving accounting were one-sided communication processes where senior accountants from Finance and Administration, making up the small minority membership of the forum, either reported on the current financial position or other major financial matters affecting the Division. The two most common responses of the sacred occupational groups to these information items was no comment or minor questions of clarification. Also, where accounting was raised during debate over various policy or operational issues, it was invariably the Finance and Administration accountants that did so, not a member of a sacred occupational group, whose response to such issues was usually minimal. The way in which accounting was used, therefore, in the minority instances where it was involved in interactions in this forum, indicate that it was regarded as marginal to the concerns of the dominant sacred occupational groups.

However, an alternative interpretation may be that the silence of the sacred occupational groups on accounting matters within the Divisional Council indicated their acceptance of the accounting positions put by the Finance and Administration accountants. Such an explanation, though, is not consistent with the reactions of Divisional Council members in those instances in which some debate on accounting implications took place.

For example, the discussion of the establishment of non-stipendiary ministers within the church (Case 8) indicates that accounting, and financial matters, were secondary to sacred ends in the Divisional Council. This issue had major financial implications for the Northern Division, particularly as it had large, sparsely populated rural Parishes. The high per capita cost of meeting the stipend of ministers in rural, and some poorer urban Parishes, meant that less funds were available for Presbytery contributions to the Division budget. Also,

Accounting Systems II 165

these Parishes often made an expenditure demand on the budget through the Home Mission Grants programme of Mission Outreach, which provided grants or loans to help with financial problems in disadvantaged Parishes. Non-stipendiary ministry, therefore, had the potential for a significant positive financial impact on the budget by reducing both these effects, the need for which was heightened by the Division's financial crisis. However, the sacred occupational groups explicitly argued against the consideration of this option on such grounds, and none of the accountants at the meeting challenged this view. The sacred dimensions of non-stipendiary ministry were proposed as the only criteria sufficient to make a decision on this innovation in one of the most critical areas for the achievement of the mission of the church. If economic benefits were realized also, this would be a bonus, but they should not affect the making of the decision. Accounting and financial issues, therefore, were regarded as secondary to sacred ends.

Case 8 - Non-Stipendiary Ministry

A major item of business at the May meeting of the Divisional Council was the discussion of a report from national church level Committee for Mission on the possible establishment of non-stipendiary ministers. Non-stipendiary ministry involved the creation of part-time ministers, particularly for rural areas, who would retain their secular jobs or independent income sources and act as ministers of the word at no, or minimal, financial cost to the church. The report gave a wide variety of reasons for this option, but submissions from Presbyteries and comment at the meeting made it clear that the dominant perceived reason was the difficulty of meeting the cost of supplying full-time ministers. As one submission stated the "..paper assumes that the answer is in developing a non-stipendiary ministry for economic reasons". However, the submissions and meeting discussion, while supportive of the concept, argued strongly that economic consequences - the cost to the church - were not the grounds on which its suitability should be decided, no matter how severe the problem. The concept should be decided on the basis of its relevance to the mission strategy of the church. This position was endorsed by the Divisional Council without dissent.

However, the apparent general acceptance of the secondary position of accounting does not indicate a unity of views on this matter, as indicated by the role of the accountants above in raising accounting matters in this forum. In Case 9, the views of the Finance and Administration Director, the most senior accountant, suggest that he saw a much more active role for accounting within the Division. He wanted Presbytery representatives to more actively consider the resource implications of the budget and provide input on the financial planning of the Division. Also, he saw a greater role for the budget in

166   *Managment Control in a Voluntary Organization*

the centralization of the control and allocation of resources. Accountants, therefore, appeared to promote the greater significance of accounting to the sacred occupational groups and its use in decisions on sacred issues.

Case 9 - A 'Church View' on Financial Resources

In two separate discussions the Director of Finance and Administration put arguments that there needed to be a church view of the allocation of financial resources within the Division:

The first was a dispute between Mission Outreach and Welfare Services over the formal responsibility for Hospital Chaplaincy. Mission Outreach currently had sole formal responsibility through its mission outreach functions, but Welfare Services retained an active interest by contributing funds to the budget for this activity and its responsibility for church hospitals. The Director of Finance and Administration used this discussion to talk about the budget process, arguing that Finance and Administration was trying to encourage everyone to see resources as the resources of the church to be allocated by the church as a whole. The implication was that it was not the role of specific sections of the church to direct where funds should be expended or only to provide funds with specific covenants.

Later in the same meeting the Director of Finance and Administration reported on progress with the 1988 budget preparation and pointed out problems being experienced in eliminating a deficit at this time. He put a challenge to Presbyteries to look at ways of raising more funds and to evaluate their priorities for the direction of resource usage. The Director of Welfare Services commented that many Presbyteries financially assist individual Parishes but this was not recognised in the budget. For example, a wealthy Parish may assist a disadvantaged Parish because members have personal knowledge of its problems. The Director of Finance and Administration responded by arguing that he wanted Parishes, Presbyteries and church agencies to put funds into the Division budget and allow the church to choose priorities. The Director of Welfare Services replied that all Presbytery fund raising was effectively hidden from the church as a whole. No action was recommended by the Divisional Council from this discussion.

Within Case 9, the potential for opposition to greater usage of accounting was also indicated. There was some feeling that the centralization of resource allocation went against the 'rights', under the church's decentralized governance ethos, of Parish and Presbyteries to control their own management (this issue is considered further in chapter 6). Also, it was felt that giving may be depersonalized, as contributions would not be seen as linked to specific mission activities. It, therefore, appeared that the greater role for accounting promoted by accountants was not supported by the sacred occupational groups.

In summary, accounting was of minor significance in the Divisional Council, and to the sacred occupational groups that

Accounting Systems II 167

dominated it. It was infrequently used, and even when it was, accounting was seen as subordinate to the sacred ends of the Division. The sacred and secular divide appeared to act strongly through the sacred occupational groups to marginalize the relevance of accounting in this forum. Also, as inferred in the previous subsection, there was an indication that the accountants in the Division shared this view of the general relation of accounting to sacred ends. However, again as in the previous subsection, there appeared to be differing occupational interpretations of how much accounting should be marginalized, with accountants promoting a more active and central role for accounting.

III. USES OF ACCOUNTING BY ACCOUNTANTS

This section analyses the uses of accounting by the accountants within the Department of Finance and Administration. As in the previous section, the aim of the analysis is to understand to what extent, how and why accounting practices are used. This will provide a picture of the level of significance of accounting for accountants, and the possible reasons for this significance, building upon the analysis in the previous section. As before, the analysis is in two parts. First, process measures of the usage of accounting are presented. Then the analysis uses overall qualitative observational assessments and key issue cases to consider in more depth how and why accounting is used by accountants.

Before proceeding, a limitation of this analysis must be addressed. As explained in the introduction to this chapter, the focus here is on accountants located within a department with a financial secular support role. Therefore, any observed level of significance of accounting could arise from a combination of two factors. First, as argued in chapter 2, a significant usage of accounting may reflect the occupational orientation and training of accountants. Second, the structural orientation of the department on secular financial management functions also may influence the level of usage of accounting. As there were no other secular support departments within the Northern Division, it was not possible to attempt to separate these two effects. Therefore, the emphasis in the analysis is on occupational effects, as these can be contrasted to the actions of sacred occupational groups identified in the previous section. However, that the observed

168 *Managment Control in a Voluntary Organization*

effects may be biased towards greater use of accounting by the secular financial role of Finance and Administration should be recognised'.

As explained in chapter 3, observation for Finance and Administration concentrated on the uses of accounting by the Finance and Administration Board. All but one of the meetings during 1987 of the Board were observed. Therefore, the analysis presented is felt to be highly typical of the pattern of usage of accounting within this forum at that time. Process measures of the use of accounting during meetings of the Board were constructed using the procedures described in the previous section, and the same judgment rules were applied (the same qualifications apply to their use in this section). The results of this analysis are summarized in Table 5.3.

MEASURE	NON-ACC.	ACCOUNTING CODES					
	CODES TOT	Y	R	N	B	C	TOT
FINANCE AND ADMINISTRATION BOARD							
Frequency	128		14	8	79	44	**145**
Code %	*46.9*		*5.2*	*2.9*	*28.9*	*16.*	***53.1***
Time	582		41	28	269	225	**563**
Code %	*50.8*		*3.6*	*2.4*	*23.5*	*19.7*	***49.2***

Table 5.3: Significance of Accounting in a Forum Dominated by Accountants

The extent of use of accounting within this forum satisfies the judgment rule for high significance, with frequency of use greater than 50% and time duration almost at this level. This relative level of significance of accounting is distinctly higher than that previously reported for the Divisional Council and Educational Activities Board, but about the same as the Directorate. However, it is slightly lower than that observed for the Finance Committee. Like the latter, and unlike the cyclical emphasis on the budget in the Directorate, this forum evidenced a broad spread of usage of various accounting practices. Although the budget was still the dominant practice, as it was in all other forums. Also, this pattern of usage was highly consistent across all meetings of the Finance and Administration Board. Thus, it terms of process measures, high (but not the highest) significance seems to be given to accounting by accountants, who used a wide range of accounting practices, with budget discussions the most used.

How accounting was used by the accountants in these interactions reinforced and increased the impression of its significance in this forum. First, they regularly reviewed the MACS monthly

Accounting Systems II 169

reports for all three departments covered by the system; Finance and Administration, Educational Activities, and Mission Outreach. The focus was usually on deviations from budget of the two sacred departments, as they were perceived as the key potential area for problems. When potential final budget achievement could be more clearly assessed later in the year, such discussions were longer, with more questions or comments being made. Thus, emphasis was given to the use of the MACS reports for financial management and control, a use that was only evident for the sacred occupational groups in the Finance Committee.

Second, like the sacred occupational groups, there were many operational decisions where only minimal concern was shown for accounting implications by the accountants, even though there were clear financial effects. In some such cases, no accounting numbers were provided. However, this disregard of accounting only applied to minor decisions. In all major decisions with significant financial implications, active use was made of accounting during decision-making. For example, during 1987 the Division commenced work on a new administrative building to consolidate the physical location of its departments. During discussions of this, a project budget was actively used by the accountants to consider cost areas and revise the building design to fit expenditure limits. In major decisions, therefore, accounting was actively used as a 'rational' decision-making aid by the accountants.

Third, there were many instances where concerns were voiced on financial control within the Division, particularly that in the sacred departments. Both the commitment and ability to execute financial control of the sacred occupational groups was questioned. This was often the prime concern when Finance and Administration had to approve aspects of the projects of sacred departments (for example Mission Outreach's Seven Year Plan and Educational Activities' joint publication of its magazine with another Division), even more than whether the project was financially viable. The accountants viewed accounting as a relevant discipline for the operation of the Division, and actively expressed the perception that sacred occupational groups did not share this view. This concern with financial control commitment and ability, therefore, evidences an importance given to accounting by accountants that was not generally evident for sacred occupational groups.

170　　　　　　　*Managment Control in a Voluntary Organization*

Finally, more emphasis was placed in budget discussions on its use as a 'rational' planning device for allocating the resources of the Division and determining the programmes of the departments. In fact, a special meeting of the Board was called in October primarily for this purpose. A concern with 'balancing the budget', the official Division policy, was heightened in budget discussions by the cuts in real terms resulting from the financial crisis. Also, this was exacerbated by there being a sizeable deficit in the first draft of the 1988 budget (see chapter 6 for more details). During these discussions, disquiet was again expressed about the sacred occupational groups, with statements that they had not fulfilled their departments' budget responsibilities by exceeding the budget parameters (thus causing a draft deficit) and failing to identify areas for cuts when requested (see Educational Activities discussion above). The accountants felt that the budget should be used more pragmatically and rationally to choose between sacred mission priorities within the outlined resource limits.

The indications, therefore, were that accounting was regarded as highly significant by the accountants in Finance and Administration. Accounting was frequently used, and in a manner that suggested it was viewed as relevant to the functions of the department. Accountants displayed active interest in the MACS reports; in major decisions they used financial analysis to guide choices; they had a significant concern with financial control; and they applied a pragmatic financial focus to the budget deficit resolution process. As for use of accounting by sacred occupational groups within the Finance Committee, part of this significance may have resulted from the secular financial responsibilities of Finance and Administration, and the accountants' concerns with the financial crisis (see chapter 4). However, the way in which accountants approached these responsibilities was qualitatively different than the sacred occupational groups in similar circumstances. They evidenced much more of a commitment and belief in the utility of a strong financial rationality for solving these secular control problems.

However, to view the use of accounting by accountants in Finance and Administration as simply a strong financial rationality flowing from their occupational knowledge base and ideology is not totally consistent with all the ways in which accounting was used by them. It has already been argued in the previous section that the accountants accepted the sacred and secular divide. This acceptance of

Accounting Systems II 171

boundaries on the relevance of accounting was also evident in Finance and Administration activities.

In Case 10, the factors considered in the sale of NBS evidence a mixture of secular and sacred concerns. Undoubtedly, the poor financial performance of NBS was a prime motivation in the issue being considered in the first place. However, of prime concern in deciding if and how to proceed with its sale were the sacred ends of the church, particularly the conflict between a commercial operation and such ends, and the specific concerns of Christian literature sales. In an interview with the Finance and Administration Director, he was questioned on the relative importance of the financial issues. He strongly argued that he would have put the view of the mismatch between commercial ventures and church goals regardless. Such recognition of the dominance of sacred ends by the accountants was observed in all major decisions within Finance and Administration that had sacred implications for the church. In major decisions, therefore, the primary position of sacred ends was generally accepted by accountants.

Case 10 - The Sale of NBS

The Northern Book Shop (NBS) had for many years been the main commercial operation of the Northern Division and a source of funds for the Division budget, but had recently been in severe financial difficulties (see chapter 4). NBS was also a focus for the sale of Christian literature and was still very successful at this activity. During 1987 Finance and Administration evaluated the options for NBS's continued operation, eventually recommending its sale to the Divisional Council. A report by the Finance and Administration Director on restructuring options for NBS summarized the main problem as given "...the current position of NBS and an assessment of the future prospects, it appears to be essential for the church to consider what it expects of NBS and what action should be taken to achieve the church's goals in the sale of Christian Literature and the provision of finance to the..." Division budget. The rationale for the selected sale alternative was; the tough commercial environment for the medium term; NBS was mainly a commercial operation, the majority of customers were not church members; the church management/accountability structure inhibited commercial decision-making; the department's management energy could be better used to serve the mission of the church; and the investment of the sale proceeds would give a more stable financial return to the Division.

During discussions, the Director put quite strongly an argument about the mismatch between the commercial nature of NBS and the goals of a church. He saw a significant problem in maintaining a reasonable balance between commercialism and serving the church. In particular, he stressed that NBS was so commercial that there was really little service to the church. This issue was the prime focus of the debate, including what alternative arrangements could be made to meet the existing service to the church - Christian literature sales. The financial dimensions of the issues and the effects for the Division budget were not raised in the debate.

172　　　　　*Managment Control in a Voluntary Organization*

In parallel with the acceptance of the dominance of sacred ends, there was also a view that accounting could be actively used to assist sacred ends. A very explicit example of this was the promotion of the budget through the 'Before the Next Step' programme (see Case 11). The focus was on how contributions to the budget supported the work of the church. The budget was portrayed by the accountants as enabling the pursuit of a wide range of mission activities within the Division. Such promotion creates a more significant, although still secondary, role for accounting. It is argued by accountants to be a 'tool for mission', rather than a secular technique that conflicts with sacred functions. In this sense, such views are attempts to 'sacredize' accounting and weaken its subordination under the sacred and secular divide. However, this is not to give it a dominant position, just to reduce resistance to its use.

Case 11 - The 'Before the Next Step' Programme

The Before the Next Step programme, initiated by Finance and Administration, involved the promotion of the Division budget to individual church members, Parishes and Presbyteries through visits by staff from all Division departments, and the wider distribution of a pamphlet explaining and promoting the budget. The aim of the programme was to promote the strong connection between the performance of the mission of the church and contributions to the budget.

The pamphlet contained statements from the Division Secretary promoting how the budget had furthered the work of the church in worship and ministry, evangelism and discipleship, and community concern. Some quotes give a feeling for the active promotion given to the budget:

"Many of these things have been made possible, and have been continued through the..." budget.

"One feature of the life of the Mainstream Church is the way each congregation shares its resources so that it and other congregations may receive support and services which are beyond the resources of the local congregation to provide. In financial terms, this sharing takes place through the" budget.

"The ..[budget].. is the primary way in which Parishes enable the whole church to undertake the work of mission and the activities of service which it is not possible for individual Parishes to undertake themselves".

In summary, the aim of this section has been to analyse the significance of accounting when it was used by accountants within Finance and Administration, and to consider explanations for the way in which they used accounting. Process measures indicated that accounting appeared to be regarded as highly significant by

Accounting Systems II 173

accountants. When the way in which accounting was used was considered, this impression of the significance of accounting was increased. Very active use was made of accounting in decision-making, there was a strong concern with financial control, and a pragmatic financial rationality was applied to the budgeting process.

Three potential explanations exist for the high significance of accounting, the formal secular support role of Finance and Administration, its management by accountants, and accountants' concerns over the financial crisis. The first meant that managerial action was focused on secular control problems, particularly financial management and budgeting issues. The financial rationality and means-ends analysis of accounting practices may appear highly relevant to such functions. Accountants are likely to be very active in applying such solutions, and promoting their use by others. Also, the existence of the financial crisis would have supported the accountants' perception of the need for accounting solutions, particularly through the budgeting process. Therefore, a strong view of the high relevance of accounting permeated this department.

However, some similar effects were seen for sacred occupational groups within the Finance Committee. While the process measures of the extent of usage by accountants were lower than for the sacred occupational groups in that setting, the much stronger financial rationality evidenced in the way that accounting was used by accountants suggests that they saw it as much more significant than the sacred occupational groups. The financial rationality based on the occupational views of accountants, therefore, appeared to be the dominant source of the high significance given to accounting by accountants, with the other factors being reinforcing context.

The accountants also supported the sacred and secular divide, with the secondary position of accounting to sacred ends being accepted. As argued previously though, accountants had a different interpretation of the necessary extent of the subordination of accounting. This was expressed in their view that accounting should be a 'tool for mission'; that is, that accounting could be actively used to promote sacred ends and did not necessarily conflict with them. This view seemed to be at its most extreme in discussions of the budget, where the use of a financial logic to help choose between sacred priorities was advocated. It is not clear in such situations whether accounting was being used as a tool for mission, or was being used to

174   *Managment Control in a Voluntary Organization*

dominate it. Certainly, the analysis in the previous section suggests that the sacred occupational groups took the latter view. Also, the possible effects of the financial crisis, with the accompanying perception of a need for budget cuts, in the adoption of this extreme position by the accountants should not be ignored. The conflict and debate around different interpretations of the role of accounting in the budgeting process is considered further in chapter 6.

IV.   TENSIONS BETWEEN OCCUPATIONAL GROUPS

In the previous two sections the general acceptance of the dominance of sacred ends over accounting by both accountants and sacred occupational groups has been argued. However, it was also proposed that accountants had a different interpretation of this relationship than sacred occupational groups, and that this may lead to conflict and debate over the significance of accounting within the Northern Division. In this section, interactions between senior Division staff in meetings of the Senior Management Group are analysed to provide further insight into these issues. As discussed in chapter 3, the formal role of the Senior Management Group is as an integration device for the management structure. It is composed of the four department Directors, the Division Secretary and the three Chairpersons. An analysis of interactions involving accounting in the Senior Management Group will allow access to the extent of tension between the views of accountants and sacred occupational groups, as represented by these key senior staff from these two groups.

MEASURE	NON-ACC.	ACCOUNTING CODES					
	CODES TOT	Y	R	N	B	C	TOT
Frequency	142	1			81	11	**93**
Code %	*60.4*	*0.4*			*34.5*	*4.7*	***39.6***
Time	685	6			236	28	**270**
Code %	*71.7*	*0.7*			*24.7*	*2.9*	***28.3***

Table 5.4: Significance of Accounting in the Senior Management Group

As previously, process measures of the meetings observed were calculated. The meetings observed were concentrated around the discussions of the budget formulation process (see chapter 3). As identified in the two previous sections (and in chapter 4), this was the key accounting practice around which tensions between the accounting

Accounting Systems II 175

and sacred occupational groups became expressed. These observations, therefore, are regarded as typical of situations where such tensions were actively expressed. The overall level of the significance of accounting in the Senior Management Group was low at 39.6% of frequency of use and 28.3% of time duration (see Table 5.4). Almost all of this usage of accounting was budget related (approximately 87%). In particular, there were two lengthy discussions aimed at balancing the budget that occurred before and after the Budget Conference. The discussion below focuses on these two events.

In the first budget discussion (see Case 12) the Senior Management Group considered the way in which clear options could be put to the Budget Conference for programme cuts, or increased income, to balance the budget. The Finance and Administration Director argued that programme cuts were the only feasible solution. His position was that mission activities had to be rationally evaluated within the budget structure, allowing choices to be made about which sacred ends should (and could) be pursued. The position of the Directors of the sacred departments (the senior representatives of sacred occupational groups) was the opposite; being concerned with ways of avoiding programme cuts. They argued that such cuts were inconceivable, that there were no programmes that could be discontinued or reduced. This was a rejection of a 'rational' budget logic of accountants for one that was totally focused on the achievement of sacred ends. From this perspective, the problem with the budget was the lack of income, which should be increased so that there was no interference with sacred functions.

While these views of both the accountants and the sacred occupational groups may support the dominance of sacred ends over accounting logic, the potential for conflict between them is significant. The accountants' view argues that choices need to be made between sacred ends because of the financial crisis, and that the logic of the budget can assist in making the rationally best choices. Sacred occupational groups reject the relevance of such choice processes. Sacred ends to them should be protected, not rationally reduced. The budget could only assist them by highlighting the need for, and in assisting in the finding of, additional resources. Interactions to reduce a budget deficit, therefore, brought the different views of the occupational groups on the relevance of accounting directly into conflict.

176   *Managment Control in a Voluntary Organization*

Case 12 - 'Constructing Clear Options'

The meeting was considering the draft budget for consideration at the Budget Conference. The Finance and Administration Director outlined that after cutting all new programme requests there was still a budget deficit of $320,000. He felt that there was no hope of getting enough extra funds from Presbyteries to cover this, therefore, balancing the budget meant either increasing department income or programme cuts. He concluded by stating that he wanted the departments to put clear options to the Budget Conference so that it would have to make the hard decisions.

Some of the figures were then examined for 'padding', but no-one felt this really existed. The Educational Activities, Mission Outreach and Finance and Administration Directors then, in turn, outlined what income increases or cuts they felt they could propose. Educational Activities argued that there did not seem to be any area where cuts could be made in the short-run. All programmes were considered necessary and things like theological education needed more time for any change to be planned and implemented. At one point the Finance and Administration Director interjected that Educational Activities had to face the reality that it would have less money and ask; What is this in terms of people? What are your options?

Mission Outreach started its discussion by complaining that its biggest cost increase was Finance and Administration' accounting charges and that they could not cut these as they were outside their control. The Finance and Administration Director responded that the charges were less than the cost of processing. Mission Outreach continued by outlining that it also did not see any areas for significant income increases and that all existing programmes were essential and already operating on the margin. The Finance and Administration Director emphasised again that the departments had to put clear options to the Budget Conference.

The Finance and Administration Director then outlined in detail the expenditure areas of his department and a number of expenditure cutting and income increasing options. For example, cancelling the 1988 Annual General Meeting and increasing service fees to off-budget church agencies. None of the options considered reducing the programmes of this department, except a suggestion that the Director's position could be cut.

There was then limited discussion of options in all departments. This did not progress towards identifying a package of options to be put to the Budget Conference as agreement could not be reached on the need for cuts with Educational Activities, and Mission Outreach. The members then agreed that the discussion was getting nowhere and it was ended without having clarified how the deficit could be addressed.

The conflict, and incompatibility, between the differing occupational views of the relevance of accounting was stronger after the Budget Conference (see Case 13), when programme cuts had been imposed by the accountants. This can be seen in challenges to the right of accountants to take such actions independently of the sacred occupational groups. Also, the sacred occupational groups portrayed themselves as losers and the accountants as winners. Therefore, the

Accounting Systems II

sacred occupational groups did not accept the application of a rational budget logic, but openly resisted cuts to their sacred activities.

Case 13 - 'Balancing the budget'

The Budget Conference had considered programme cuts and income increasing options for the three departments. It recommended mainly income increasing options for Finance and Administration and programme cuts for the two sacred departments. However, a balanced budget had not been achieved and final consideration of options had been referred to the Senior Management Group. Before this could occur the Finance and Administration Board met and decided on the global figures that it would use as a basis to recommend a balanced budget to the Annual General Meeting. The budget discussion here commenced with the Finance and Administration Director advising the other members of his Board's recommendations. He circulated the global income and expenditure amounts for each department and advised that it was now the departments' responsibility to specify the areas of cuts. He finished by stating that the figures were generally in line with the Budget Conference, except for an extra $60,000 cut to Mission Outreach.

The first question asked was why the Finance and Administration Board had acted on this matter before the meeting of the Senior Management Group. The Finance and Administration Director responded that his Board saw it as their responsibility to recommend the budget to the Annual General Meeting. The Mission Outreach Director then stated that he thought it was unfair that the whole additional balancing problem had fallen on his department and that the two sacred departments had taken the majority of cuts. The Division Secretary then commented that we have to take seriously that we don't have the funds and look at options.

There was then extended discussion of the role of the departments. During this discussion the Division Secretary stated that "we are not really talking about figures today, we are talking about the work of the kingdom". The discussion generally went over a range of issues about why departments were necessary and reasons for the lack of resources. There was general recognition that this was a very complex issue that impacted on many levels of the Division, but no clear picture emerged of how the budget situation could be dealt with.

Finally, the Division Secretary asked where we were getting on the budget. The Mission Outreach Director responded, 'nowhere, the money has to go so there is no point talking about it here'.

This situation also indicates that accountants, and accounting, may be perceived as inappropriately intruding into and trying to dominate sacred functions, even when this was not their intention. The Finance and Administration Director saw his position in these interactions as helping to solve the secular control problems resulting from the financial crisis by maximizing the sacred ends that could be pursued within limited resources. However, the sacred occupational groups would not accept any role for accounting where it, even partly, directed sacred ends. Thus, the accountants' interpretation of the

178 *Managment Control in a Voluntary Organization*

sacred and secular divide seemed to reject any fundamental tension between accounting and sacred functions, accounting could be used as a tool for mission. In the interpretation of sacred occupational groups, such tension was endemic to accounting practices.

The discussion above of the conflicting interpretations of accountants and sacred occupational groups on the relevance of accounting lends support to a proposition that the views of accountants on the role of accounting in management indicate a preference for the substitution of management control technologies, such as a budget, for trust within management relations, and that sacred occupational groups may hold the opposite position. In interviews with senior staff at the end of the study (see chapter 3), many of them raised concerns about the relationship between trust and the use of accounting.

Trust issues were raised explicitly by six of twenty staff interviewed from sacred occupational groups and by two of four accountants[8]. Sacred occupational groups felt that greater trust between staff was needed in the Division, not greater use of the budget or accounting controls. They felt that accounting had taken on an exaggerated importance in the budgeting process, and in the running of the Division more generally. One person expressed this quite strongly, stating that there needed to be more trust of people, and less of Finance and Administration acting as the 'big stick'. Implicitly, similar views on trust versus accounting were held by another six members of sacred occupational groups who argued that too much emphasis was placed on accounting in decision-making. Accountants were stated to be a group preventing the 'real work' of the church. In addition, one person stated that the tendency for accounting to control the mission of the church led to distrust of the accounting systems and the accountants. This is consistent with Fox's (1974) argument that the distrust embedded in management control technologies breeds distrust in those at whom they are directed. Sacred occupational groups, therefore, favour trust over accounting controls and resent the imposition of such controls on sacred activities.

In contrast, one accountant saw the issue as more of a trade-off between trust and formal controls such as accounting, as Armstrong (1989a) argued. The other stated that trust was fine when everything was going well, but accounting needed to be more important when the Division was in trouble, as it was now. These accountants, therefore, favoured the substitution of accounting controls for trust, particularly

Accounting Systems II 179

when there was a perceived need for financial discipline in times of financial crisis.

In summary, this section has analysed the differing interpretations of the relevance of accounting under the sacred and secular divide held by accountants and sacred occupational groups. When such views were brought into conflict through the budgeting process, their basic incompatibility was revealed. Accountants viewed accounting as a tool for mission that could assist in rationally choosing between sacred ends to meet the perceived imperatives of secular financial control problems. In this sense, accounting was seen as a substitute for trust in management relations, acting as a form of management discipline in times of financial crisis. The focus of sacred occupational groups was on sacred control problems. They viewed secular financial control problems as constraints that should be removed, as suggested in chapter 4, not imperatives to which rational adjustment should be made. Trust was their preferred basis of management relations and the imposition of accounting discipline by accountants was resented. The differing views of these occupational groups, therefore, were important in the promotion of, and resistance to, accounting within the Division.

V. CHAPTER SUMMARY

In this chapter, the level of significance of accounting within the Northern Division has been examined. Significance was assessed by considering the extent to which, and the ways, that accounting was used by accountants and sacred occupational groups. Explanations for the observed significance and uses of accounting by each occupational group were proposed. The analysis focused on occupational groups because, while comparisons could be made across departments with differing sacred orientations, it was not possible to make such comparisons across departments with different secular orientations. There is a potential bias in the findings for accountants, therefore, as their usage of accounting may reflect both their occupational orientation and the financial management function of the department within which they were located. The conclusions from this analysis are summarized below.

One measure of significance presented was quantitative process measures of the extent of use of accounting by accountants and sacred

180 *Managment Control in a Voluntary Organization*

occupational groups in various forums. These measures enabled a consistent basis of comparison across forums, but their interpretation was limited by the absence of any comparative measures for other organizations. The findings summarized here, therefore, should be seen as only indicative within the limitations of the judgment rules applied to gauge significance. From these measures, accounting appeared to have a variable significance within the Northern Division. In the Divisional Council and the Educational Activities Board, sacred occupational groups appeared to regard accounting as of low significance. Within the Educational Activities Directorate, the significance of accounting varied, with the sacred occupational groups treating it as high when the budget was discussed, but low at other times. Consistent high significance for accounting appeared to exist for the sacred occupational groups in the Mission Outreach Finance Committee, which regularly used a broad range of accounting practices. In the Finance and Administration Board, the accountants seemed to regard accounting as of high significance. However, this was less than that evidenced for the Finance Committee, although they had a similar pattern of usage of accounting across a broad range of practices. Also, the process measures indicated that the budget was consistently regarded as the most important accounting practice across all forums and both occupational groups. In terms of how much use was made of accounting, therefore, it varied between low and high significance for sacred occupational groups and was of high significance for accountants, with the budget being the most important accounting practice for both.

As an extra check on the reasonableness of the patterns suggested by the process measures, and as a means of extending their implications to forums where observational evidence was limited, the frequency of references to accounting (classified in a similar manner to the process measures analysis) in the agendas, supporting documents and minutes of all meetings of the Divisional Council and the Boards of the four departments during the same 1987 time period were calculated[9]. The results of this analysis are summarized in Table 5.5.

The findings for the first three forums (the Educational Activities Board, the Divisional Council and the Finance and Administration Board) support the pattern previously found for the process measures. Accounting related agenda items or references are minimal for the Educational Activities Board and the Divisional

Accounting Systems II   *181*

Council, suggesting low significance. Similarly, the high significance for the Finance and Administration Board is supported by much higher levels of references in this forum. The low references to accounting for the Mission Outreach and Welfare Services Boards, forums not covered by the process measures analysis, suggest that low significance for accounting can be generalized to these forums. The low significance finding for Mission Outreach suggests that the high significance for its Finance Committee was restricted to the particular financial management orientation of this forum, as argued earlier in the chapter. This analysis suggests, therefore, that the process measures findings are reasonable and may be more widely applicable to other arenas where sacred occupational groups and accountants were active.

Forum	Receiving of Financial Statements	Budget Matters	Accounting Data & Concepts Used	Total Acc. Uses (%)	Total Agenda Items
Educational Activities	10	7	9	26 (17.9)	145
Divisional Council	4	6	10	20 (14.4)	139
Finance and Administration	19	13	22	54 (50)	108
Mission Outreach	17	10	5	32 (19.0)	168
Welfare Services	0	2	4	6 (4.4)	137

Table 5.5: Frequency of References to Accounting in Documents of Various Forums

The pattern of a variable significance of accounting was also supported by the more detailed qualitative evidence and key issues cases presented on the use of accounting by sacred occupational groups and accountants. The general tendency was for sacred occupational groups to treat accounting as a secondary criteria in discussions and decision-making, while accountants made very active use of accounting and treated it as a major concern. While both occupational groups recognised the primary position of sacred ends, they had differing interpretations of the extent to which accounting should be regarded as secondary.

Sacred occupational groups were primarily concerned with sacred control problems. They tended to regard accounting as

182 *Managment Control in a Voluntary Organization*

irrelevant to such matters, resisted its intrusion upon the pursuit of sacred ends, and resented the distrust in their commitment to responsible management embedded in the use of accounting control technologies within the Division. Even for the budget, where more significance for accounting seemed to be indicated for sacred occupational groups, the general reaction was for resistance to the financial logic of the budget. As sacred occupational groups dominated the management structures of the Division, except for Finance and Administration, accounting, therefore, tended to play a limited and marginalized role in its operations.

This tendency was also evident in the Finance Committee. Even though sacred occupational groups paid more attention to accounting matters in this setting, it was not allowed to determine whether sacred ends should be pursued. Accounting was seen as only an implementation constraint, with decisions being made on the basis of their fulfilment of sacred priorities. The secondary position of accounting was related to the poor financial position of Mission Outreach, which had a significant debt burden. This perception of a major secular control problem, which was exacerbated by the Division's financial crisis, appeared to be the main reason accounting was resorted to by sacred occupational groups. However, the limitation of such use to this arena represented the partitioning of such financial concerns from the sacred activities of Mission Outreach by sacred occupational groups. By this partitioning, and by limiting the use of accounting to an implementation constraint, sacred occupational groups still subordinated accounting to sacred ends.

One partial exception to this marginalization of accounting was the pressure placed on financial control by the accountants. One reflection of this was the resentment by sacred occupational groups of the intrusion of accounting into the achievement of sacred ends, and of the replacement of trust with accounting controls in management relations. Another was the significant use of the Management Accounting Control System reports for this purpose by the sacred occupational groups in the Finance Committee, mentioned above. Pressure by accountants, therefore, for financial control may have been one area of some significant impact of accounting on sacred occupational groups within the Division.

In contrast, accountants evidenced a high concern with financial control, and applied a pragmatic financial logic to control problems.

Accounting Systems II 183

They promoted the greater use of accounting as a tool to aid the pursuit of sacred ends, particularly through rational choice of sacred priorities within the budgeting process. Also, this different interpretation of the relevance of accounting to sacred ends by accountants supported the greater use of accounting controls to discipline the activities of sacred occupational groups. This created the possibility that the promotion of accounting by accountants more widely within the Division, particularly within the budgeting process, could lead to greater intrusion on the activities of sacred occupational groups in the name of the support of sacred ends. Therefore, the actions of accountants, and conflict and debate between their views and the opposing views of sacred occupational groups, were important in understanding the higher significance given to accounting in some circumstances.

The sacred and secular divide was proposed as a major factor explaining the variable significance of accounting. The general tendency to marginalize accounting was found to be related to the dominance of sacred ends over secular concerns, such as accounting. The sacred and secular divide was stronger for the sacred occupational groups. Sacred control problems were their dominant concerns, and accounting was regarded as a profane secular intrusion into the sacred activities of their departments. The accountants were more concerned with secular control problems, particularly financial management issues. This specific secular orientation enabled greater relevance to be perceived for accounting, even though the sacred and secular divide still acted to limit the ways in which accounting was used. The sacred and secular divide, therefore, influenced the attitudes of accountants and sacred occupational groups on the significance of accounting.

The differing interpretations of the relevance of accounting held by accountants and sacred occupational groups led to conflict between these two groups when accounting challenged sacred ends. In such conflict, accounting itself seemed to, at times, affect how this conflict took place. It acted as stocks of knowledge and moral orders within the organization that both enabled and constrained how accountants and sacred occupational groups conceived of the ranges of action, including resistance to accounting, open to them (as discussed in chapter 1). In particular, sacred occupational groups tended to conceive of the resistance to the budget in terms of the financial rationality promoted by accountants. Also, the adoption of the Seven Year Plan by Mission Outreach to address its secular financial control

184 *Managment Control in a Voluntary Organization*

problem, enabled a detailed financial visibility of the sacred programmes of this department that was not previously available. This allowed the accountants to more concretely challenge the financial justification of these sacred activities. The structuring of action by accounting, therefore, also affected how accounting was used.

Finally, the financial crisis of the Division affected the perceived relevance of accounting. It prioritized secular financial control problems, and appeared to support the promotion of the greater use of accounting in the name of financial control and 'rational' decision-making by accountants, such as the pressure for programme cuts in the budget. However, the impinging of such programme cuts on the pursuit of sacred ends also meant that the financial crisis acted to increase the resistance of sacred occupational groups to such a financial logic. The financial crisis, therefore, both increased the relevance of accounting and resistance to it.

The analysis in this chapter, therefore, has indicated that accounting is of variable significance in the Northern Division, and that this is related to the interaction of the actions of accountants and sacred occupational groups, the effects of the sacred and secular divide, and the impacts of the Division financial crisis. In particular, the conflict between accountants and sacred occupational groups within the budgeting process has been indicated to be a central area of tension between the use of accounting and sacred ends within the Division. These issues are considered further in chapter 6.

Notes

[1] Sacred occupational groups were also significant within the deliberations of the Annual General Meeting. However, the only major use of accounting in this forum was the budget. Discussion of the role of occupational groups in this forum, therefore, is deferred until the budget analysis in the next chapter.

[2] The initial coding scheme distinguished between accounting and non-accounting interactions, operational and strategic decisions (as the forums observed had a mixture of operational and policy responsibilities), and use of accounting system outputs and 'other' accounting practices. These categories were then refined and enlarged by pilot coding of a random selection of meetings until the code categories stabilized.

[3] In cases where more than one code formed part of a single timed interval, the total time was split proportionally unless the field notes indicated clearly that a non-proportional sharing was appropriate. For example, two code classifications share a time interval but

Accounting Systems II

one is marked in the field notes as a minor interjection into an otherwise continuous discussion of the other code.

[4] The reason for this was that the Business Manager had been busy supervising the completion of the building of the department's new student hostel and had had no time to prepare summaries for the Board.

[5] While often dealt with in this order, not all meetings followed this exact sequence.

[6] A 'Scheme of Arrangement' is a voluntary management plan entered into by companies when faced with severe liquidity problems instead of going into liquidation. Its focus is the payment of the debts of the firm through continued trading, rather than liquidating all assets.

[7] Following the arguments in chapter 2, it is felt that a secular department with a different focus (for example, personnel) would experience similar tensions with sacred orientated departments. However, this tension would be around a different occupational focus, not necessarily accounting. The general literature on voluntary organizations supports such a contention (Harris 1990; Kramer 1981; Mellor 1985; Weiss 1988).

[8] It should be stressed that trust issues were raised independently by the subjects. The trust dimension had not been incorporated in the theoretical framework at the time this data was collected.

[9] Such detailed documents were not available for the Educational Activities Directorate and the Mission Outreach Finance Committee.

Chapter 6
Accounting Systems III: The Dynamics of the Budgeting Process

I. INTRODUCTION

In chapter 5 it was concluded that accounting was generally of low, but variable, significance in the Northern Division. The Budgeting System was identified as a primary area of accounting practice responsible for such variance, being the most significant across both sacred and secular forums. The budgeting process appeared to be the central arena where sacred ends and accounting came into direct conflict, and thereby where accounting had potential to have a significant impact upon the Division. Also, it was the site of confrontations between the differing interpretations of the role of accounting held by accountants and sacred occupational groups. Accountants promoted the greater significance of accounting in the budgeting process, while sacred occupational groups resisted the intrusion of this financial logic on their pursuit of sacred ends. Finally, the relevance of accounting and the views of the accountants were particularly prioritized within the budgeting process by the financial crisis of the Division, which focused attention on the budget as a means of fitting mission programmes within limited resources. However, this also acted to increase the resistance of sacred occupational groups to such 'rational' use of the budget. In this chapter, the significance of the Budgeting System and its impacts upon the Northern Division are considered in more depth.

The first section of the chapter discusses historical trends in the budgeting process in the Northern Division. It analyses the historical importance of the budgeting process, the issues and problems that have

188 *Management Control in a Voluntary Organization*

surrounded it, and the practices that have been employed to address these issues and problems. The second section uses this context base for a discussion of the formulation of the 1988 budget as a critical case. This analysis considers more specifically the conflict between sacred ends and accounting, and the confrontations between sacred occupational groups and accountants identified in chapter 5. The chapter concludes with a summary of the dynamics of the budgeting process in the Northern Division.

II.   HISTORICAL TRENDS IN THE BUDGETING PROCESS

In chapter 4, the association of the financial crisis with a long history of the perception of budget crises within the Division was discussed. This suggests that the impacts of the Budgeting System also may have a long history within the Division. Therefore, this section examines historical trends in the budgeting process of the Division, thereby providing an assessment of the continuities and discontinuities in the significance, issues, problems and budgeting practices that have existed.

The analysis is based on the 1978 to 1987 annual budgets reports to the Annual General Meeting by the Budget and Finance Board, and the Department of Finance and Administration, its successor, and the reports of several committees and task groups directly associated with the budgeting process[1]. The major features of the budgeting process identified from these reports are summarized in Table 6.1.

These major features of the budgeting process have been fairly consistent over the whole ten year period and reflect two dominant concerns; the maintenance of a participatory, consultative budget formulation process, and the need to address the perception of a series of budget crises. They have also been related to two major aspects of the Northern Division; the ethos within Mainstream Church governance structures for high levels of grass-roots involvement (see chapter 3), and the relation of the budget crisis to the financial crisis of the Division and Parish support for the budget. These relationships are explored below.

Accounting Systems III

Budget Conference: The Budget Conference was seen as the primary forum where the budget problems had to be addressed. This was because the resolution of budget problems was always seen as having to be a process of consultation and consensus. The Budget Conference was always the 'representative body' for Presbyteries, departments and the responsible budget authorities to have their say on the budget, although the formal way in which it was constituted did change. The key role of the Budget Conference is evidenced by the very minor alternations made to budgets by the Annual General Meeting.
Structure of the budget: For most of the time period the budget submissions consisted of two main schedules. That always shown first was the 'financial supply' which specified the expenditure approvals for the departments and Presbyteries. This was followed by the 'Ways and Means Plan' which set out the income sources which were to fund the 'financial supply'. This structure symbolically constructs the view that sacred ends, as represented as expenditure approval, takes precedent over financial resources, as represented as income sources. This structure was dropped for the 1986 and 1987 budgets to one of 'recurrent expenditure' followed by 'recurrent income'. This new structure still exhibits some residue of the symbolic support of mission over resources.
'A balanced budget': The 'official goal' of the budgeting process was that a balanced budget be presented to the Annual General Meeting for approval. This was articulated in the first budget submission and continually surfaced over the period. A budget catch cry became 'we must live within our means'. However, despite this goal, in 6 out of the 10 years deficits were recommended and approved.
'Reducing budget demands': The 'operational goal' of the budgeting process became budget reduction. This had two faces. First, there were views that the services supported by the budget were too costly and that the total size of the budget needed to be reduced. Second, pragmatically, the budget process was always one of expenditure containment as department and Presbytery submissions continually exceeded estimated income by considerable amounts.
Setting budget priorities: One of the key budget practices aimed at budget containment and reduction was the setting of priorities. This was seen as the only 'rational' way in which the 'unlimited needs' of the Division could be matched to the its 'limited financial means'. However, the pursuit of such priorities proved very difficult and they were never satisfactorily implemented.
Promotion of the budget: There was a constant perception across the time period of the need to promote the budget to the Parishes. The view was 'our people' did not understand the mission work undertaken through the budget. If this could be communicated to them then resistance to giving would be reduced and the resultant increase in income would solve at least part of the budget crises. The most tangible outcomes of budget promotion were Operation Breakthrough, the special projects scheme, the name change to the 'Mission and Service Fund' and the establishment of the Communication Services Unit.
Centralization of accounting control: Some of the practices introduced over the period to control budget outcomes and to make more 'efficient use of church resources' effectively centralized control within the Division head office structure. These practices were the centralization of administrative functions, particularly accounting, within the Department of Finance and Administration; the establishment and changes to the operation of the Division Reserve Fund; the development of 'user pays' concepts for administrative services; and the centralization of department funds under Division accounts managed by the Department of Finance and Administration.

Table 6.1: Major Features of the Budgeting Process in the Northern Division

190 *Management Control in a Voluntary Organization*

The relationship between the grass-roots governance ethos of the church and the budgeting process is summarized in Figure 6.1. One consequence of this ethos is the dominance of a view that decision-making should be via processes of consultation and the seeking of consensus. Another is the recognition of the Parish as the key level for the fulfilment of the mission of the church. This ethos becomes expressed through the underlying nature of the structure of negotiations within the Division, that is the processes and means by which negotiation takes place and decisions are arrived at. One major and important dimension of such structures of negotiation in all organizations is the extent to which decision-making processes are centralized or decentralized (for example, March and Simon 1958; Robbins and Barnwell 1989; Thompson 1967). Within the Northern Division, the dominance of the grass-roots ethos has resulted in a general tendency for decentralized structures of negotiation to be preferred. In chapter 3, the manifestation of such tendencies in the general governance structures of the Mainstream Church and the management structure of the Northern Division were discussed. Also, the primary position of the Parish was recognized through the importance given to a broad representation of Parish laity in all decision-making forums. In chapter 2, the tendency to favour decentralized decision-making and the broad involvement of members in decision-making was also observed for voluntary organizations more generally (Gerard 1983; Leat 1988; O'Connell 1988; Rothschild-Whitt 1979).

Budgeting processes are one major manifestation of the underlying structure of negotiations in organizations. The preference within the Division for decentralized decision-making has been expressed in the concern in its budgeting process with the maintenance of a participatory, consultative process. The primary budgeting practice by which this has been achieved is the Budget Conference. The aim of this body has been to bring together representatives of the Presbyteries (Parishes) and departments to discuss budget strategies for the Division, and to determine the form of the budget to be recommended to the Annual General Meeting. It has been used as a forum to resolve conflict over budget allocations and to allow Parish level input into the mission programmes of the departments. The original intentions were that any residual conflict would be referred to the Annual General Meeting for resolution, as the most representative

Accounting Systems III 191

forum of the Division, and this was done when necessary. However, from 1986, any residual conflict has been referred first to the Senior Management Group. As part of the new management structure (see chapter 3), the Senior Management Group represents more an executive, corporate model of decision-making with a department focus, than the grass-roots ethos of the Budget Conference and the Annual General Meeting. The budgeting process, therefore, has emphasized a broad based participation of the Division through the Budget Conference, however, in recent years some of this role has been taken over by the more narrowly focused Senior Management Group, which is against the preference for decentralized decision-making.

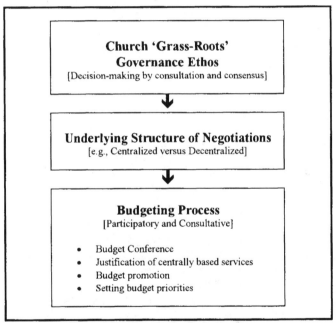

Figure 6.1: A Consultative Budgeting Process

Emphasis on the importance of the views of Parishes has also resulted in pressure within the budgeting process for the justification of the level of Division-based (central) services. During the period there have been continued concerns expressed from the Parishes about the cost of centrally based services and the ability to support them. This has resulted in an operational focus within the budgeting process on

192   *Management Control in a Voluntary Organization*

reducing budget demands, and greater accountability for services to Parishes. Another outcome has been a concern to promote the relevance to, and necessity for, mission of centrally based services supported by the budget to the Parishes. The Division's newspaper and its replacement magazine have regularly over the ten year period carried advertisements and stories stressing the linkages between mission and the budget[2]. A third outcome has been a series of enquires into the organization of centrally based services. One result of these enquires was the establishment of the Presbyteries-Division Co-ordinating Team (PDCT), which was set-up as a means of making the Division departments "...much more sensitive to the requirements of Parishes and Presbyteries" (Northern Division 1979a, p.275). It was to be a forum where Presbytery and department representatives "...may meet and consult in a spirit of partnership ... to clarify priorities in mission" (Northern Division 1979a, p.280). The budgeting process, therefore, has also been concerned with the accountability of budget supported activities to the Parishes and Presbyteries, and efforts to support their relevance to the mission of the church.

Therefore, the grass-roots governance ethos of the church and the recognition of the importance of Parishes in fulfilling the church's mission have been manifested through a preference for decentralized structures of negotiation within the Northern Division. The budgeting process, as one type of such structures, has also tended to reflect such preferences with its participatory, consultative nature[3]. This has resulted in budgeting practices such as the Budget Conference, budget promotion and broad participation in the setting of budget priorities.

Another major set of relationships in the budgeting process was between the concern with the need to address the perception of a series of budget crises, and the context factors of the financial crisis and Parish support for the budget. As argued in chapters 4 and 5, the financial crisis was associated with the heightening of the conflict between sacred ends and the budget, through the potential for cuts in mission programmes. Despite this conflict the budget reports usually stressed the role of the budget in facilitating the achievement of the mission of the church. Before 1985, this was tangibly expressed in the budget documents, where the 'financial supply' (expenditure budget) was shown as supported by the 'Ways and Means Plan' (income budget). From 1986 (after the adoption of the new management structure and the employment of professional managers), a more

Accounting Systems III 193

'neutral' accounting language of 'Recurrent Expenditure' followed by 'Recurrent Income' was used, but still mission preceded resources. Also, concern was shown within budget discussions with the need to support mission activities even if the financial resources were not available. Thus, the sacred and secular divide was reflected within the budgeting process in the subordination of financial resources to their use to support mission activities.

Such subordination, however, resulted in a tension between mission activities and the availability of financial resources because of the budget crises. As discussed in chapter 4, the budget was continually concerned with needs to cut expenditure programmes due to limited resources. This created the impression that mission activities supported by the budget must accommodate, at least in part, to the dictates of financial resources. This tension was heightened by the prevalent view from the Parishes that the budget was an excessive demand on their resources. As discussed previously, Parishes were concerned with accountability of centrally based services. Budget reports frequently mentioned concerns with the 'extent, effectiveness and cost' of such services. Also, it was reported that Parish members viewed their contribution to the budget as a 'tax' rather than a positive opportunity to support the mission activities of the Division departments. This is a significant Parish attitude, as it indicates an apparent strong negative Parish (the core of the mission activities of the church) view on the sacred and other functions of the departments. Budget contributions seemed to be seen within the Parishes as penalties to be borne because of the existence of the 'unnecessary' and 'costly' head office activities. The perception of a penalty was also increased by the diversion of scarce Parish funds away from their own mission activities. The budgeting process, therefore, was permeated with feelings of tensions between the need to support mission activities, particularly those directly supporting the Parishes, and the constraints of a limited pool of financial resources.

First, the Budget and Finance Board, and later Finance and Administration, as the responsible budget authorities, felt that part of the cause of these tensions was the 'poor' stewardship of Parish members. The shortage of financial resources was argued to be because members did not see the connection between giving to the budget and their commitment to Christ, as was expressed in their view of contributions as taxes. If they did, then the negative Parish views on the budget would be overcome and the financial crisis of the Division solved, at least in part, through greater giving. These views were another motivation for the budget promotion activities discussed previously. However, there was little evidence during the ten year period that the generally negative views of Parish members had been changed by such actions, and thus there was little motivation for improved stewardship to support the budget[4]. This meant that solutions to the budget crisis were conceived in terms of expenditure reduction, not increasing income or the 'exercising of faith' in Parish members to support the work of God.

The negative views of Parish members towards greater support for the budget, the financial crisis, and the resultant series of budget crises set a negative tone for the budgeting process as it was always striving to find solutions to reduce the tension between mission activities and limited financial resources. As discussed in chapter 4, the official budget policy of the Division had always been to balance expected income with expenditure. As indicated above, the operational policy had become 'living within our means' and reducing budget demands. Together these two policies would seem to indicate that the budget acted as a significant constraint on mission activities. However, this rarely occurred to a total extent as in six out of the ten budgets, deficits were approved. In many of these cases the budget reports stated that it was felt that 'the work of the church' could not be cut any further to obtain a balanced budget. This indicates that the pursuit of sacred ends often overrode budget criteria, even in the face of budget crises[5]. However, this view seems to have weakened since 1985 under the new management structure and the takeover of budget responsibility by Finance and Administration from the Budget and Finance Board, with balanced budgets being recommended to the Annual General Meeting since that time. The budgeting process, therefore, has been couched in the negative terms of restricting mission activities, although the dominance of sacred ends over financial criteria has usually been evident. However, in recent years this dominance may have been reduced.

One of the major budget practices associated with this negative construction of the budgeting process was the search for mission (budget) priorities. A key role of the PDCT, as mentioned above, was to set 'priorities in mission' for the Division[6] through consultations between representatives of the Presbyteries and the departments. The

Accounting Systems III   195

establishment of this body separate from the activities of the Budget and Finance Board (responsible for budget formulation at that time) represents the effects of the sacred and secular divide. This sacred function, setting mission priorities, was partitioned off from the secular concerns of budget formulation. However, the PDCT still appeared to be dealing with a rational budgeting issue, resource allocation priorities. Over several years the PDCT tried many methods to determine mission priorities; for example, listings of all mission functions in the Division, rankings of sets of mission functions, and functional budgets. However, it was never able to compare mission activities across departments and Presbyteries, and rationally choose which sacred ends had the highest priority. From its attempts, the PDCT concluded that there was no clear correlation between mission activities and resource priorities, and that there was no simple way that the setting of mission priorities could lead to rational resource allocation within the budgeting process. Attempts within the budgeting process, therefore, to reduce its negative overtones and the tension with mission activities by setting mission priorities to determine the use of limited resources were perceived as failing because such priorities and rational allocation were argued to be incommensurable.

The PDCT was one outcome of the series of 'management' enquires, mentioned previously, into the extent of centrally based Division activities and the ability of the Division to support them. Another outcome was the centralization of aspects of accounting control within the Division; all administrative and accounting functions of the departments were centralized under the Department of Finance and Administration; charges were initiated for services on a user pays basis; and all department funds were centralized into one set of accounts under the control of Finance and Administration. All these changes were argued for in the name of efficiency, and making the best use of limited resources. However, they also reduced the financial and operating autonomy of the sacred departments, and ran counter to the decentralization favoured by the grass-roots governance ethos, as expressed in Figure 6.1. Decision-making power in the area of financial policies was shifted to Finance and Administration in the name of solving the budget crises. The negative overtones of the budgeting process, therefore, were implicated in some increase in the potential influence of Finance and Administration within the Division, which was a significant departure from the favoured decentralization approach for other policy areas.

The interaction, therefore, of the perception of budget crises, and the Division's financial crisis and Parish views on the budget resulted in the budgeting process generally being perceived as a process of constraining sacred ends to fit limited financial resources. The impacts of such constraints, though, were limited by a parallel view that financial concerns must be subordinated to sacred ends. This was particularly reflected in the approval of deficit budgets despite a policy of balancing the budget, and in attempts to establish mission priorities. Even though the latter represented some attempt to approach the budget as a rational allocation process, the way in which this failed illustrated the perception of an incommensurability of choosing between sacred ends and a rational budgeting process. However, there were some indications that this resistance flowing from the dominance of sacred ends had lessened in recent years. There had been some centralization of financial control under Finance and Administration in the name of greater efficiency, and more of an accounting language had permeated the budgeting process. Also, since 1985, no deficit budgets have been approved. Therefore, there was potential for increasing tension between the support of sacred ends and rational budget solutions to the Division's financial crisis.

In summary, this section has analysed historical trends in the continuities and discontinuities in the significance, issues, problems and practices that have existed within the budgeting process of the Northern Division. Many continuities have been evident throughout the ten year period examined. A highly participatory, consultative approach has been the norm. This has reflected the preferred decentralized structure of negotiations in the Division, and the grass-roots governance ethos of the church. Also, the recognition of the importance of Parishes in fulfilling the mission of the church has led to pressure being placed on the size of the budget, and the justification of the centrally based Division activities it supports. This concern with reducing budget demands has also been heightened by the Division's financial crisis, and a perception of an inability to increase stewardship in support of the budget. The result has been a construction of the budgeting process within the Northern Division as a negative process of constraining sacred ends to fit within the dictates of limited financial resources. However, there has not been a total domination of

Accounting Systems III 197

mission activities by the budget. In general, the decision process has supported the primary position of sacred ends. Overall, the budgeting process has tended to reflect a tension between mission activities and limited financial resources, where Parish, Presbytery and department groups seek to 'live within their means' while still prioritizing sacred ends.

However, there were also some discontinuities in this general tendency. In recent years there has been an increase in the ability of Finance and Administration to influence the operations of the budgeting process. In part, this increase has arisen from solutions sought to the budget crises in the name of greater financial and management efficiencies. In particular, since the financial crisis worsened significantly after 1983, and the new management structure was adopted in 1984, there has been more rigorous adherence to the official balanced budget policy. This may indicate greater use of a financial logic in the budgeting process. If this is so, then the negative tone of the budgeting process can be expected to increase due to greater direct conflict between sacred ends and adherence to the balanced budget policy. This greater centralized influence of Finance and Administration can also be expected to led to tensions with the preferred decentralized structure of negotiations. The budgeting process, therefore, would appear to be a critical arena for significant impacts of accounting on the Northern Division.

The formulation of the 1988 budget represented a further development of these recent trends towards a more negative tone for the budgeting process, greater overt conflict between sacred ends and a financial logic, and the increased influence of Finance and Administration on the budgeting process. The further insights into the dynamics of the budgeting process revealed by this 'crisis' budget are discussed in the next section.

III.   A CASE STUDY OF THE BUDGETING PROCESS UNDER FINANCIAL STRESS

In this section, the formulation of the 1988 budget of the Division is analysed. In many ways, this budget was typical of the dynamics of the budgeting process identified in the previous section. The general commitment to a participative, consultative budgeting process was evident. The 1988 budget process commenced, as usual,

198 *Management Control in a Voluntary Organization*

with the departments and Presbyteries submitting their plans on the basis of Finance and Administration promulgated parameters (a proposed reduction of 5% in real terms for 1988, see chapter 5). After initial discussions between sacred department, Presbyteries and Finance and Administration, a Budget Conference was held to evaluate priorities, decide how to balance the budget and put recommendations to the Annual General Meeting. The tensions between limited financial resources and mission activities were again a central focus of this budget formulation process. However, the 1988 budget also saw the continuation of the more recent trends away from the domination of sacred ends and the greater sway of a financial budgeting logic. As discussed in chapter 4, the financial crisis had greater effects on the post 1985 budgets, with reductions in real terms in the level of expenditure and cuts to the programmes of the departments, particularly Mission Outreach and Educational Activities. When this greater financial stress was combined with trends in recent years to more strictly enforce the official balanced budget policy, the 1988 budget was the first budget since the new management structure was introduced where significant cuts to the basic programme infrastructure of the sacred departments was proposed, particularly in terms of staff positions. Thus, the 1988 budget became a 'crisis' budget, where the tensions between the secular and sacred dimensions of the budgeting process were more emphatically revealed. The aim of the analysis in this section, therefore, is to provide further insight into the dynamics of the budgeting process of the Division and the conflict between accounting and sacred ends as revealed by a critical case.

The analysis is based on non-participant observation of the budget formulation discussions in a range of Division forums[7], commencing with the Divisional Council Consultation in February 1987, through the Budget Conference and Annual General Meeting debates, to the eventual finalization of the budget by the Finance and Administration Board in December 1988 (see chapter 3 for details of forums observed). This observational data was supplemented by analysis of various budget and department documents and interviews with staff. From this data, a budget chronology with three fairly distinct stages can be discerned, of which the first and last were the most significant. The first stage deals with the discussions leading up to, and including, the Budget Conference, where initial budget options were considered and the first clear outcomes for the 1988 budget were determined. The second stage covers the initial reactions of the sacred departments to the proposed cuts in their programmes that arose in Stage One. The third stage commenced with a critical point in the budget process, the decision by Finance and Administration to balance the budget independently of the sacred departments (see chapter 5). It covers the resistance that this decision invoked from sacred departments, the effects of this on the formal budget adoption at the 1987 Annual General Meeting, and the final adjustments necessary to balance the 1988 budget after its formal adoption by the Annual General Meeting. These three stages are discussed in the following three subsections.

Stage One - Constructing Clear Options

During the first stage of the 1988 budget process, the departments and Presbyteries prepared and submitted their budget submissions to Finance and Administration. Then, strategies for meeting the official balanced budget policy were identified and discussed. This initial series of debates climaxed in attempts to resolve different strategies at the Budget Conference. The major phases in this stage are summarized in Table 6.2.

The budget process commenced with a Divisional Council Consultation on the theme - "Towards 2000: Missional Imperatives for the Parish". Over two and a half days, the Consultation attempted to identify the broad mission goals to which the Division should give its attention in the next decade. While the financial crisis was discussed, it was stated that the Consultation should ignore economic restrictions and focus on the critical 'missional imperatives' that would determine where the Division should be directing its resources. During the discussions, it soon became evident that various aspects of ministry were the major concerns of most participants, such as the quality of ministers and the level of stress they worked under. A particular concern was the current level of recruitment of theological students. Based on the current average ratio of confirmed members to ministers, it was estimated that an additional 68 ministers (currently 225 in Parish settlement) would be needed by the year 2000 if the church maintained its current share of its region's population. In addition, the Division had an aging ministry, with a high percentage in their 50s who would retire during the same time period. Filling this demand for new ministers would require at least an immediate doubling of the current yearly graduation of 3 or 4 students (and similar level of intake) and its maintenance for the next decade. Ministry in general, therefore, was identified as the most critical issue facing the Division over the next decade, and training of new ministers as a potential sacred crisis unless recruitment could be significantly increased. These concerns were communicated widely within the Division.

Phase 1 Divisional Council Consultation	27 Feb to 1 Mar	Consultation reviewed problems of the Division with funding and ministry. A critical emphasis on ministry for the next decade identified.
Phase 2 Educational Activities Board	8 Apr	Draft budget discussed. Discussion of use of gambit budget versus a 'church approach'.
Phase 3 Educational Activities Directorate	8 May	Budget submission reviewed by Finance and Administration. Had not been asked to redo even though a deficit. Finance and Administration was looking to ways to reduce deficit. Educational Activities and Mission Outreach want to put challenge to Presbyteries. Detected a positive approach to budget this year.
Phase 4 Finance and Administration Board	11 May	Director reported he had been tempted to ask departments to redo their budget submissions due to a deficit of $470,000. Now looking at some combination of income increases and expenditure cuts. Also favoured putting challenge to Presbyteries to increase contributions.
Phase 5 Divisional Council	26 May	Finance and Administration Director explained draft budget deficit. Asked Presbyteries to consider increased contributions and their areas of service priorities for the Budget Conference. Also, issue of reducing off-budget transfers of funds between Parishes and putting them into budget to allow Church to choose priorities.
Phase 6 Finance and Administration Board	6 July	Budget submissions adjusted to eliminate all new work, except one new full-time Presbytery Officer, but still maintain existing programmes. Adjusted deficit of $231,000 still unacceptable. Need combination of income increase and expenditure cuts. Asking departments for 'cut scenarios' of $50,000, $75,000 and $100,000 for Budget Conference. Felt Division 'can't have a deficit'.
Phase 7 Senior Management Group	7 July	Adjusted budget deficit outlined as discussed previous day at Finance and Administration Board. Directors asked to prepare 'cuts scenarios'.

Table 6.2: A Chronology of Stage One of the 1988 Budget Process

Accounting Systems III 201

Phase 8 Educational Activities Directorate	17 July	Discussion of 'cut scenarios' for department. Concern expressed over affects on staff positions and number of theological students. Felt could not make this level of cuts and maintain existing activities. Felt pressure of a 'balanced budget' leading to unrealistic figures.
Phase 9 Senior Management Group	21 July	Discussion of draft budget for consideration by Budget Conference. A deficit of $320,000, Finance and Administration Director felt no hope of increased Presbyteries giving covering this deficit. He wanted Budget Conference to make 'hard decisions' on areas of cuts. Finance and Administration, Educational Activities and Mission Outreach outlined cut areas. Educational Activities and Mission Outreach Directors argued that the required levels of cuts could not be made, needed all present areas of services. Finance and Administration argued must face financial reality, departments must put 'clear options' to Budget Conference on their priorities. Mission Outreach raised concern over accounting charge being outside their control. Meeting ended without deficit issue being resolved.
Phase 10 Finance and Administration Board	3 Aug	Finance and Administration 'cut scenarios' considered. Little scope seen due to user pays nature of most services and committed overheads nature on much of rest. Four income increasing and expenditure cutting options accepted.
Phase 11 Budget Conference	4 Aug	Deficit of $360,969 to be eliminated. Department and Presbyteries groups to evaluate options. <u>Mission Outreach group</u> - concern over accounting charge. Series of options put but resistance to staff or programme cuts. Aim of options was to maintain existing infrastructure. Options sought to trim existing activities to the bone. Cuts of $75,000 proposed. <u>Plenary discussion</u> evaluated group options. Presbyteries resisted giving full commitment to level of increased pledges. Also, off-budget funds raised again. Call for centralizing of funds to allow departments to assess priorities. Feeling that identified group items not complete, needed to list other activities. Some options not felt to be feasible. Problem of funding of ministerial education a major concern. Deficit of $102,262 left. Educational Activities volunteered to take options to balance budget. Finance and Administration Director not happy with this way of balancing budget. Wanted Senior Management Group to consider further options.

Table 6.2: A Chronology of Stage One of the 1988 Budget Process - Continued

Surprisingly, these sacred concerns were not strongly obvious during the remainder of the initial budget discussions leading up to the Budget Conference, although some anxiety over support for theological students was expressed. The main emphasis of this stage was attempts

202   *Management Control in a Voluntary Organization*

by the accountants in Finance and Administration to get the sacred departments to construct clear options for budget cuts to be presented to the Budget Conference. The sacred departments resisted this approach, as previously indicated in chapter 5. However, the sacred concerns identified at the Consultation were not actively used as a basis of this resistance. Before the Budget Conference, the sacred departments did not appear to treat the prospects for budget cuts as 'real', despite the clear signals from Finance and Administration that there had to be a cut of 5% in real terms. The sacred occupational groups seemed either unable or unwilling to approach the budget in terms of such a financial logic, where the impacts of such cuts would have had to have been assessed. Their initial resistance was an ignoring of the accountants' financial logic of the budget, and arguments for an income increasing strategy until the 'reality' of programme cuts became clearer. Therefore, the sacred occupational groups saw no apparent need to draw on sacred control problems and priorities as sacred activities were not initially perceived as under threat. This acted to delay the playing out of the conflict between the accountants and sacred occupational groups over the 1988 budget process. However, there was still some tension between the two occupational groups during the first part of this stage.

From the start of the budgeting process, the accountants evidenced a strong belief that the balanced budget policy must be adhered too, that a deficit was unacceptable. The Finance and Administration Director regularly argued in meetings that the deficit had to be eliminated by some combination of income increases and expenditure reductions. He put the challenge to Presbyteries to increase their contributions, but the main strategy adopted by Finance and Administration was for Educational Activities, Mission Outreach and Finance and Administration to identify options for reducing their demands on the budget by scenarios of $50,000, $75,000 and $100,000[8]. These reductions were after all 'wish lists' and new programmes, except a new full-time Presbytery Officer, had been eliminated; that is the budget was basically the activities of the previous year adjusted for inflation. The accountants put the view that significant increases in the income side of the budget were unlikely, and that the sacred departments had to face this 'reality' and identify how they were going to cope with the reduced resources[9]. In particular,

Accounting Systems III 203

they argued for the formulation of a 'realistic, achievable' budget through the rational consideration of clear options for programme cuts.

In contrast, the sacred occupational groups in the two sacred departments argued that other budget strategies had to be found. They felt that income increasing solutions had to be pursued as the option of the cuts scenarios was not realistic. Their main basis of judging 'realism' seemed to be the existing level of their sacred activities. Whenever the cuts scenarios were discussed, the sacred departments put the view that there was no room for any reductions in their programme structures[10]. However, despite the call for an income focus, no real budget strategy for replacement of the accountants' position was proposed. The response of the sacred occupational groups was solely to contest the viability and validity of the programme cuts strategy.

In the lead up to the Budget Conference, therefore, the perceived need to address the financial crisis by reducing budget askings and balance the budget led to conflict between accountants and sacred occupational groups. The latter attempted to defend their sacred programmes by arguing that the budget problem should not be constructed as an expenditure problem. Instead, solutions that supported, rather than intruded upon, sacred ends should be employed, but concrete options were not provided. Accountants promoted rational financial solutions to the budget problem. Sacred ends were important, but they could not all be supported because of the income constraints of the financial crisis. The 'logical' solution was for the Budget Conference to choose between sets of priorities.

The Budget Conference was structured by the accountants to match their views of how the budget problem should be solved. It was chaired by the Finance and Administration Director, who introduced the discussions by outlining the deficit problem and putting the case that it was an expenditure reduction problem. He then split the participants into four working groups, one each for Finance and Administration, Educational Activities, Mission Outreach and the Presbyteries, to consider cuts scenarios of between $100,000 and $200,000. Also, the structure of the budget documents supplied to participants favoured comparisons in terms of department versus department, as they were in a department cost centre format. After each group constructed options, a plenary session was to select the cuts that balanced the budget. The Budget Conference, therefore, was

204   *Management Control in a Voluntary Organization*

organized to function as a rational evaluation of competing department programme reductions.

However, the Budget Conference did not actually function in this manner. In the Mission Outreach working group[11], the department's staff strongly resisted discussion of the restructuring or reduction of their programmes, particularly any involving staff cuts. They also blamed Finance and Administration for some of their funding problems through the level of charges for accounting services. Very little of the discussion actually involved consideration of expenditure reductions options, being mainly concerned with explaining why reductions were not (should not be) possible. When all the groups reported back, none had developed options of the level requested, with Educational Activities the only group identifying reductions over $100,000 (total of $128,000). Also, the plenary discussion failed to evaluate priorities between those limited options identified, with the focus being on whether they were feasible rather than which were priorities. The Budget Conference, therefore, failed to implement the accountants' budget strategy as sacred occupational groups spent most of the discussion time challenging its desirability. However, it also did not consider any alternative income increasing solutions to the budget problem.

The end result was that when the meeting ran out of time, all identified options were accepted as they were almost sufficient to eliminate the budget deficit, resulting in sizable expenditure reductions for the sacred departments. It should also be noted that the outcomes for Finance and Administration were all internal income increasing strategies, no reductions in its activities were proposed. The Finance and Administration Director closed the Conference by stating that he was not happy with the overall solution arrived at, and that he wanted the Senior Management Group to consider further options. Such disquiet was with the irrational way the solution had been was arrived at, however, not the form of the outcome.

Therefore, the first stage of the 1988 budget process was mainly concerned with conflict between accountants and sacred occupational groups over suitable strategies for balancing the budget. The participative, consultative nature of the Division's budgeting process made possible a contested terrain where alternative views of the role of the budget could be debated. The accountants promoted a role for the budget as a rational tool for choosing between sacred priorities. This

Accounting Systems III 205

was expressed through an expenditure reduction strategy as the financial crisis was perceived as making income increases unrealistic. The sacred occupational groups resisted the intrusion of such a financial logic on their sacred activities. They promoted expenditure reduction as unrealistic, and called for income increasing strategies instead. However, surprisingly in mounting this resistance they did not relate their activities to the critical missional imperatives of ministry identified to be facing the Division. In the initial attempts to balance the budget, there was significant disagreement on viable and valid strategies between occupational groups.

However, it is not being claimed that this resistance of the sacred occupational groups was solely a product of their sacred orientation. Resistance to budget cuts by operating sections, or any other type of organizational unit, is probably the norm in all organizations (for example, Wildavsky 1975). In this sense, the 1988 budget process of the Division is no different to previous research findings. However, some features of voluntary organizations in general, and of churches more specifically, probably do alter the form of such resistance. As discussed in chapters 1 and 2, voluntary organizations usually have a significantly modified form of wage labour relations. In particular, the sanctions of dismissal and demotion are usually not available, or are significantly attenuated. As a result, the nature of organizational control and the conflict resolution processes surrounding the budgeting process are different. Under such conditions, ideology (such as sacred orientation in churches) becomes a more central issue. For example, in his analysis of resistance to resource redistributions in an Anglican Diocese, Harris (1969) pointed out that while resistance was not based on the church's belief system, but the specific interests of the Parishes affected, the protection of such interests was often justified in terms of the belief system (see Booth 1993). The sacred orientation of the sacred occupational groups, therefore, is relevant in understanding the nature of the resistance process, even though it is not its sole source.

Despite the resistance of the sacred occupational groups, and the fact that the accountants' rational approach to the budget was not followed, a critical result at the end of this first stage of the 1988 budget process was that expenditure reductions were proposed for the sacred departments. This occurred because the accountants controlled the structure of the Budget Conference discussions, and tried to limit

206   *Management Control in a Voluntary Organization*

them to their expenditure reduction view of the nature of the budget problem. Also, such a view was probably acceptable because of the strong history of such a focus in the Division's budgeting process. Finally, the imposition of cuts was also made possible by the failure of sacred occupational groups to propose any alternative budget strategies during the Budget Conference. The setting for the next stage of the 1988 budget process, therefore, was that sacred department programme cuts seemed likely but that they did not accept the justification for these reductions.

Stage Two - Marshalling Resistance

The second stage of the 1988 budget process was a short interlude of a month between the outcomes of the Budget Conference and the decision of the Finance and Administration Board to independently impose expenditure cuts to balance the budget. During this time, the sacred departments considered their options on how to respond to the Budget Conference outcomes, and identified various resistance strategies. The major phases in this stage are summarized in Table 6.3.

Phase 12 Divisional Council	4 Aug.	Maintenance of Ministry Task Group report recommended that all ministerial support be centralized under oversight of Finance and Administration through a committee of 'experts'.
Phase 13 Educational Activities Directorate	7 Aug.	Reviewed Budget Conference outcomes. Prime issue was student allowances, needed to move off-budget. Outlined options for cuts. Looking for new income sources and new way of funding ministerial education. Raised Division's need for more ministers. Decided needed to get Annual General Meeting to change budget. Felt there was no way to make agreed staff cut.
Phase 14 Educational Activities Board	18 Aug.	Explained Budget Conference outcome. Felt only department that had identified requested 'cut scenarios' and had consequently been hardest hit. Explained why some cuts could not be met. Issues not resolved.

Table 6.3: A Chronology of Stage Two of the 1988 Budget Process

The resistance of Educational Activities to the possibility of programme cuts arising from the Budget Conference has already been discussed in chapter 5. As discussed there, their main strategies of resistance were to; a) look for financial solutions that did not affect the

Accounting Systems III 207

infrastructure, b) to more actively consider income increasing solutions for the budget problem, such as establishing an independent funding source for ministerial education and moving it 'off-budget', and c) to decide to challenge the budget at the Annual General Meeting and have the cuts changed. The dominance of sacred ends was still the primary decision-making criteria in this sacred Department. However, the financial rationality within which the budget problem had been constructed by accountants, and the resultant outcomes of the Budget Conference, had resulted in the greater use of such a rationality by sacred occupational groups, though this was to resist rather than support the accountants' position. While no direct observation of Mission Outreach reactions was possible in the same time period, their previous reactions at the Budget Conference, and their arguments for very similar strategies of resistance during stage 3 (see next subsection), suggest that their position at this time was also one of marshalling resistance to the possibility of sacred programme cuts.

In the same period, what was to turn out later to be a significant event took place. During a Divisional Council meeting (Phase 12), a special task group report on ministerial support was considered. This recommended that the responsibilities of the Ministerial Stipends Committee (an independent body composed of Presbytery members reporting directly to the Annual General Meeting) for setting stipends and theological student allowances be centralized under Finance and Administration, which had responsibility for all other matters of ministerial support (for example, superannuation and moving expenses). The Divisional Council decided to recommend to the Annual General Meeting that a committee under the oversight of Finance and Administration be established for control of all aspects of ministerial support. This centralization of control of theological student allowances within Finance and Administration was to have a significant effect on 1988 budget outcomes.

Immediately following the Budget Conference, therefore, sacred departments considered ways to resist the rational financial logic promoted for the solution of the budget problem by Finance and Administration, as the programme cuts this prioritized were perceived as conflicting with the dominance of sacred ends. However, the time for this resistance to be marshalled was to prove to be very short.

Stage Three - Enforcement of Budget Discipline

The commencement of the third stage of the 1988 budget process was marked by the decision of the Finance and Administration Board to impose expenditure cuts to balance the budget without consultation with the other departments. This represented a significant departure from the historical patterns of the Division's budgeting process, and much stronger moves to enforce budget discipline by Finance and Administration in the period leading up to the formal adoption of the budget at the 1987 Annual General Meeting. This period also involved further moves by the sacred departments to resist this budget discipline. However, such resistance was to prove only partly successful. The major phases in this stage are summarized in Table 6.4.

The decision of the Finance and Administration Board to independently determine the allocation of resources necessary to balance the budget was a significant departure from the participative, consultative budgeting process of the Division. Even though there had been a tendency to contain the resolution of residual conflict within the management structure (via the Senior Management Group) in recent years, it was a major centralization of budget prerogative for Finance and Administration to assert its formal responsibility to present the budget to the Annual General Meeting. However, the actual decision was not a significant departure from that arrived at during the Budget Conference. The general parameters of the options identified through that consultation process were adhered to, with the only major change being an extra $60,000 cut to Mission Outreach. Also, the decision only set the global budget figure for each Department, their rights to determine how their programmes were affected, and for the Annual General Meeting to arbitrate on priorities, were recognized. Thus, the Finance and Administration decision can be seen as an attempt by accountants to get the sacred departments to face what they saw as the financial reality of the budget.

However, the sacred occupational groups still did not accept the relevance of such a rational accounting view of the budgeting process to their activities. They heatedly challenged the right of Finance and Administration to make such decisions, and their effects. In particular, Mission Outreach and Educational Activities argued that they were losers, as they had borne all the cuts necessary to balance the budget,

Accounting Systems III   209

and Finance and Administration was a winner as it had only had to increase its net contribution to the budget (see chapter 4). Again, sacred occupational groups argued for income increasing strategies, but identified the problem more concretely as poor stewardship by Parish members. Their major response was to develop strategies of

Phase 15 Finance and Administration Board	31 Aug	Budget Conference considered. Decided to balance budget. Reduced Mission Outreach by further $60,000 and recommended global figures for departments and Presbyteries.
Phase 16 Senior Management Group	1 Sep	Finance and Administration Director reported on budget decision, explained that saw as their responsibility and felt it unfair that Senior Management Group had to make hard decisions. Mission Outreach felt it unfair that they had taken all cuts to balance budget and two sacred departments majority of cuts at Budget Conference. Role of departments extensively discussed. No clear picture emerged of how to deal with budget problems. Finance and Administration wanted Annual General Meeting to look seriously at hard decisions needed in balancing the budget.
Phase 17 Senior Management Group	15 Sep	Stewardship identified as major problem across whole Mainstream Church. Giving less than 5% of single aged pension.
Phase 18 Mission Outreach Board	29 Sep	Effects of balanced budget decision discussed. Problem of income growth identified. Also, need for trade-offs with new programmes. Despair expressed over staff cuts, especially in Regional Education and Mission Officers. Worry over Finance and Administration making decisions about goals of this department. Stewardship felt to be central problem. Felt to be plenty of excess resources in Parishes. Decided needed to put cuts that would hurt to Annual General Meeting and strongly argue effects of budget cuts.
Phase 19 Finance and Administration Board	8 Oct	Special meeting on budget. Heated feelings of sacred department Directors at Senior Management Group reported. Some adjustments agreed to reduce Mission Outreach cuts ($10,000). Worry that Mission Outreach would put sensitive cuts to Annual General Meeting and get change in budget. Felt that would be able to convince Annual General Meeting to stay with balanced budget. Problem of student allowances and increased student numbers identified. Felt could not refuse students, but need to restructure allowances. Ministerial training said to be too costly. Decided to have special appeal to fund 5 extra students, but also to force Educational Activities to look at options.

Table 6.4: A Chronology of Stage Three of the 1988 Budget Process

210   *Management Control in a Voluntary Organization*

Phase 20 Annual General Meeting	10 Oct	Day 1: Importance of ministry and increased student numbers outlined by Chairperson. Problem was to find the funds.
	12 Oct	Day 3: Finance and Administration presented budget to be adopted on Day 6. Emphasized had been operating beyond our means for many years and problem of level of Parish giving. Concluded it was not a nice budget, but could not afford more. Educational Activities discussion raised problems of financial constraints, particularly in relation to ministerial education. Specific concern by some on level of student allowances. 'Finances felt to be ruling policy of the church'.
	13 Oct	Day 4: Mission Outreach discussion identified staffing problems and its many areas of service to Division. Stewardship emphasised as a problem area. However, no discussion of budget effects during policy debates.
	14 Oct	Day 5: Community Service discussion did not raise budget issues. Same outcome for Finance and Administration discussion later in day.
	15 Oct	Day 6: Adoption of budget debated. Motions calling for greater support for students. Proposal to increase Presbyteries contributions by 2% defeated. Approved idea of Educational Activities, in consultation with Finance and Administration, exploring options for funding extra students and reporting on method to Divisional Council. Mission Outreach spoke on effects of cuts on their activities. Echoed by Educational Activities. Some support for 'anguish' felt by departments. Again, need for better stewardship mentioned. However, budget passed without further alteration. Also, the new Ministerial Support Funds Committee under control of Finance and Administration established.
Phase 21 Finance and Administration Board	2 Nov.	Extra students above budget, now 10 not 5, budget shortfall of $100,000. Felt needed to resolve level of allowances as were too high. Also needed to run a special funding appeal and get Educational Activities to look at the cost of ministerial education. Saw these as solutions for 1988, but did not solve problem for next budget.
Phase 22 Finance and Administration Board	7 Dec.	Director reported on decision to reduce theological student allowances and that remaining deficit was $85,000, less $35,000 already pledged to special appeal. Mission Outreach request for longer range planning on budget discussed. This felt to be the ideal, but could not be achieved at present. Felt guarantees could not be given.

Table 6.4: A Chronology of Stage Three of the 1988 Budget Process- Continued

Accounting Systems III 211

resistance that would highlight the negative effects of the budget cuts on sacred ends. These were primarily to challenge the budget at the Annual General Meeting and emphasize the necessity of their sacred activities to its members. Discussions in Mission Outreach went as far as to suggest that it could use its discretion to recommend cuts that 'would hurt the most' to have maximum impact at the Annual General Meeting[12]. The effect of Finance and Administration decision, therefore, was not for the sacred departments to rationally face the financial reality of the budget, but for them to actively construct the budgeting process as a political arena within which they could protect their sacred activities from the intrusion of secular concerns.

It would seem from the position of Finance and Administration on the 1988 budget to this point, that they advocated the dominance of secular financial concerns over sacred ends. Their position, however, was more complex than such a simple dichotomy. As argued in chapter 5, accountants promoted accounting as a tool to support mission. It was only their view of the income constrained nature of the financial crisis, and the need to balance the budget, that led them to argue that 'the financial reality' must be faced through reductions in sacred activities. The accountants' acceptance that sacred ends were normally dominant was evidenced during this stage in their reaction to an unexpected increase in theological student numbers. Five students had been allowed for in the budget[13], but in response to the need for ministers identified at the Divisional Council Consultation, ten candidates were now expected. On the basis of current funding of student allowances this would require an extra $50,000 to maintain a balanced budget. Given the potential sacred crisis identified for ministers within the Division, Finance and Administration made a commitment that no student would be refused on financial grounds. In part, the accountants still applied a financial logic to this new problem, arguing that theological training was too costly and student allowances too high. However, they also evidenced a willingness to abandon their budget strategy of expenditure containment by considering a special appeal to Parishes to raise the extra funds. The accountants, therefore, promoted the restriction of sacred activities in the name of facing 'financial reality', but also recognised limits on the extent to which such secular concerns could intrude on sacred ends.

The promotion of, and resistance to, the budget reached a culmination with its presentation to the 1987 Annual General Meeting.

212 *Management Control in a Voluntary Organization*

Part of the tone for this debate was set on the first day when the retiring Chairperson, in his final address to the Division, stressed the importance of the missional imperatives identified at the Divisional Council Consultation and the 'blessing' of the increased numbers of theological students. This theme was continued by Educational Activities in its report to the Annual General Meeting. Ministerial education was the main focus of this report, which led to extended debates about the need for, and level of, student allowances. There appeared to be strong support from the majority of members of the Annual General Meeting for ministerial education. During this debate, the Head of the Theological College stated that he felt 'finances were ruling the policy of the church'. This statement openly expressed a view held by many of the senior staff in sacred occupational groups[14], indicating that there was considerable tension between the budget strategy promoted by the accountants and the preferred position of the sacred occupational groups, especially around the issue of ministerial education.

In a similar budget ploy, Mission Outreach also made its contributions to sacred ends the focus of its report to the Annual General Meeting. They particularly emphasized the effects the budget cuts would have on services to Parishes, and the loss of Regional Education and Mission Officers (REMOs) in some Presbyteries. In contrast to the Educational Activities report, there was little reaction to these problems, although support for the important work of REMOs was voiced. However, it appeared that there was no significant support for the budget problems faced by Mission Outreach.

Before the formal budget adoption, therefore, it appeared that the resistance from Educational Activities may be successful in the area of ministerial education, but that Mission Outreach was unlikely to be similarly successful in avoiding any budget cuts. The general lack of significant reaction to the loss of sacred activities, except for ministerial education, is consistent with the historic Parish views on the budget discussed previously. These generally viewed the extent of Division-based services as excessive, and favoured their reduction. Therefore, with the majority of Annual General Meeting members being Parish ministers and laity, it seemed that there was little broad sacred support for many of the cuts to department sacred activities, except for ministerial education which was a significant sacred priority and had strong potential Parish level impacts.

Accounting Systems III 213

This pattern of support was maintained during the budget adoption debate. The two sacred departments again emphasized the negative effects on their sacred activities. Also, many speakers commented sympathetically on the problems and anguish that was being faced by these departments. However, no motions were made to alter the budget and seek solutions other than expenditure reduction, except in the area of theological students. Several motions seeking to address this issue were debated. There was strong support for the need to accept all students, and for them to have a reasonable level of financial support. Initially it was proposed that Presbyteries be required to increase their contributions by 2%. However, Finance and Administration opposed this as unrealistic, and instead proposed its option of taking further time to review the cost of allowances and investigating a special appeal to cover the increased costs. This option also included an upper limit of ten on the student intake. Eventually, this motion was supported, although the limit on numbers was removed; all suitable students were to be accepted and supported. The Annual General Meeting, thus, approved the general budget strategy of Finance and Administration. The only resistance to addressing the financial crisis through expenditure cuts was the strong support for the critical sacred end of ministerial education, with which the accountants agreed.

This support for theological students was also an issue in the following report to the Annual General Meeting of the Ministerial Stipends Committee, which recommended that the current student allowances system apply for 1988. These recommendations were opposed by the Divisional Council motion for the abolition of the Ministerial Stipends Committee and its replacement with a Finance and Administration controlled Ministerial Support Funds Committee. This was approved, but its membership was expanded to include a lay representative from each Presbytery (consistent with the preferred structure of negotiations in the Division). However, as these Presbytery representatives would mainly be corresponding members, the effective control of the Committee still resided with Finance and Administration. The potential for Finance and Administration to address its perception of the financial dimension of the theological student problem was thus made possible.

After the Annual General Meeting, Finance and Administration used this new control over ministerial support to attempt to find a

214   *Management Control in a Voluntary Organization*

'financially realistic' solution to the support of theological students, a problem which had now expanded to a potential $100,000 budget deficit with 15 new students expected. The new Ministerial Support Funds Committee was constituted as quickly as possible, and given the mandate to review (reduce) the level of allowances[15]. However, this only minimally reduced the deficit, and Finance and Administration continued with its planned departure from its general budget strategy by using a special appeal to fund the remaining deficit. This decision might appear to be inconsistent with the previous arguments of the accountants that increases in income were unlikely and that the budget strategy had to be based on fitting expenditure within income estimates. However, the 'faith' placed in increased Parish stewardship for this problem was seen only as a short-term solution. The uncertainty of income levels was still stated to be a problem for the 1989 budget. Special appeals and faith in increased giving still were not regarded as a rational basis for solving the general budget problem, which had to be addressed through more financially realistic assessments of funding availability.

In summary, during the third stage of the 1988 budget process, there was conflict between the budgetary discipline promoted by accountants and the protection of sacred ends promoted by sacred occupational groups. Accountants generally supported the importance of sacred ends, but argued that the financial reality of the financial crisis had to be addressed by expenditure cuts. To balance the budget, such cuts had to be imposed on sacred departments. Sacred occupational groups strongly resisted this intrusion on their sacred activities, and constructed the budgeting process as a political arena for challenging budget cuts. From the normal dominance of the sacred and secular divide, such strategies of resistance may have been expected to have been successful. However, they were not generally successful because, historically, the sacred activities of the departments did not have broad Parish support. Thus, it was not that the views of the accountants were totally accepted, but that Parish members preferred to keep resources for Parish sacred ends rather than increase support of Division activities. The exception was the critical sacred ends of ministerial education, where the secondary nature of financial concerns was clearly signalled by Parish members. Accounting views of the budget, therefore, appeared to generally dominate the 1988 budget outcomes, but the limits for this was the level of sacredness of

Accounting Systems III 215

the ends it challenged. When these were critical, and had broad support, the intrusion of accounting was not tolerated.

However, the accountants also accepted this subordination of accounting for such critical sacred ends. They still, though, constructed the support of such ends within a financial rationality. This was evidenced by a concern with the 'costliness of support', and their application of a financial rationality to the funding of ministerial education through the new central control over ministerial support. While the dominance of sacred ends was not questioned, how they were to be resourced was subjected to an accounting gaze, as it had been defined as a secular concern. Also, the adoption of the extra-budget appeal strategy for this problem appeared to replace the accountants' income constrained view of the budget with one of faith in an income increasing strategy. This would have been a significant change, as it would have sustained the sacred departments' views of how the budget should support their sacred ends. However, instead it was defined as a one-off crisis solution, the success of which did not challenge the income constrained view of the budget crisis now, and in the future. Therefore, future budgets were still seen by the accountants as facing the same financial crisis, with increased stewardship as an unlikely (and thus, risky) solution, and rational, financially realistic budgeting the only option.

IV. CHAPTER SUMMARY

This chapter has examined both the historical and contemporary dynamics of the budgeting process in the Northern Division. The budgeting process was selected for detailed analysis as it was identified in chapter 5 as the most significant accounting practice across all areas of the Division. It was argued to be a contested terrain between the differing interpretations of the role of accounting held by accountants and sacred occupational groups. Also, the budget was the key accounting practice through which the secular control problems prioritized by the financial crisis came into direct conflict with sacred ends. In particular, the 1988 budget was typical of historical trends for a participative, consultative budgeting process, and the increasing tension in recent years between mission activities and the financial crisis. However, it was also a critical case, as it was the first budget where this tension became highly overt, with significant reductions to the mission activities of the sacred departments. Therefore, the significance of the Budgeting System was potentially a major indicator of the impact of accounting upon the life of the Division.

Historically and contemporarily, the Budgeting System was identified as a source of some significant impacts of accounting on the Northern Division. The official policy had always been a balanced budget, but this policy had been more rigorously adhered to since 1985. Also, the income constrained view of the budget promoted by accountants in recent years had resulted in programme reductions in the sacred departments, particularly in the 1988 budget. In addition, the budgeting process had been associated with some centralization of accounting control over a number of years in the name of more 'expert management' and 'greater effectiveness', with more moves in this direction in recent times. In particular, there was a tendency for a movement away from the broad participative, consultative basis of the Budgeting System towards a more restricted, head-office, Finance and Administration dominated process. Also, several areas of financial policy had come more securely under the control of Finance and Administration, for example, ministerial support. Overall, the Budgeting System seemed to have some highly significant effects on the Division, and to have been associated with greater influence by accountants in its management.

Sacred occupational groups strongly resisted this greater significance of accounting within the budgeting process, and its intrusion on their pursuit of sacred ends. As argued in chapter 5, they opposed the relevance of a rational financial approach to the management of their sacred priorities. This was reflected in their rejection of the secular control emphasis of the accountants on balancing the budget through expenditure reduction. In part, this rejection was contingent on the way in which the budget was used. If the budget had been used to support sacred ends, such as through using it as a means to identify income increasing options to fund mission activities, it may have been accepted. However, to the sacred occupational groups accounting was clearly a secondary concern to the primacy of sacred ends. Their response to its intrusion on sacred ends was to resist budget cuts by emphasizing the negative effects on their mission activities. Therefore, the sacred and secular divide was strongly embedded in the orientation of sacred occupational groups

Accounting Systems III 217

within the sacred departments, and in the form of their resistance to the Budgeting System.

The accountants, as argued in chapter 5, also supported the sacred and secular divide, but in a weaker form as their focus was on the secular control problem presented by the financial crisis. Their financial rationality constructed the relation of the financial crisis to the budget as one of income constraint. Financially responsible and realistic management, therefore, was seen as requiring a budget strategy of expenditure reduction, which, unfortunately, meant that sacred ends had to be rationally fitted within the limited financial resources available. The promotion of this approach was aided by the advantageous organizational structure position of Finance and Administration, which gave them formal control of the budgeting process, and enabled them to formulate the budgeting process as a rational expenditure reduction exercise. Thus, the ability of accountants to effectively articulate the budgeting process as one of rational expenditure reduction enabled them to impose budget cuts against the resistance of the sacred occupational groups.

However, the promotion of accounting solutions by the accountants did not appear to be sufficient in itself to overcome the tendencies of the sacred and secular divide. A critical factor was the general inability of the sacred occupational groups to marshal significant support for their resistance efforts. This was because historically there was not broad sacred support for the activities of the departments within the Parishes. The Parishes generally favoured the reduction of central Division activities to allow greater resources to be diverted to Parish activities. From this, it may be proposed that there is an additional axis of tension within the sacred and secular divide, with local activities favoured over central activities. This is consistent with the previous findings of Harris (1969) and Laughlin (1984) (see Booth 1993), but the evidence here is only suggestive and further research is required to develop this possibility.

The importance of the extent of sacred support for the success of resistance to the financial logic of the budgeting process was evidenced in the case of ministerial education. This critical sacred end had broad Parish support, and its primacy over secular concerns was acknowledged by both the sacred occupational groups and the accountants. Sacred ends had to be perceived as critical by a wide support base, particularly at the Parish level, to be exempted from the

218 *Management Control in a Voluntary Organization*

dominant budget strategy of expenditure reduction. However, the accountants still evaluated this sacred control problem within a financial rationality, and attempted to construct its exemption status as once-off and special so that the budget strategy could be maintained for future budgets. Thus, the tension between mission activities, the financial crisis and the financial rationality promoted by accountants was likely to continue as part of the dynamics of the budgeting process within the Northern Division.

Notes

[1] The Budget and Finance Board and Finance and Administration were the primary bodies responsible for budget formulation. Also important were the reports of the Presbyteries-Division Co-ordinating Team, responsible for a period for formulating budget priorities. See Northern Division 1977, 1978, 1979a, 1979b, 1980a, 1980b, 1981a, 1981b, 1982a, 1982b, 1983a, 1983b, 1984a, 1984b, 1985a, 1985b, 1986a, 1986b. These budget related reports contained substantial narratives on budget formulation issues and outcomes.

[2] The 'Before the Next Step' Programme discussed in chapter 5 was another example of budget promotion.

[3] It is also recognised that such practices within the budgeting process may be one of the ways in which the underlying structure of negotiations and the grass-roots ethos of the Division are reproduced in terms of Giddens' (1984) conception of the duality of structures and action. However, such effects are not directly relevant to this analysis.

[4] One exception to this was Operation Breakthrough. As stated in chapter 4, this budget promotion resulted in a significant rise in income in 1983. Operation Breakthrough was an one-off exercise aimed at increasing members' stewardship by making them see budget activities as more personal commitments to mission. It involved a significant campaign of leaflets, promotional videos, Parish based task groups and Parish visits by department staff. Part of this was the symbolic change of the budget name to the 'Mission and Service Fund'. Despite this programmes' success, no similar efforts were made in later years.

[5] The continued ability to resist the budget crises in this way may also have been related to the fact that the final result of many of these budgeted deficits was substantially reduced by unexpected increased contributions from various Division agencies during the budget year.

[6] There were no mentions in budget reports before this time of the use of any system of priorities in budget cutting actions.

[7] It should be noted that this data represents only sections of the total 1988 budget process. Many discussions undoubtedly took place outside the data collection patterns of

Accounting Systems III

this study. However, the discussions observed were significant ones as they covered the major formal department and Division based decision points through which the budget passed.

[8] A department could reduce its use of budget funds by increasing its own independent sources of income or reducing expenditure. As the two sacred departments had no income sources capable of raising the required levels of funds, they were largely limited to expenditure reduction.

[9] Accountants also emphasised the expenditure side of the budget because most items were fairly fixed, being staff wages or associated costs. Thus, once programmes were approved, it was very difficult to alter the budget during the year.

[10] The maintenance of the existing level of infrastructure may also have been related to the relatively new identity of each department, which had only achieved the full establishment of their structures in 1986.

[11] It was decided to observe one discussion group for all its discussions rather then move from group to group and only get incomplete data on each. The Mission Outreach group was selected as less previous observation had been possible of the views of its staff.

[12] These were felt to be Regional Education and Mission Officer (REMO) positions which were the primary avenue of department services to the Parishes. These were the final choice for the required cut in 2 staff positions, but this choice was affected also by convenience as two REMOs were expected to resign anyway.

[13] This would have been more than adequate given intakes in recent years.

[14] This was determined from observations of their positions during the budgeting process and confirmed in the final debriefing interviews (see chapter 4).

[15] The Committee reduced the level of allowances by breaking their linkage with the ministerial stipend, basing them instead on the Federal government's tertiary study student allowances, and introducing means testing for future years. This only reduced the deficit by a small amount for 1988, but more importantly it restated the Division's policy on support of theological students to one of providing some financial assistance, not a total living allowance.

Chapter 7
Conclusions

I. INTRODUCTION

This study has addressed the basic problematic - how does accounting achieve and maintain a position of organizational significance (Hopwood 1983)? This problematic is important because accounting has obtained and continues to maintain a significant position in the affairs of a wide array of modern organizations. To address this problematic, accounting was analysed as a situated practice (Chua 1988) in an effort to add to the increasing body of research on accounting in action. In doing so, the traditional, dominant perspective in the accounting literature that accounting possesses inherent functional imperatives that are useful in organizations was rejected as a starting premise (Burchell et al 1980), as it limits the consideration of why and how accounting is used in organizations. It was replaced with a view that the significance of accounting in organizations is socially constructed, and a concern to identify the actual outcomes and consequences of the use of particular types of accounting practices. Any analysis must question the various uses of accounting that exist, their effects and the nature of their organizational and social settings. Thus the 'purposefulness' of accounting itself becomes part of the problematic of study.

In chapter 1 it was argued that the purposefulness of accounting was linked with the rationalization of management in modern organizations. These ideas were developed further in chapter 2. A critical structuralist framework was used to propose that the organizing problems of business organizations around the extraction, realization and allocation of surplus value were a major focus of the rationalization process. Accounting, as a highly developed abstract

221

222 Managment Control in a Voluntary Organization

financial measurement and communication system, had various objective and subjective characteristics which provided a particular form of visibility into and of these economic means-ends relationships, and thus were potentially useful for the management of such problems. However, accounting was not the sole, or even obviously the 'best', way in which these organizing problems could be addressed. Such organizing problems were argued to be the province of management, which is composed of a range of occupational groups with differing expertise competing for the dominance of management hierarchies via the promotion of alternative solutions to these organizing problems. This competition may be aided by the real, and ideologically emphasized, effects of economic crises. Therefore, it was stated that accountants within firms, and the accounting profession more generally, play a significant role in constructing accounting as a 'better' solution than those of other occupational groups. At the present time, this can be seen in the concerns within parts of the profession, at least in the U.S.A. and Australia, with the management accounting issues surrounding 'relevance lost' (Johnson and Kaplan 1987) and Japanese accounting practices (Williams et al 1990). Also, in part the actions of accountants are aided by the institutionalization of accounting ideas in modern industrial societies. In enabling managers to think about and act upon economic means-ends relations, accounting also may constrain their ability to use other ways of thinking and acting by constructing and propagating restricted views of rationality and moral orders within firms. From these perspectives, the significance of accounting in capitalist firms was argued to be related to its characteristics, the organizing problems to which these may be relevant, and the occupational groups that promote and/or resist its use.

It was argued in chapter 1 that the problematic be focused on accounting in churches, as a subset of voluntary organizations, as extreme cases of the potential conditions under which accounting may be purposeful in organizations. The process of rationalization has spread beyond profit-making firms to encompass a wide range of organizations in the state and civil society. In chapter 2, it was established that the diffusion of ideas involved in this process has led to a general tendency towards increasing homogeneity of organizational forms and management practices in all sectors of modern societies, but at the same time there are also other pressures

Conclusions 223

towards divergence of practices. Within this context, the use of accounting and control systems, and the measurement of the success of work performance on the basis of financial criteria, have become increasingly difficult for any large scale organization to avoid. However, even within business organizations the process of rationalization is not complete and can meet with significant resistance. It was argued that this may be particularly so for organizations in the state and civil society, where alternative non-calculable bases of organizational legitimation are found. It was proposed in chapter 2 that the commitment of voluntary organizations to the values of community and democracy represent a highly non-calculable basis of organizational legitimation which is a direct challenge to rationalization. Also that churches, because of their generally altruistic form of membership involvement and the extreme non-calculable basis of their religious ends, were potential sites where rationalization would be least legitimate and the purposefulness of accounting very open to question.

In chapter 2, therefore, an adaptation of the critical structuralist framework to the specific context of churches to consider such issues was developed. Churches were argued to face two major types of organizing problems, which represent the sacred and secular divide in such organizations, to which management solutions have to be found. The dominant organizing problems are those concerned with the maintenance of the sacred dimensions of the organization, and these potentially act as a significant source of resistance to the process of rationalization and the significance of accounting in churches. Secular organizing problems, however, which are concerned with administrative and financial support activities for the sacred, provide space for rationalization and accounting in churches, but are subordinated to the sacred. Competing solutions to these organizing problems may be promoted by the various occupational groups involved in the management of churches. In particular, the clergy are structurally cast in a role of protecting the sacred, and would be expected to promote the sacred and secular divide and be the major source of resistance to rationalization and accounting. On the other hand, accountants would promote accounting solutions to secular organizing problems. To overcome the resistance of the sacred and secular divide they may also attempt to 'sacredize' such solutions. Also, the resistance to solutions may be affected by various crises faced by churches. Sacred crises, such as declining membership, will increase the resistance to rationalization and decrease the significance of accounting solutions. Secular crises, such as financial shortages, may increase the space for rational management solutions and the use of accounting practices. The potential outcomes may be more indeterminate, however, when sacred and secular crises and organizing problems become intertwined. In summary, the space for rationalization and accounting may be related to the promotion and resistance around the organizing problems flowing from the sacred and secular divide. The variable significance of both will be affected by sacred and secular crises, and the actions of competing occupational groups promoting their own occupational solutions to these organizing problems, particularly the clergy and accountants.

This framework was applied to a case study of accounting practices in the Northern Division of the Mainstream Church. Chapter 3 outlined some background context of the Mainstream Church and its Northern Division. Chapter 4 described and analysed the formal operations of the accounting systems of the Northern Division. The effects of the financial dynamics of the Division were also considered. Chapter 5 considered the differential uses of accounting in practice by sacred occupational groups and accountants within the Division. Chapter 6 focused on the dynamics of the budgeting process, and how it was related to processes of negotiation within the organization, as the budget was the focal accounting practice of the Division. The first section of this chapter overviews the major findings of the study in terms of the framework outlined above. In the next section the findings are compared to some general trends in voluntary organizations, and specifically to the findings of previous studies on churches. This comparison is provided to give some indication of the ability to generalize from this case study, and potential directions for future research. The study concludes with some brief overview comments.

II.   MAJOR FINDINGS

The problematic of this study required that two general questions be addressed. First, how significant was accounting in the Northern Division of the Mainstream Church. This includes a consideration of current significance and any trends over time. Then, how and why did this level of significance occur; that is, what

Conclusions   225

explanation(s) can be offered for the observed uses and effects of accounting within the Northern Division. Both these questions have been considered side-by-side in the analysis in chapters 4, 5 and 6. In this section, first the evidence relating to the level of significance of accounting within the Northern Division is reviewed, then the critical structuralist explanation proposed in the analysis is contrasted to several other competing explanations. Also, it should be restated at this point that this study has only focused on the head office operations of the Northern Division. Therefore, the discussion below relates only to that level of analysis. The broader applicability of the findings is assessed in the next section.

Assessing any overall level of significance of accounting within the Northern Division is a difficult task. Three different types of measures of the importance of accounting have been presented in chapters 4, 5 and 6. First, a fairly crude measure of significance was gauged from the sophistication of the technical design of the Division accounting systems. There is a general assumption in much of the accounting literature that the less developed an accounting system, the less its potential importance in an organization (for example, Anthony and Young 1984; Chandler and Deams 1979; Kaplan 1984; Laughlin 1984; Loft 1986). Second, the extent of the use of accounting in decision-making, in terms of frequency of use and time duration of use, was used as a process measure of the potential impact of accounting within the Division. In relative terms, the higher these measures, the higher its significance. However, due to the absence of any previous research using such simple quantitative measures, the absolute level of significance was based on ad hoc judgement rules. It is hoped that future research will build on this novel measurement approach so that benchmark criteria can be established. Finally, outcome measures were provided in terms of extensive qualitative assessments of how accounting was used in decision-making and key issue cases. The indications for each of these are reviewed below.

First, the Northern Division accounting systems in 1987 were assessed to be fairly sophisticated. The Management Accounting Control System was a highly developed responsibility accounting system with a strong budgetary control focus for departments and cost centres. Its features, such as depreciation allocations to departments, nominal interest charges to enforce 'responsible financial management' by departments and the use of the quarterly forecast

226   *Managment Control in a Voluntary Organization*

column to enforce regular revisions of the budget scenario, were indications of the use of standard business control technologies. The Budgeting System also followed a fairly standard business form of practice with its bottom-up, participative process. The focus of the process on establishing priorities and allocating scarce resources between the departments emphasized the importance of financial dimensions of the activities of the Division. Therefore, both the Management Accounting Control System and Budgeting System of the Northern Division were technically modern and followed many business practices.

The sophistication of the Management Accounting Control System also appeared to have increased over time. The basic structure of the Management Accounting Control System was adopted in 1979, but its functions were refined further after the new divisional management structure was implemented in 1984. In particular, the introduction of more advanced techniques such as depreciation allocations, nominal interest charges and revised budget forecasts occurred during this later period. The basic design of the Budgeting System seemed to have been fairly consistent since 1977. However, a change towards more centralized control of the process under the Department of Finance and Administration since 1985, and final priority determination through the Senior Management Group in 1986, had occurred. These seemed to indicate a trend towards more reliance on professional managers. There were some indications, therefore, that the technical design of the accounting system of the Northern Division had been becoming more sophisticated in recent years.

The Management Accounting Control System and the Budgeting System, therefore, potentially enabled a very standardized and monetarized gaze into, and thereby financial control over, very detailed levels of the operations of the departments of the Northern Division. It had sophisticated accounting systems with a tendency for an increase in this sophistication. From a technical design perspective there appeared to be a reasonable potential for accounting to be significant in the Division.

Second, the process measures of the use of accounting revealed a more variable realization of the potential significance of the accounting systems within the Northern Division:

i) Sacred occupational groups generally made limited use of accounting. Within the Divisional Council and the Department of

Conclusions 227

Educational Activities Board, the frequency and time duration of use of accounting was less than 30%, except for frequency in the Board which was 31%. This was judged to indicate a low significance for accounting (secondary analysis of meeting documents confirmed this pattern and suggested it also applied to the Department of Mission Outreach and the Department of Welfare Services Boards). The pattern was similar for the Educational Activities Directorate when the budget was not being discussed. However, when the budget was considered by sacred occupational groups in this forum, the extent of use of accounting appeared to be of high significance. High significance for accounting was also indicated when it was used by sacred occupational groups within the Department of Mission Outreach Finance Committee, with both frequency and time duration greater than 60%. Also, a wide range of accounting practices were used in this forum. Therefore, the significance of accounting, in terms of process measures, to sacred occupational groups appeared to be variable. It was generally low, but was higher when the budget was discussed (this was to a lesser extent than in the Directorate but still applied across all forums), and in the Finance Committee.

ii) Accountants evidenced a generally higher use of accounting than sacred occupational groups. Within the secular financially orientated Department of Finance and Administration Board, accounting was frequently used (53%) and took up about half the time of discussions (49%) (secondary analysis of meeting documents confirmed this pattern). This indicated a high significance for accounting, but lower than that for the Finance Committee. Like that forum, usage by accountants was more evenly spread over the Management Accounting Control System, budget and accounting ideas more generally. Also, the budget again was dominant, being about half of all accounting usage. Accounting, therefore, appeared to be of high significance to accountants, but not pervasive.

iii) Within the Senior Management Group, a forum concerned with interactions between accountants and sacred occupational groups, 40% of items and 28% of time involved accounting. The budget accounted for almost all of these uses, at 87% for each. This indicates a generally low significance for the use of accounting during interactions between accountants and sacred occupational groups, with the budget being the key focus of interactions concerning these occupational groups.

228 *Managment Control in a Voluntary Organization*

For the process measures, therefore, it appeared as if accounting had a tendency to have a limited impact on sacred occupational groups within the Division. However, there were two exceptions to this tendency. First, the budget was the most significant accounting effect across all forums, and was even more significant at certain points in time. Second, accounting appeared very significant in the Department of Mission Outreach Finance Committee, which may be expected given its secular financial support function within this sacred department. The tendency was for accounting to have a much higher impact for accountants within the secular financial orientated Department of Finance and Administration. Again, the budget was also the major concern of accountants. Accounting, therefore, appeared to be of variable significance in the Division, both within and across occupational groups.

The first two measures of the significance of accounting give an apparently inconsistent picture. The technical sophistication of the Division accounting systems indicates a reasonable potential for accounting to be significant, but this does not seem to be realized in terms of the extent of use of accounting, except for the accountants, sacred occupational groups in one setting, and the budget. However, as the process measures weight all uses equally, they could understate the significance of accounting in terms of outcomes. The impacts of accounting in terms of outcomes was gauged by overall qualitative assessments of how it was used and through key issue cases. Again the picture here was mixed:

i) While generally the Management Accounting Control System reports seemed to be little used, the accountants in the Department of Finance and Administration did place strong emphasis on financial control. The performance of all departments was regularly reviewed and pressure was placed on them addressing any negative trends. Strong evidence of this effect was the establishment and operation of the Department of Mission Outreach Finance Committee, where the sacred occupational groups were highly concerned with the previous poor financial performance of this sacred department. However, it should be noted that another effect of this Committee was to partly partition such concerns from the sacred operations of the department. This emphasis on financial control also represented a favouring of management control techniques over trust in managerial relations by the accountants. That this had some impact was reflected in sacred

Conclusions 229

occupational groups resentment of the lack of trust in their management and the intrusion of accounting controls into their achievement of sacred ends. Therefore, there seemed to be evidence of some impact of the Management Accounting Control System in the area of budgetary control.

ii) Aspects of the Budgeting System also indicated some significant accounting effects. Historically, while the official goal was a balanced budget, this had not been enforced in the period 1977 to 1985, but had been for the three budgets since then. Also, in the last two budgets the income constrained view promoted by the accountants in the Department of Finance and Administration had resulted in programme cuts, particularly for the 1988 budget. However, this increased impact of accounting within the Division was not unchallenged. The sacred occupational groups in the sacred departments did not accept the income constrained view of the accountants and argued instead for an income increasing approach. It is recognised that such resistance to budget cuts may be expected in any budgeting process. However, the particular nature of wage labour relations in churches, and voluntary organizations in general, where sanctions are more difficult to apply, mean that ideology (sacred orientation) becomes a more central issue in understanding the nature of the resistance process. This resistance, while vigorous, was unsuccessful, and the accountants' definition of the situation and its solution prevailed. There were also indications of a movement away from the strong historical consultative basis of the Division budgeting process towards a more centralized, accounting orientated process since 1986. In addition, the solution of the 1988 budget crisis had enabled the movement of all the financial aspects of ministerial support under the oversight of the Department of Finance and Administration. The Budgeting System then appeared to have highly significant outcomes for the Northern Division, and to have been associated with greater influence by accountants in its management.

iii) However, where accounting was used, the way in which decisions were made in the Northern Division indicated major limits on the significance of accounting. The general outcome was that accounting was clearly secondary as a decision criteria to sacred ends. The only exception to this was basic operational decisions that did not appear to have any direct mission effects. This subordination of accounting was accepted by both sacred occupational groups and

230   *Managment Control in a Voluntary Organization*

accountants, but the latter did promote greater use of accounting in terms of the financially realistic pursuit of mission. This was evidenced in the much greater use of accounting reports and ideas in the Department of Finance and Administration, a secular domain, and the higher weighting given to these information sources. Also, it emerged in the budget domination by the accountants discussed above. The income constrained and expenditure cuts budget strategy was promoted as it was seen as the only financially responsible solution to support sacred ends through the budget crisis. It was not proposed to promote the dominance of accounting. The alteration of the strategy to incorporate an income increasing solution for the high sacred priority of extra ministerial students in the 1988 budget emphasized this acceptance of the dominance of sacred ends by the accountants. Therefore, there were clear limits placed on the significance of accounting within the Northern Division as it was seen as secondary to mission. This view was particularly used by sacred occupational groups managing the sacred departments, but existed in a weaker form for accountants in their secular department. They promoted the partial subordination of the sacred to accounting in the name of being financially realistic and responsible.

Therefore, in terms of outcomes measures, even in those instances where significant use was made of accounting, the general tendency was that its significance was restricted by a subordinate position to sacred ends. This tendency was stronger for sacred occupational groups than accountants. Also, it seemed to be the same for sacred occupational groups regardless of the different sacred orientations of the three departments within which they were located, except that the Departments of Mission Outreach and Educational Activities were more concerned with the budget as they were the ones directly affected by it. A similar comparison cannot be made for the secular orientation of a department, as the Department of Finance and Administration was the only example within the Division. It is possible that the findings for accountants are a product of both their occupational orientation and the financial management responsibilities of the department within which they were located. Despite these tendencies, however, accounting still had some significant effects on the management of the Division through a strong budgetary control logic and the accountants' dominance of the Budgeting System. In particular, the enforcement of the accountants' income constrained

Conclusions 231

strategy to solve the budget crisis resulted in a significant intrusion of accounting into the realm of mission activities.

Overall, this study has found a variable significance for accounting in the Northern Division. While the accounting systems of the Division were sophisticated, the extent of their impact on its management appeared limited. For the sacred occupational groups, accounting generally had little impact, and where used it was treated as secondary to sacred functions. Usage of accounting was more significant for accountants, but still the subordinate position to sacred activities appeared to exist. However, they promoted a more active role for accounting as a necessary support function for sacred activities. Therefore, as sacred occupational groups dominated the management structure, the tendency was for accounting to play a limited and subordinate role in the management of the Division.

However, there were two partial exceptions to this tendency. First, accountants were able to exert considerable pressure for financial control on the sacred departments through the Management Accounting Control System. This use of accounting had increased since the adoption of the new management structure and the greater role of Finance and Administration in the financial oversight of Division operations. This created some tension with sacred occupational groups because they saw this as distrust of their management, as conflicting with the subordinate role of accounting, and as an intrusion into their rights to pursue their sacred functions as they saw fit. While they had to deal with such concerns, they tried as much as possible to partition accounting off from sacred functions. Second, the dominance of accountants in the Budgeting System allowed them to enforce accounting solutions to the budget crisis on the sacred departments. The control of this strategic resource allocation process under a time of resource shortage enabled accounting to have a significant impact on the ability to pursue mission programmes by the sacred departments. This also generated considerable resistance from the sacred occupational groups, but this was unsuccessful as they could not offer what appeared to be viable sacred solutions to the budget crisis. Through these two critical areas, therefore, accounting did have a significant impact and accountants played a greater role in the management of the Northern Division.

What explanations can be offered for these findings? In the first two chapters, a general distinction was made between efficiency and

232 *Managment Control in a Voluntary Organization*

control processes based explanations of the significance of accounting in modern organizations. Efficiency explanations, which in general argue for the significance of accounting in terms of it offering the most efficient solutions to the uncertainties faced by modern organizations in particular periods, were argued to be insufficient as they used an overly narrow economic conception of organizational action and thereby did not account for the actual actions of management. Control processes explanations, such as the critical structuralist approach adopted in this study, provide such insight as they focus on the actions of management, and competing occupational groups, in their attempts to dominate within organizations. Can any efficiency explanations be offered for the findings on the significance of accounting within the Northern Division of the Mainstream Church?

First, a simple efficiency based explanation could be proposed in terms of the functional orientation of the organization and its change over time. The 'non-business' nature of the majority of the activities and concerns of a church could be argued to lead to a lack of any functional use for accounting. The low overall significance of accounting within the Northern Division, therefore, would be explained by arguing that there was no comparative advantage for the inherent attributes of accounting in solving the dominant organizing problems of such organizations. It could also be argued that those instances where accounting was more significant was due to the more 'business' nature of the management activities in these areas. While the nature of the tasks undertaken may indeed offer some explanation of the variance in the use of accounting across operational units within the Division, overall such a simple efficiency argument is insufficient for at least three reasons. It provides no explanation for the resistance to, and active subordination of accounting in situations where it was potentially relevant such as dealing with budget cuts in the sacred departments. Also, it does not account for different levels of significance in accounting between forums in sacred and secular departments which had similar formal responsibility for financial matters. Finally, no insight is offered for the observed role of different occupational groups in the variable significance of accounting. The functional orientation of the Northern Division, therefore, is rejected as an alternative explanation.

A second efficiency explanation may be based on the scale of the organization - the larger the organization the greater its need for

Conclusions 233

administrative support and more sophisticated control systems, and thus the greater the significance of accounting. The Northern Division was argued to be a large organization with significant financial flows. The scale of the organization, therefore, may offer a partial explanation of the technical sophistication of its accounting systems and the emphasis on budgetary control, but is inconsistent with the low overall significance of accounting. Also, scale cannot account for the observed areas of the increase in the significance of accounting in recent years as the Division has been relatively constant in size since 1977 and the size of head office operations in financial terms has contracted since 1984 (see chapter 4). Finally, again the scale argument offers no explanation for the resistance to accounting and the role of occupational groups. Therefore, a scale effect is also rejected as an alternative explanation of the findings.

Overall, then an efficiency explanation of the findings of this study is rejected. Efficiency arguments fail to explain the variation in the significance of accounting observed, its connection to processes of resistance and promotion, and the associated actions of occupational groups.

Another alternative explanation of the findings, part way between the efficiency and control processes approaches, may be some form of diffusion argument. In general, such an argument would propose that there is a spread of managerial technologies from mainstream to marginal organizations within a society. This could be because such technologies are efficient in mainstream organizations and are copied in marginal organizations even though their efficiency is not as obvious in such settings. Alternatively, diffusion could result from the imposition of dominant forms of control through legitimation processes. In either case, the simplest form of a diffusion argument would propose the incremental spread of accounting into organizations such as churches. This could be an explanation of the increases in the sophistication of the accounting systems of the Northern Division since 1977. Also, if such sophistication was a result of copying or legitimation processes, it may also explain the overall low significance of accounting, with its adoption just being symbolic. An alternative form of the diffusion argument, where incremental spread is replaced by intrusions in response to crises affecting organizations, may explain the budget and financial control findings, as there was found to be a correlation between the financial crisis in the Division and these

234   *Managment Control in a Voluntary Organization*

effects. However, both these arguments offer no explanation for the variation in the significance of accounting across forums, its higher significance in the budgeting process and the imposition of financial control, the subordination of accounting to sacred ends, or the actions of occupational groups. Therefore, a diffusion argument may be a partial explanation for some of the findings of this study, but still fails to provide an integration of the total pattern of the significance of accounting within the Northern Division.

In contrast, it is proposed that a control processes form of explanation, of which the critical structuralist framework used in this study is one analytic variant, is capable of providing a useful insight into the overall pattern of the variable significance of accounting within the Northern Division. It includes the concern of efficiency explanations with the solving of control problems, but rejects their simple view of functional adjustments in favour of the analysis of the actions and knowledge of occupational groups within management. Also, the concerns of diffusion explanations with the general tendency of rationalization across organizations and the effects of crises can be incorporated. However, these effects are not taken as fait accompli, but are related to the dynamics of organizational action. The main insights for this study offered by such an explanation are summarized below in terms of the three broad propositions set out at the end of chapter 2.

The first proposition was that despite the pressures for rationalization upon churches, and an associated tendency to increase the significance of accounting, the dominance of sacred control problems would lead to resistance to the use of accounting and its treatment as a secondary concern. The diffusion of rational management control strategies, and perhaps scale effects, may be part of the explanation for the sophistication of the accounting systems of the Division and its management structure, but the subordination of secular control problems to sacred control problems provides an explanation of the overall pattern of the limited, but variable, significance of accounting within the Division.

The resistance to accounting within the Division was evidenced in the dominance of the sacred and secular divide in all aspects of the Division's operations. The dynamics of the operation of the sacred and secular divide were found to be complex, with the perception of the sacred varying from direct to indirect across settings. When sacred control problems were being directly affected then resistance to

Conclusions 235

accounting was high and its use was subordinated to the achievement of mission activities. This type of situation was particularly evident in policy making activities and the budgeting process. Also, the generally lower significance of accounting in the sacred departments was consistent with this effect. In such settings, accounting was perceived as constraining and disciplining sacred functions. In contrast, the higher significance of accounting in the Department of Mission Outreach Finance Committee, and the Department of Finance and Administration was related to the greater relevance of secular control problems in these forums, and a perception that effects on sacred concerns were less direct. In addition, the sacred and secular divide acted to partition off and subordinate some aspects of decisions or operations from direct sacred effects. For example, sacred concerns could be dealt with at the decision-making or policy stage, which then acted as background constraints for what were perceived as more secular issues during the implementation phase. Accounting could play a more active role during the latter phase, but its significance had already been limited by subordinating financial issues to the implementation phase. The sacred and secular divide, therefore, partly explains the overall pattern of findings of the variable significance of accounting within the Northern Division.

The dominance of the values of community and democracy, their emphasis on trust, and the extreme non-calculable, particularly non-monetary, basis of the transcendental goals of churches, as represented in sacred functions and concerns, therefore, served as a significant source of resistance to the use of rational, means-end, low trust orientated management control techniques such as accounting, as represented in secular functions and concerns. The overall effect was for accounting to be seen as secondary to sacred activities and for its use to lead to tension with sacred ends.

The second broad proposition was that there would be conflict between the clergy and other sacred occupational groups and accountants over the use of accounting in churches. Specifically that the clergy would be the main source of resistance to accounting and accountants its main promoters. The clergy and the other occupational groups, such as religious educationalists, involved in the management of the sacred departments were seen to actively promote the dominance of sacred functions and the subordinate position of accounting. They saw the management of the Division in terms of sacred control

236   *Managment Control in a Voluntary Organization*

problems and promoted sacred solutions to these problems. The use of accounting was only tolerated for operational decision situations or when it was seen as supporting mission activities. This resistance to the intrusion of accounting into sacred concerns was strongest during the budgeting process, when accountants sought to impose programme cuts on the sacred departments. The accountants in the Division promoted accounting as a tool for the support of sacred functions. They accepted the concept of the sacred and secular divide, but had a different interpretation of it, where accounting was still secondary to sacred concerns, but there was less, or even no, tension between them. This was based on a strong financial rationality orientation, where accounting was a means of applying a necessary 'financially realistic' discipline to the pursuit of sacred activities. Accountants focused on the secular organizing problems of the Division and promoted secular solutions to them. However, emphasis was placed on the necessity of both these problems and their solutions for the support of the sacred. Greater significance of accounting thus was promoted by accountants, but in a 'sacredized' way. The actions of accountants and sacred occupational groups, therefore, were directly involved in the variation of the significance of accounting.

Also, resistance to accounting was related to differences in the orientation to the role of trust in managerial relations between accountants and sacred occupational groups. A sacred orientation favoured high trust relationships while medium to low trust seemed typical of a secular orientation[1]. Accounting financial control techniques were typical of the secular orientation to trust, and their intrusion into sacred functions was thus resented and resisted.

The importance of the actions of occupational groups was most evident for the Budgeting System, which appeared to be a contested terrain for the promotion of the differing occupational views of the sacred and secular divide, and the importance of accounting. There was considerable conflict between the accountant and sacred occupational groups over the use of an accounting solution to balance the budget. The financially realistic view of the accountants led them to promote an income constrained perspective of the budget situation, where sacred functions had to be constrained to fit the 'limited' financial resources of the Division. The sacred occupational groups attempted to resist this accounting strategy, as its programme cuts impinged on mission activities. They promoted an income increasing

Conclusions 237

solution aimed to protect sacred functions. It would have been expected that the sacred and secular divide would have favoured the success of the solution of the sacred occupational groups. However, there were several specific factors in the Division which seemed to work in favour of the actual outcome, the success of the accountants' view. First, the historical opposition of Parish members to the support of central Division services weakened sacred support for the sacred departments. Second, the construction by the accountants of the budgeting process within a narrow financial discourse strongly discounted the viability of any income increasing strategies. Third, the pre-existing strong position of the accountants within the management structure with respect to financial management and their official responsibility for presenting a balanced budget, legitimated their control of the budgeting process. Therefore, the contests between occupational groups were important in determining the level of significance of accounting in particular settings.

The role of occupational groups in the resistance to and promotion of accounting, therefore, was also part of the explanation for the variable significance of accounting within the Division. The clergy and other sacred orientated occupational groups resisted accounting and supported the operation of the sacred and secular divide. Accountants also supported this divide, but promoted their own accounting solutions to secular control problems. This contest between occupational groups was particularly important because, as seen for the Budgeting System, it could lead to the, at least partial, breaking down of the sacred and secular divide.

The third and final broad proposition was that the existence of sacred and/or secular crises would prioritize sacred and secular control problems and solutions respectively. The former would aid the actions of the clergy (and others) and increase resistance to accounting, and the latter would aid the actions of accountants (and others) and have the opposite effect. In the case of the Northern Division, a secular crisis in the form of a strengthening financial crisis since 1983 influenced the potential significance of accounting. This crisis made more visible the financial dimensions of sacred activities, and legitimated the need for their financial support and the application of accounting solutions. It enabled accountants to promote tighter financial control through the Management Accounting Control System, and the use of the income constrained budget strategy. The

238   *Managment Control in a Voluntary Organization*

existence of a secular crisis, therefore, aided the activities of accountants in promoting greater significance of accounting in specific settings.

It should be emphasized that such an outcome was not inevitable. Some form of financial stringency had been associated with the budgeting process since 1977. It was necessary for the financial situation to be perceived as extreme, in the sense that there were insufficient resources to support all sacred functions, and for accountants to promote an income constrained budget strategy as the only solution to this situation, before accounting orientations were able to impose on the scared. This situation led to sacred and secular organizing problems being seen as overlapping, and the sacred being defined in a partly financial way. This both restricted the ability to propose sacred solutions and increased the legitimacy of accounting. In addition, the possibility of this intrusion was increased by a historical lack of wide Parish support for central Division mission activities. This was not the case for the potential sacred crisis of a future shortage of ministers, and the associated need to support the increase in the number of ministerial students in the 1988 budget. This sacred control problem had a high priority within the Division and wide Parish support. The accountants accepted the priority of this sacred problem and initially tried to fit it within their income constrained budget solution. However, when it became clear that this would not be possible, then an income increasing solution for this part of the budget was adopted, even if still within a strong financial logic. The increased significance for accounting legitimated by the financial crisis, therefore, was dependent on its extent, the actions of accountants and the level of support for the sacred function intruded upon.

Both sacred and secular crises, therefore, affected the significance of accounting within the Northern Division. A financial secular crisis was the most important in increasing the significance of accounting, but such secular control problems could become intertwined with sacred control problems. How this paradox was sorted out was not predetermined, it depended on the sacredness of the problems, the extent of the secular crisis and the actions of occupational groups.

Finally, in chapter 3 it was stated that some observation of Presbytery meetings and interviews with Presbytery and Parish treasurers were conducted to provide a partial assessment of the

Conclusions 239

applicability of the above findings to these other structural levels of the Division. The indication from this data was that the accounting systems at these levels were very rudimentary, being mainly simple cash income and expenditure recording systems and associated cash annual budgets. At the Presbytery level, these accounting systems appeared very marginalized. This is consistent with the explanation above, given the dominant sacred pastoral role of the Presbyteries. Accounting seemed to have a higher usage at the Parish level, but it was still only tangential to the main sacred orientation of the Parishes. The uses that existed were mainly to ensure that sufficient income was available to pay for support of ministers and manses, and to meet the budget commitment to the Division. There is some indication, therefore, that the general tendencies of the Division level findings and explanation may be applicable to other levels of the Division.

In summary, a number of competing explanations for the findings of this study on the variable, but overall limited significance of accounting in the Northern Division have been considered. It has been argued that a control processes explanation provides a more satisfactory explanation than the various efficiency and diffusion arguments canvassed. A control processes explanation is also more consistent with the existing literature on the development and variety of management control strategies in organizations. The critical structuralist variant of such an explanation used in this study stressed; (i) the importance of the different control problems of churches, particularly the tension between dominant sacred religious values and goals, and the ends of more secular coordination and administrative support functions; (ii) the actions of competing occupational groups, particularly conflict between the occupational views of the clergy and accountants; and (iii) the opposing prioritizing effects of sacred and secular crises in providing a means of understanding the use of accounting within churches. The next section considers the applicability of this explanation to voluntary organizations more generally.

III. A COMPARISON WITH TRENDS IN VOLUNTARY ORGANIZATIONS

In chapter 2, the development of the theoretical framework of this study narrowed the focus from management control issues in

240   *Managment Control in a Voluntary Organization*

voluntary organizations to the specific case of churches. The rest of the study, and the overview of the conclusions in the previous section, narrowed this focus further by considering the case of one church. Such a specific focus was necessary for this study. However, the final task of this study is to partly reverse this process by briefly exploring whether the control processes explanation and critical structuralist framework used here may be applied more broadly for understanding the development and variety of management control in voluntary organizations. It was argued in chapter 3 that it was possible to generalize from a single case study by abstracting from the details of the specific case analysis to a broader theoretical explanation. This provided a basis for arguing the wider applicability of that explanation in terms of the more general nature of its concepts and relationships via a process of theoretical inference (Mitchell 1983). It is proposed that there is a potential ability to generalize the findings of this case study to voluntary organizations more generally, and other churches more specifically, on the basis of the generality of the basic framework of analysis outlined in chapters 1 and 2, and on the broad agreement of this form of explanation with the previous literature on each. However, the wider applicability of the specific findings of the study needs to be established by further comparative research.

The discussion in this section is organized around the general trends in the nature of management control in voluntary organizations reviewed in chapter 2. Within each trend, more specific comparative evidence is drawn from two other studies of financial issues in churches. Laughlin's (1984, 1988) study of the Church of England is the only available detailed work on accounting practices in such a context (see Booth 1993). This work has many overlaps with this study, but there are also significant differences[2]. Still, Laughlin's work provides the only source of direct comparative material on accounting in churches. In an attempt to find other evidence, a search was made for more general discussions of the finances of churches. Several discussions of the finances of the Catholic Church were found, with the latter being particularly of interest to many writers because of the myths about its great wealth (for example, Gollin 1971; Pallenberg 1971; Tarling 1980). However, most of these were either very vague references in more general works, or poorly argued and supported, some even dealing in sensational journalism. In contrast, Gollin's (1971) work on the finances and financial administration of the

Conclusions 241

Catholic Church in the U.S.A., did provide an interesting insight into the general financial administration of this church. While this work attempted to evaluate the myths of the wealth, financial prowess and power of the Catholic Church, it was based on direct evidence of the financial practices of the church from interviews and documents. However, it must still be interpreted with care as the author tends to use strong normative overtones based upon his views of 'good modern management practices', and the leap from evidence to conclusion sometimes appears to be based on assertion rather than direct inference. Laughlin's and Gollin's work, therefore, form the main sources of comparative evidence on churches as voluntary organizations.

The first general issue that should be considered is the level of significance of accounting in voluntary organizations. No direct indication of this was found in the literature reviewed in chapter 2. The tendency of greater rationalization of management practices in the voluntary sector may reflect increasing significance for accounting. There was an intimation that this had happened where government funding was involved (Kramer 1981; Milofsky 1988c; O'Neill and Young 1988b). However, there were also indications that there was resistance to any increase in business management control techniques in voluntary organizations, which would be expected to decrease the significance of accounting. Also, it has been proposed in the not-for-profit accounting literature that there is a tendency for a lack of 'adequate' accounting practices in such organizations, although much of this literature has been concerned with the public sector, and it is often strong on assertion and short on evidence. Thus, there are indications for both low, and increasing, significance of accounting trends in voluntary organizations[3]. It is proposed at this time, therefore, that given the equivocal indications of current research evidence, and the diversity in the type and scale of activities covered by organizations within the voluntary sector, that it is probably unlikely that there is any clear trend towards low or high significance for accounting across all voluntary organizations.

However, this does not appear to be the case for churches. As discussed in chapter 2, Laughlin (1984) concluded that accounting had been marginalized in the life of the Church of England and overall was of secondary importance. A similar conclusion was reached by Gollin (1971) for the Catholic Church. He disputed the myth of its financial

242 *Managment Control in a Voluntary Organization*

prowess. While specific instances of strong, entrepreneurial financial management could be found, overall he argued that the Catholic Church were lucky they 'had God on their side'. Parish and Diocese income and expenditure management were argued to be amateurish and inefficient by business standards, and that they approached their financial responsibilities in a non-professional manner. While specific details were not given, Gollin argued that Parish accounting systems were rudimentary and financial control and planning very dependent on the whims of the pastor. Also, while more developed accounting systems existed at the Diocese level, which had more extensive financial responsibilities, their use was described as haphazard. Budgeting was stated to be casual and to have little to do with establishing priorities. Overall, Gollin assessed the financial management systems and practices of the Catholic Church as 'irrational', with little 'useful, usable financial information', and suffering from 'financial inflexibility'. Finally, the indication in this study was also that overall accounting was of limited significance, and of a secondary nature in the Division's management. Together, these findings seem to indicate that there is a tendency within churches for accounting to be seen as of low significance in their management.

Within voluntary organizations, therefore, any general trend in the level of significance of accounting cannot be discerned with the available evidence. At least for churches there does seem to be a tendency for accounting to be of low significance. However, as was argued in chapter 1, perhaps for other voluntary organizations, such as those who charge directly for their services, for example not-for-profit hospitals, use of accounting may be more significant. It remains for further comparative research to determine the actual range of variation of the significance of accounting in voluntary organizations. However, the result for churches does indicate that there may be some systematic form to such variation. It may be that any variation is related to the types of ends pursued by the organization, which leads the discussion to the next general trend in voluntary organizations.

A major distinctive feature of management control in voluntary organizations argued in chapter 2 was the dominance of their altruistic and qualitative, non-monetary gaols in the evaluation of appropriate management systems and techniques (for example, DiMaggio 1988; O'Connell 1988; Rothschild-Whitt 1979). This was argued to create a tension with business management control strategies which relied

Conclusions 243

more heavily on both concepts of hierarchy, which conflicted with the democracy and community ethos of voluntary organizations, and on quantitative means-ends control techniques, which conflicted with the pursuit of qualitative, non-monetary goals. It is this tension flowing from the qualitative, values based nature of the ends in voluntary organizations that was proposed as an explanation for the subordination of business management control strategies in such organizations.

The concept of the sacred and secular divide was proposed by Laughlin (1984) to explain the subordination of accounting in the Church of England (see chapter 2). This concept was integrated into the theoretical framework of this study, and proved equally useful in explaining the same type of finding. Support for this concept can be found also in Gollin's (1971) work on the Catholic Church. He discussed the training and attitude of priests to financial management and described them as 'economic innocents'. Theological educators argued that trainees wanted a 'theology of love, not how to balance a checkbook'. Also, many examples were given of what Gollin saw as irrational financial decision-making by Pastors, where 'local sentiment' determined purchasing from local congregation members, and 'faith or needs' drove building programmes rather than systematic financial evaluation. At a more general level, Gollin also referred to the conflicting roles of clergy as religious leaders, and as administrators and managers. "Throughout this entire study of the Roman Catholic ecclesiastical economy, we've seen many instances of the tension between the need for gain and the need to do good. ...[at all levels]..., we've watched as priests struggle to be efficient businessmen and yet not merely men of business" (Gollin 1971, p.487). Gollin painted a picture where the clergy were not only poorly equipped to be financial managers, but also not interested in becoming so. This theme is also raised by Bolton (1980) in his history of the Salvation Army in Australia, another religious voluntary organization. Since its foundation in Australia in the 1880s, the Salvation Army has struggled to fund its mission activities. Yet the view of the Salvation Army seems to be that the needs of mission must come before concerns about financing them.

> "Usually the first thought of those who launch a new charity is: 'What will the government give us?' and if there be refusal on the part of the executive good work is allowed to lapse. We believe that the truly Christian plan is to set about the work in the best possible way; and if the work be of God, He will make it prosper, and the

244 *Managment Control in a Voluntary Organization*

means will be sent along to provide for it" (statement on Salvation Army policy, quoted in Bolton 1980, p.178).

Also, money was commonly referred to as the 'ammunition for the Salvation war'. This, and the above policy, represent the subordination of finances to sacred concerns. It also appeared that finances were only 'sacredized' when clearly in a support function. For example, the accumulation of wealth per se was described as a 'temptation' and 'evil' which must be avoided by all Salvationists. The indication is, therefore, that the sacred and secular divide is a tendency across churches and other religious organizations, and is useful in explaining the secondary position assigned to accounting.

The sacred and secular divide can be interpreted as a special case of the tension between the altruistic and qualitative, non-monetary ends of voluntary organizations and business management control strategies. If so, then it is reasonable to propose that the marginalization and secondary position of accounting will be a general tendency in voluntary organizations, despite the lack of current empirical support discussed above. However, this is not an argument that accounting is always subordinated. It is conceivable that the strength of this ends tension may vary across voluntary organizations. For example, a neighbourhood collective may place more emphasis on democracy than a not-for-profit hospital, and the goals of the former may be less easily reduced to quantitative surrogates than the latter. Thus some variation would be expected. Still, the general proposition would remain that in voluntary organizations there is a fundamental conflict between their non-calculable ends and the use of accounting.

It may be that greater theoretical purchase, and potential generality, can be gained on this issue by the application of Weber's (1947) distinction between substantive and formal rationality. Briefly, formal rationality is the evaluation of a course of action by the application of quantitative or accounting techniques, particularly in monetary terms, and substantive rationality is the evaluation of a course of action in terms of any given set of ultimate values. Weber argued that some degree of incompatibility always exists between these two forms of rationality because some part of substantive rationality can never be reduced to formal calculation, but must always rely on an appeal to its specified absolute values or ends. According to Weber, the range of values that were substantively rational could be indefinite. A feature of all is that they evaluate the outcomes of action, with one result being that "...the merely formal calculation in monetary terms

Conclusions 245

may seem either of quite secondary importance or even as fundamentally evil in itself' (Weber 1947, p.186). The non-calculable ends of voluntary organizations, therefore, can be argued to form the basis of substantively rational evaluations of actions in such organizations. The formal rationality of accounting practices may seem to have little relevance under such circumstances. The concepts of substantive and formal rationality, and the tensions between them, therefore, may offer a way of integrating the concept of the sacred and secular divide with the broader means-ends tensions in other voluntary organizations, and thereby provide a more general theoretical base for further research on this major issue in management control in voluntary organizations.

A third major management control issue in voluntary organizations is the potential for conflict between differing occupational groups involved in their management, particularly between professional staff directly involved in goal accomplishment and administrative support staff (for example, Harris 1990; Kramer 1981; Weiss 1988). Professional staff are more likely to promote management control solutions based on substantive rationality as their occupational views can be expected to be closely aligned with the ends of voluntary organizations. In contrast, administrative staff, such as accountants, are more likely to apply formal rationality based solutions flowing from their occupational views. The contestation between these two broad occupational groupings can be expected to play a significant part in the significance of accounting, and other formal management control technologies, in voluntary organizations.

In Laughlin's (1984) study, the clergy, particularly at the Parish level, were argued to be the prime supporters of the sacred and secular divide, and the main promoters of the irrelevancy of accounting within the church. The same implication follows from Gollin's (1971) discussion of the attitudes of Catholic Church clergy to finance and the omission of management skills from their occupational training. This primary role of the clergy also occurred in this study. As well, other closely associated 'religious orientated' managers were found to play a similar role. The organizational literature on churches (see Booth 1993) indicates that such tendencies are common for all clergy and other occupational groups who have a sacred orientation. As these occupational groups are those most directly involved with the accomplishment of the primary goals of churches, and the use of a substantive rationality, these findings provide further evidence of the tendency within voluntary organizations of resistance to management control techniques, and accounting, flowing from professional staff groups.

The contestation of accountants, and their emphasis on formal rationality, with the views of the clergy was found in this study. There was also a partial indication in Laughlin's (1984) work that accountants brought their own occupational views to bear. However, Laughlin argued that accountants in the Church of England supported the dominance of substantive rationality in the Church of England, and a similar argument was presented in this study[4]. However, a clearer indication was found that there was a strong tendency for accountants to apply formal rationality to the evaluation of courses of action affecting sacred areas of the church, despite their acknowledgement of the importance of substantive ends. Again, therefore, the pattern for voluntary organizations more generally seems to be supported.

The voluntary organization literature also points to the possibility of contestation between professional occupational groups whose occupational views on appropriate methods of substantive goal achievement may conflict (see chapter 2). The tensions between Parish and central orientations of clergy indicated in Laughlin's work, and similar concerns found in this study may be an example of such contests. This adds another dimension to the potential effects of occupational groups on management control strategies and accounting in voluntary organizations which needs to be addressed further in future research. As has been argued, an analysis of the actions of occupational groups, the occupational views that they bring to the organization, and the relation of these to notions of substantive and formal rationality, must play a central part in understanding the variable significance of accounting in voluntary organizations.

The final management control trend in voluntary organizations is the effects of financial pressures on the greater use of formally rational management control strategies. There has been some discussion in the literature that greater concern with financial resources, through either the demands of major fund providers or a decreasing funding base, have been associated with greater formalization of management control in voluntary organizations (for example, DiMaggio 1988; Gerard 1983; Wilson 1989). This may occur through the perception of financial crisis leading, in turn, to the

Conclusions 247

greater perception of the monetary dimension of actions in voluntary organizations. This may increase the possibility of the perceived relevance of formal rationality based control techniques, as can be seen with the greater concerns with issues of efficiency in voluntary organizations in the last two decades (for example, DiMaggio 1988; Wolfenden Committee 1978).

Such an effect was seen in this study in terms of the greater impact of accounting through the budgeting system as the financial crisis of the Division worsened. Laughlin (1984) also reported that the use of accounting systems had increased in recent years with the increasing financial stress experienced by the Church of England[5]. Similarly, Gollin (1971) reported that increasing financial stress during the 1960s, caused by the outstripping of income growth by expenditure, particularly the cost of running religious schools, had been associated with attempts to 'modernize' management structures and accounting systems, and the centralization and rationalization of financial holdings, insurance and purchasing arrangements in some Dioceses in the Catholic Church. Within churches, therefore, there is some support for the role of financial crises in prioritizing the greater use of formal rationality over substantive rationality.

For voluntary organizations, therefore, the effects of financial crises on the level of significance of rational management control techniques and accounting should be investigated further. However, this should be expanded in future research on voluntary organizations to include the concept of a sacred crisis, introduced in this study for the case of churches. For voluntary organizations more generally, a sacred crisis may be re-conceptualized as a substantive ends crisis. This may involve some direct threat to the values or goal attainment of the organization, or the loss of commitment of its members. The understanding of the development and variety in substantive and formal rationality orientated management practices, and the significance of accounting, may be assisted by a consideration of the effects of both types of crises.

Overall, the discussion in this section has indicated that there is a significant level of overlap between some of the major issues running through the literature on management control in voluntary organizations, and the control processes explanation of the variable significance of accounting used in this study. These comparisons, therefore, may indicate some of the basic ideas of a model of the

248 *Managment Control in a Voluntary Organization*

dynamics of management control, and the role of accounting, in voluntary organizations. In summary, these basic ideas are, (i) the dominance of substantive rationality in the evaluation of action in voluntary organizations, (ii) the tension between this and the use of formal rationality, on which many modern management control techniques, including accounting, are based, (iii) the playing out of this tension in the contests between occupational groups involved in voluntary organizations, the occupational views of some supporting substantive rationality and of others favouring formal rationality, and (iv) the way in which the occurrence of 'substantive ends' and financial crises, and their interaction, may differentially prioritize the use of each form of rationality, and the actions of occupational groups. The arguments in chapter 2, and the analysis in this study, have suggested some of the ways in which these ideas may interact for the specific case of churches, but the limited level of understanding at present of management control in voluntary organizations makes their more general specification difficult. The confirmation of the relevance of these ideas, the addition of other major concepts, and the formulation of their interaction requires further research.

IV. CONCLUDING COMMENTS

Overall, this study has attempted to demonstrate that any understanding of the significance of accounting in an organization must go beyond the consideration of its technical nature and investigate how it is actually used in practice (Chua 1988; Roberts and Scapens 1985). As such, it has sought to add to the growing body of research on accounting in action. However, despite the significant progress that has been made in recent years, our substantive knowledge of how accounting is used in organizations is still limited. One of the major problems in this regard is that there have been few attempts to build models of the dynamics of accounting and management control in organizations based upon systematic empirical investigations, especially through programmes of comparative research. The argument in the preceding chapters has sought to demonstrate that a useful way in which this may be done is through a research programme focused on one type of organization, particularly where the focal type is selected on the basis of its theoretical significance, as was the case for voluntary organizations in this study.

Conclusions

Detailed case studies have much to add to our substantive knowledge of accounting practices, but only a systematic programme of comparative research can lead to the theoretical integration of this knowledge. It is hoped that this study has contributed a small step in that direction in the case of voluntary organizations.

Notes

[1] Although it should be recognized that high trust can exist for such orientations, for example, between top management (Fox 1974).

[2] They overlap in that both analyse accounting as a situated practice and relate it to its organizational and social context. Also, both emphasize the importance of religious beliefs in understanding the significance of accounting. Major differences are; (i) Laughlin's emphasis on the origins of and avenues for change in accounting systems while this study has considered more the uses of accounting systems in practice; (ii) Laughlin's use of a critical theory analytic framework; (iii) differences in organizational structures - the Church of England is a national church while the Mainstream Church is a federation; (iv) Laughlin's greater concentration of analysis at the Parish level; and (v) the different funding arrangements of the two churches, particularly the sizable income from endowments of the Church of England.

[3] Another possibility is that there is some form of cyclical trend. When voluntary organizations are formed they may place more emphasis on their ideals and values, leading to a low reliance on accounting. However, as voluntary organizations grow and/or face various crises they may experience increasing pressure for greater use of accounting.

[4] No indication of the role of accountants was available from Gollin (1971).

[5] However, Laughlin (1984) argued that accounting systems in this regard acted as anxiety reducing mechanisms. Thus, while their use increased, it did not impinge on substantive ends domains but rather tended to isolate these areas from these formal rationality concerns. This may indicate that while financial crises may increase the use of accounting, this may be in a restricted way.

Appendix
Management Accounting
Control System Reports

The accounting reports shown in the following pages are summarized versions of the regular monthly and quarterly accounting reports produced by the Northern Division's Management Accounting Control System. The exact structure and form of reporting are shown and the numbers are illustrative of those reported during the period of this study. However the names of departments and their cost centres have been disguised at the request of the subject church.

251

Account Name	Item	This Month			Year To Date			Total Year	
		Actual	Budget	Variance	Actual	Budget	Variance	Forecast	Budget
Aboriginal Liaison	Income								
	Expense	$802	$885	$82	$4,491	$4,209	($282)		$4,209
	RESULT	$802	$885	$82	$4,491	$4,209	($282)		$4,209
Home Mission	Income	$4,195	$16,750	($12,554)	$67,702	$66,000	$1,702		$66,000
	Expense	$33,032	$28,654	($4,378)	$98,099	$98,431	$331		$98,431
	RESULT	$28,836	$11,904	($16,932)	$30,396	$32,431	$2,034		$32,431
Hospital Chaplaincy	Income	$11,731	$12,448	($716)	$152,901	$145,426	$7,475		$145,426
	Expense	$14,188	$14,079	($109)	$154,948	$145,426	($9,522)		$145,426
	RESULT	$2,457	$1,631	($826)	$2,046	$0	($2,046)		$0
Actual reports would have a full alphabetical listing of cost centres in the Department. Three centres for the Department for Mission Outreach have been shown for illustrative purposes. The Forecast column is used to show revisions of budget expectations during the year. While it had always been part of the system, its use had only been required for 1987 and future years. Positive numbers in column totals indicate a 'net income' overall result and negative numbers an overall 'net expense' result.									
TOTAL	RESULT	$14,898	$12,061	$2,837	($167,895)	$3,029	($170,924)		$3,029

Department Monthly Income Report (Month of December, 1986)

Account Name	This Month			Year To Date			Total	Year
	Actual	Budget	Variance	Actual	Budget	Variance	Forecast	Budget
Ministerial Education								
ME General	$4,550	$2,895	($1,655)	$3,820	$19,094	$15,243		$7,785
Hostel	$1,280	$0	($1,280)	($111)	$0	$111		$0
ME Total	$5,830	$2,895	($2,935)	$3,708	$19,064	$15,355		$7,785
Administration								
General	($535)	$383	$918	($4,685)	$1,692	$6,377		$2,490
CEM Fund	($2,239)	($1,702)	$537	($15,113)	($6,808)	$8,305		($20,400)
Memorial Lecture Fund	($9,085)	$0	$9,085	($9,095)	$0	$9,095		$0
University Chaplain	$138	$100	($38)	$420	$678	$257		$0
Ecumenical Chaplain	($458)	$36	$494	$4,200	$242	($3,958)		$0
Administration Total	($12,179)	($1,183)	$10,996	($24,272)	($4,196)	$20,076		($17,910)
Publication Services								
General	($1,605)	($180)	$1,425	($15,863)	($5,057)	$10,806		($18,176)
Pub. Serv. Total	($1,605)	($180)	$1,425	($15,863)	($5,057)	$10,806		($18,176)
Example shown is for the Department of Educational Activities. Account sections represent the major cost centres of the department, with three illustrative cost centres shown. Negative amounts in actual and budget columns represent surpluses.								
TOTAL	($1,794)	($2,588)	($793)	($68,780)	($6,969)	$61,811		($60,296)

Department Monthly Surplus/Deficit Summary (Month of April, 1987)

| Account Name | Start of Year Balance | This Month Balance | Changes in Balances | | | | | Annual Budget |
| | | | This Month | | Year To Date | | | |
Summary of Assets			Actual	Budget	Actual	Budget	Variance	Budget
Current Assets								
Administration	$142,648	$134,297	$57,531	$0	($8,350)	$0	$8,350	$0
Evangelism	$850	$4,188	$3,282	$0	$3,338	$0	($3,338)	$0
Home Mission	$1,034	($472)	$441	$0	($1,507)	$0	$1,507	$0
Resource Centre	($16)	($155)	($54)	$0	($139)	$0	$139	$0
World Mission	($2,601)	($12,224)	($1,242)	$0	($9,622)	$0	$9,622	$0
Conference Centres	$770	$1,416	$166	$0	$645	$0	($645)	$0
Total Current Assets	$142,685	$127,048	$60,124	$0	($15,636)	$0	$15,636	$0

This structure is repeated for the remaining major asset categories of Loans & Deposits, Investments, Fixed Assets, Provision for Depreciation, and for the liabilities categories of Current Liabilities, Deposit Accounts, Long Term Liabilities and Special Funds & Trusts. Total asset and liability figures, and net assets for each major cost centre and in total are also given. The Department of Mission Outreach have been shown here for illustrative purposes. Credit balances can appear in assets because of the notional Department cash balances. If these are overdrawn they show as negative assets.

Net Assets								
Net Assets								
Administration	($42,337)	($436,228)	$23,834	$0	($393,890)	($14,000)	$379,890	($14,000)
Evangelism	$34,938	$15,447	$20,737	$0	($19,490)	$0	$19,490	$0
Home Mission	$238,530	$214,907	($91,698)	$0	($73,622)	$15,000	$88,622	$15,000
Print Shop	$8,439	$9,761	($2,495)	$347	$1,322	$4,164	$2,842	$4,164
Resource Centre	($482)	($622)	($54)	$0	($139)	$0	$139	$0
World Mission	$49,921	$37,980	$5,819	$125	($11,941)	$1,500	$13,441	$1,500
Conference Centres	$11,196,907	$11,269,628	($8,649)	$4,222	$72,720	$70,395	($2,325)	$70,395
TOTAL NET ASSETS	$11,535,917	$11,110,975	($52,506)	$4,694	($425,041)	$77,059	$502,100	$77,059

Cost Centre Monthly Balance Sheet Summary (Month of December, 1986)

Bibliography

GENERAL REFERENCES

AAA (1989), *Measuring the Performance of Nonprofit Organizations: The State of the Art* (Report of the Committee on Nonprofit Entities' Performance Measures, AAA Government and Nonprofit Section; Saratosa, Florida: American Accounting Association).

Abdel-Khalik, R. and B. Ajinkya (1983), "An Evaluation of the Everyday Accountant and Researching His Reality", *Accounting, Organizations and Society*, Vol. 8, No. 4, pp. 375-384.

Albrow, M. (1970), *Bureaucracy* (London: Pall Mall Press).

Aldrich, H. (1972), "Theory Construction, Path Analysis, and the Study of Organizations: A Re-Examination of the Findings of the Aston Group", *Administrative Science Quarterly*, Vol. 17, No. 1, pp. 26-43.

Amigoni, F. (1978), "Planning Management Control Systems", *Journal of Business Finance and Accounting*, Vol. 5, No. 3, pp. 279-291.

Anthony, R. (1978), *Financial Accounting in Nonbusiness Organizations* (Stamford, Conn: Financial Accounting Standards Board).

Anthony, R. and D. Young (1984), *Management Control in Nonprofit Organizations*, (Homewood, Illinois: Richard D. Irwin, third edition).

Argyris, C. (1952), *The Impact of Budgets on People* (New York: The Controllership Foundation).

Armstrong, P. (1984), "Competition between the Organizational Professions and the Evolution of Management Control Strategies", in Thompson, K. (Ed), *Work, Employment and Unemployment: Perspectives on Work and Society* (Milton Keynes: Open University Press), pp. 97-120.

Armstrong, P. (1985), "Changing Management Control Strategies: The Role of Competition Between Accountancy and Other Organizational Professions", *Accounting, Organizations and Society*, Vol. 10, No. 2, pp. 129-148.

Armstrong, P. (1986), "Management Control Strategies and Inter-Professional Competition: the Cases of Accountancy and Personnel Management", in Knights, D. and H. Willmott (Eds), *Managing the Labour Process* (Aldershot: Gower), pp. 19-43.

Armstrong, P. (1987a), "The Rise of Accounting Controls in British Capitalist Enterprises", *Accounting, Organizations and Society*, Vol. 12, No. 5, pp. 415-436.

Armstrong, P. (1987b), "Engineers, Management and Trust", *Work, Employment and Society*, Vol. 1, No. 4, pp. 421-440.

Armstrong, P. (1989a), "Management, Labour Process and Agency", *Work, Employment and Society*, Vol. 3, No. 3, pp. 307-322.

Armstrong, P. (1989b), "Variance Reporting and the Delegation of Blame: A Case Study", *Accounting, Auditing and Accountability Journal*, Vol. 2, No. 2, pp. 29-46.

Armstrong, P. (1991), "Contradiction and Social Dynamics in the Capitalist Agency Relationship", *Accounting, Organizations and Society*, Vol. 16, No. 1, pp. 1-25.

Arndt, T. and J. McCabe (1986), "Communicating the Financial Aspects of Church Operations", *The Ohio CPA Journal*, Spring, pp. 25-29.

Ashbrook, J. (1967), "Ministry Leadership in Church Organization", *Ministry Studies*, Vol. 1, No. 1, May, A Ministry Studies Board Monograph.

Baiman, S. (1982), "Agency Research in Managerial Accounting: A Survey", *Journal of Accounting Literature*, Spring, pp. 154-213.

Baiman, S. (1990), "Agency Research in Managerial Accounting: A Second Look", *Accounting, Organization and Society*, Vol. 15, No. 4, pp. 341-372.

Bariff, M. and J. Galbraith (1978), "Interorganizational Power Considerations for Designing Information Systems", *Accounting, Organizations and Society*, Vol. 3, No. 1, pp. 15-27.

Barnes, B. (1986), "On Authority and its Relationship to Power", in Law, J. (Ed), *Power, Action and Belief: a New Sociology of Knowledge?* (Sociological Review Monograph 32; London: Routledge and Kegan Paul), pp. 190-195.

Bartunek, J. (1984), "Changing Interpretive Schemes and Organizational Structuring: The Example of a Religious Order", *Administrative Science Quarterly*, Vol. 29, No. 3, September, pp. 355-372.

Batstone, E. (1979), "Systems of Domination, Accommodation and Industrial Democracy", in Burns, T., L. Karlsson and V. Rus (Eds), *Work and Power: The Liberations of Work and the Control of Political Power* (London: Sage), pp. 249-272.

Berger, P. (1963), "A Market Model for the Analysis of Ecumenicity", *Social Research*, Spring, pp. 77-93.

Berger, P. and T. Luckman (1966), "Secularization and Pluralism", *Sociology of Religion: Theoretical Perspectives (I)*, Vol. II, pp. 73-84.

Berry, A., Capps, T., Cooper, D., Ferguson, P., Hopper, T., and E. Lowe (1985), "Management Control in an Area of the NCB: Rationales of Accounting Practices in a Public Enterprise", *Accounting, Organizations and Society*, Vol. 10, No. 1, pp. 3-28.

Beyer, J. (1981), "Ideologies, Values, and Decision Making in Organizations", in Nystrom, P. and W. Starbuck (Eds), *Handbook of Organizational Design*, Vol. 2 (New York: Oxford University Press), pp. 166-202.

Bhasker, K. (1981), "Quantitative Aspects of Management Accounting" in Bromwich, M. and A. Hopwood (Eds), *Essays in British Accounting Research* (London: Pitman), pp. 229-273.

Billis, D. (1984), "Voluntary Sector Management: Research and Practice", *Working Paper No. 1*, The Centre for Voluntary Organization, London School of Economics and Political Science.

Billis, D. (1989), "A Theory of the Voluntary Sector: Implications for Policy and Practice", *Working Paper No. 5*, The Centre for Voluntary Organization, London School of Economics and Political Science.

Birnberg, J. and M. Shields (1989), "Three Decades of Behavioral Accounting Research: A Search for Order", *Behavioral Research in Accounting*, Vol. 1, pp. 23-74.

Birnberg, J, Shields M. and S. Young (1990), "The Case for Multiple Methods in Empirical Management Accounting Research (with an illustration from budget setting)", *Journal of Management Accounting Research*, Vol. 2, Fall, pp. 33-66.

Blau, P. (1956), *Bureaucracy in Modern Society* (New York: Random House).

Bibliography 257

Boland, R. (1982), "Myth and Technology in the American Accounting Profession", *Journal of Management Studies*, pp. 107-127.

Boland, R. and L. Pondy (1983), "Accounting in Organizations: A Union of Natural and Rational Perspectives", *Accounting, Organizations and Society*, Vol. 8, No. 2/3, pp. 223-234.

Boland, R. and L. Pondy (1986), "The Micro Dynamics of a Budget-Cutting Process: Modes, Models and Structure", *Accounting, Organizations and Society*, Vol. 11, No. 4/5, pp. 403-422.

Bolton, B. (1980), *Booth's Drum: The Salvation Army in Australia, 1880 - 1980* (Sydney: Hodder and Stoughton).

Booth, P. (1988), *Power in Organizations: Towards an Understanding of the Role of Accounting* (School of Accounting Working Paper No. 86, University of New South Wales).

Booth, P. (1993), "Accounting in Churches: A Research Framework and Agenda" *Accounting, Auditing and Accountability Journal*, Vol. 6, No. 4, pp. 37-67.

Booth, P. and N. Cocks (1990), "Critical Research Issues in Standard-Setting", *Journal of Business Finance and Accounting*, Vol. 17, No. 4, Autumn, pp. 511-528.

Booth, P. and H. Paterson (1982), "Accounting for Contributed Services: An Identification of Issues", *Accounting and Finance*, Vol. 22, No. 1, May, pp. 73-79.

Bougen, P., Ogden S. and Q. Outram (1990), "The Appearance and Disappearance of Accounting: Wage Determination in the U.K. Coal Industry", *Accounting, Organizations and Society*, Vol. 15, No. 3, pp. 149-170.

Bouma, G. (1983), "Australian Religiosity: Some Trends Since 1966", in Black, A. and P. Glasner (Eds), *Practice and Belief: Studies in the Sociology of Australian Religion* (Sydney: George Allen & Unwin), pp. 15-24.

Bourn, M. and M. Ezzamel (1986a), "Costing and Budgeting in the National Health Service", *Financial Accountability and Management*, Vol. 2, No. 1, pp. 53-71.

Bourn, M. and M. Ezzamel (1986b), "Organizational Culture in Hospitals in the National Health Service", *Financial Accountability and Management*, Vol. 2, No. 3, pp. 203-225.

Bourn, M. and M. Ezzamel (1987), "Budgetary Devolution in the National Health Service and Universities in the United Kingdom", *Financial Accountability and Management*, Vol. 3, No. 1, pp. 29-45.

Boyce, L. (1984), "Accounting for Churches", *Journal of Accountancy*, February, pp. 96-102.

Braverman, H. (1974), *Labor and Monopoly Capital: the Degradation of Work in the Twentieth Century* (London: Monthly Review Press).

Bray, M. and C. Littler (1988), "The Labour Process and Industrial Relations: Review of the Literature", *Labour & Industry*, Vol. 1, No. 3, pp. 551-587.

Bromwich, M. and A. Hopwood (Eds) (1981), *Essays in British Accounting Research* (London: Pitman).

Brownell, P. and K. Trotman (1988), "Research Methods in Behavioral Accounting", in Ferris, K. (Ed.), *Behavioral Accounting Research: A Critical Analysis* (Columbus, Ohio: Century VII Publishing Company), pp. 331-362.

Bruns, W. (1989), "A Review of Robert K. Yin's, Case study Research: Design and Methods", *Journal of Management Accounting Research*, Vol. 1, Fall, pp. 157-163.

Brunsson, N. (1982), "The Irrationality of Action and Action Rationality: Decisions, Ideologies and Organizational Actions", *Journal of Management Studies*, Vol. 19, No. 1, pp. 29-44.

Burawoy, M. (1979), *Manufacturing Consent* (Chicago: University of Chicago Press)

258 *Managment Control in a Voluntary Organization*

Burchell, S., Clubb, A. and A. Hopwood (1985), "Accounting in its Social Context: Towards a History of Value Added in the United Kingdom", *Accounting, Organizations and Society*, Vol. 10, No. 4, pp. 381-413.

Burchell, S., Clubb, C., Hopwood, A., Hughes, J. and J. Nahapiet (1980), "The Roles of Accounting in Organizations and Society", *Accounting, Organizations and Society*, Vol. 5, No. 1, pp. 5-27.

Burckel, D. and B. Swindle (1988), "Church Accounting: Is There Only One Way?", *The Woman CPA*, July, pp. 27-31.

Burgess, R. (Ed) (1982), *Field Research: A Sourcebook and Field Manual* (London: George Allen and Unwin).

Callus, R., Morehead, A., Cully, M. and J. Buchanan (1991), *Industrial Relations at Work: The Australian Workplace Industrial Relations Survey* (Canberra: Commonwealth Department of Industrial Relations / Australian Government Publishing Service).

Caplan, E. (1966), "Behavioural Assumptions in Management Accounting", *The Accounting Review*, Vol. XLI, No. 3, July, pp. 496-509.

Carchedi, G. (1977), *On the Economic Identification of Social Classes* (London: Routledge and Kegan Paul).

Carmichael, D. (1970), "Behavioral Hypotheses of Internal Control", *The Accounting Review*, Vol. XLV, No. 1, April, pp. 235-245.

Chambers, R. (1966), *Accounting, Evaluation and Economic Behaviour* (Englewood Cliffs, NJ: Prentice-Hall).

Chandler, A. (1962), *Strategy and Structure: Chapters in the History of the American Industrial Enterprise* (Cambridge, Mass.: MIT Press).

Chandler, A. (1977), *The Visible Hand: The Managerial Revolution in American Business* (Cambridge, Mass.: Harvard University Press).

Chandler, A. and H. Deams (1979), "Administrative Coordination, Allocation and Monitoring: a Comparative Analysis of the Emergence of Accounting and Organization in the U.S.A. and Europe", *Accounting, Organizations and Society*, Vol. 4, No.1/2, pp. 3-20.

Chenhall, R. and P. Brownell (1988), "The Effect of Participative Budgeting on Job Satisfaction and Performance: Role Ambiguity as an Intervening Variable", *Accounting, Organizations and Society*, Vol. 13, No. 3, pp. 225-233.

Choudhury, N. (1988), "The Seeking of Accounting Where It Is Not: Towards a Theory of Non-Accounting in Organizational Settings", *Accounting, Organizations and Society*, Vol. 13, No. 6, pp. 549-557.

Chua, W.F. (1986a), "Radical Developments in Accounting Thought", *The Accounting Review*, Vol. LXI, No. 4, pp. 601-632.

Chua, W.F. (1986b), "Theoretical Constructions of and by the Real", *Accounting, Organizations and Society*, Vol. 11, No. 6, pp. 583-598.

Chua, W.F. (1988), "Interpretive Sociology and Management Accounting Research - A Critical Review", *Accounting, Auditing and Accountability Journal*, Vol. 1, No. 2, pp. 59-79.

Chua, W.F. and P. Degeling (1989), *Health Care Control in the United States: A Case-Study of Positivity, Discipline and Resistance* (Paper presented at the first Management Accounting Research Colloquium, University of New South Wales, Australia).

CICA (1980), *Financial Reporting for Non-Profit Organizations: a Research Study* (Toronto: The Canadian Institute of Chartered Accountants).

Clawson, D. (1980), *Bureaucracy and the Labour Process: the Transformation of US Industry 1850-1920* (New York: Monthly Review Press).

Bibliography 259

Clegg, S. (1975), *Power, Rule and Domination: A Critical and Empirical Understanding of Power in Sociological Theory and Organizational Life* (London: Routledge and Kegan Paul).

Clegg, S. (1989), "Radical Revisions: Power, Discipline and Organizations", *Organization Studies*, Vol. 10, No. 1, pp. 97-115.

Clegg, S. (1990), *Modern Organizations: Organizations Studies in the Postmodern World* (London: Sage).

Clegg, S. and D. Dunkerley (1980), *Organisation, Class and Control* (London: Routledge and Kegan Paul).

Colignon, R. and M. Covaleski (1991), "A Weberian Framework in the Study of Accounting", *Accounting, Organizations and Society*, Vol. 16, No. 2, pp. 141-157.

Colville, I. (1981), "Reconstructing 'Behavioural Accounting'", *Accounting, Organizations and Society*, Vol. 6, No. 2, pp. 119-132.

Cook, J. (1988), "Managing Nonprofits of Different Sizes", in O'Neill, M. and D. Young (Eds), *Educating Managers of Nonprofit Organizations* (New York: Praeger), pp. 101-116.

Cooper, D. (1981), "A Social and Organizational View of Management Accounting", Bromwich, M. and A. Hopwood (Eds), *Essays in British Accounting Research* (London: Pitman), pp. 178-205.

Cooper, D., Hayes, D. and F. Wolf (1981), "Accounting in Organized Anarchies: Understanding and Designing Accounting Systems in Ambiguous Situations", *Accounting, Organizations and Society*, Vol. 6, No. 3, pp. 175-191.

Cooper, D. and T. Hopper (1987), "Critical Studies in Accounting", *Accounting, Organizations and Society*, Vol. 12, No. 5, pp. 407-414.

Covaleski, M. and M. Dirsmith (1983), "Budgeting as a Means for Control and Loose Coupling", *Accounting, Organizations and Society*, Vol. 8, No. 4, pp. 323-340.

Covaleski, M. and M. Dirsmith (1986a), "The Budgetary Process of Power and Politics", *Accounting, Organizations and Society*, Vol. 11, No. 3, pp. 193-214.

Covaleski, M. and M. Dirsmith (1986b), "Social Expectations and Accounting Practices in the Health Sector", *Research in Governmental and Nonprofit Accounting: a research annual*, Vol. 2, pp. 119-134.

Covaleski, M. and M. Dirsmith (1988), "The Use of Budgetary Symbols in the Political Arena: An Historically Informed Field Study", *Accounting, Organizations and Society*, Vol. 13, No. 1, pp. 1-24.

Covaleski, M. and M. Dirsmith (1990), "Dialectic Tension, Double Reflexivity and the Everyday Accounting Researcher: An Agnostic View of Qualitative Research", *Accounting, Organizations and Society*, Vol, 15, No. 6, pp. 543-573.

Covaleski, M., Dirsmith, M. and S. Jablonsky (1985), "Traditional and Emergent Theories of Budgeting: An Empirical Analysis", *Journal of Accounting and Public Policy*, Vol. 4, No. 4, Winter, pp. 277-300.

Crossman, P. (1958), "The Nature of Management Accounting", *The Accounting Review*, Vol. XXXIII, No. 1, May, pp. 222-227.

Cunningham, G. and D. Reemsnyder (1983), "Church Accounting: the Other Side of Stewardship", *Management Accounting*, August, pp. 58-62.

Daniel, W. (1959), "Church Finance and Accounting - Their Relationship to Church 'Management'", *N.A.A. Bulletin*, August, pp. 19-28.

Davis, S., Menon, K. and G. Morgan (1981), "The Images that have Shaped Accounting Theory", *Accounting, Organizations and Society*, Vol. 7, No. 4, pp. 307-318.

Day, P. and R. Klein (1987), *Accountabilities: Five Public Services* (London: Tavistock).

Demski, J. (1972), *Information Analysis* (Reading, Mass: Addison-Wesley).

260 Managment Control in a Voluntary Organization

Denzin, N. (1978), *The Research Act in Sociology*, (New York: McGraw-Hill, second edition).

Dermer, J. and R. Lucas (1986), "The Illusion of Managerial Control", *Accounting, Organizations and Society*, Vol. 11, No. 6, pp. 471-482.

DiMaggio, P. (1988), "Nonprofit Managers in Different Fields of Service: Managerial Tasks and Management Training", in O'Neill, M. and D. Young (Eds), *Educating Managers of Nonprofit Organizations* (New York: Praeger), pp. 51-69.

DiMaggio, P. and W. Powell (1983), "The Iron Cage Revisited: Institutional Isomorphism and Collective Rationality in Organizational Fields", *American Sociological Review*, Vol. 48, April, pp. 147-160.

Dirsmith, M. and S. Jablonsky (1979), "MBO, Political Rationality and Information Inductance", *Accounting, Organizations and Society*, Vol. 4, No. 1/2, pp. 39-52.

Donaldson, L. (1985), *In Defense of Organization Theory: A Response to the Critics* (Cambridge: Cambridge University Press).

Donaldson, L. (1987), "Strategy, Structural Adjustment to Regain Fit and Performance: In Defense of Contingency Theory", *Journal of Management Studies*, Vol. 24, No. 2, pp. 1-24..

Dopuch, N. (1977), "Discussion of 'Application of Quantitative Methods in Managerial Accounting'", in *Management Accounting - State of the Art* (Robert Beyer Lecture Series, University of Wisconsin-Madison), pp. 74-83.

Duncan, R. (1979), "Qualitative Research Methods in Strategic Management", in Scherdel, D. and C. Hofe (Eds), *Strategic Management: A New View of Business, Policy and Planning* (USA: Little Brown & Co).

Durkheim, E. (1976), *The Elementary Forms of the Religious Life* (translated by J. Sawin) (London: George Allen and Unwin).

Dyckman, T. (1975), "Some Contributions of Decision Theory to Accounting", *Journal of Contemporary Business*, Autumn, pp. 69-89.

Edwards, R. (1979), *Contested Terrain: the Transformation of the Workplace in the Twentieth Century* (New York: Basic Books).

Ekelund, R., Hebert, R. and R. Tollison (1989), "An Economic Model of the Medieval Church: Usury as a Form of Rent Seeking", *Journal of Law, Economics and Organization*, Vol. 5, No. 2, Fall, pp. 307-331.

Eliade, M. (1959), *The Sacred and the Profane: the Nature of Religion* (translated by W. Task) (New York: Harcourt, Brace and World).

Ellis, L. (1974), "Internal Control for Churches and Community Organizations", *The CPA Journal*, May, pp. 45-48.

Ezzamel, M. and M. Bourn (1990), "The Roles of Accounting Information Systems in an Organization Experiencing Financial Crisis", *Accounting, Organizations and Society*, Vol. 15, No. 5, pp. 399-424.

Faircloth, A. (1988), "The Importance of Accounting to the Shakers", *The Accounting Historians Journal*, Vol. 15, No. 2, pp. 99-129.

FASB (1980), *Objectives of Financial Reporting by Nonbusiness Organizations* (Statement of Financial Accounting Concepts No. 4; Stamford, Conn: Financial Accounting Standards Board).

Ferris, K. (Ed) (1988), *Behavioral Accounting Research: A Critical Analysis* (Columbus, Ohio: Century VII Publishing).

Fichter, J. (1961), *Religion as an Occupation* (New York: University of Notre Dame Press).

Figlewicz, R., Anderson, D. and C. Strupeck (1985), "The Evolution and Current State of Financial Accounting Concepts and Standards in the Nonbusiness Sector", *The Accounting Historians Journal*, Vol. 12, No. 1, Spring, pp. 73-98.

Bibliography

Flesher, T. and D. Flesher (1979), "Managerial Accounting in an Early 19th Century German-American Religious Commune", *Accounting, Organizations and Society,* Vol. 4, No. 4, pp. 297-304.

Floyd, A. (1969), "Management Accounting for Churches", *Management Accounting* (U.S.), February, pp. 56-59.

Foucault, M. (1979), *Discipline and Punish: The Birth of the Prison* (Harmondsworth: Penguin Books).

Foucault, M. (1980), *Power/Knowledge* (Brighton: Harvester Press).

Fox, A. (1974), *Beyond Contract: Work, Power and Trust Relations* (London: Faber and Faber Ltd).

Friedman, A. (1977), *Industry and Labour: Class Struggle at Work and Monopoly Capitalism* (London: Macmillan).

Futcher, T. and T. Phillips (1986), "Church Budgeting: A Secular Approach", *The National Public Accountant,* Vol. 31, September, pp. 28-29.

Gambino, A. (1979), *Planning and Control in Higher Education* (New York: National Association of Accountants).

Gambino, A. and T. Reardon (1981), *Financial Planning and Evaluation for the Not-For-Profit Organization* (New York: National Association of Accountants).

Gerard, D. (1983), *Charities in Britain: Conservatism or Change?* (London: Bedford Square Press / National Council of Voluntary Organizations).

Giddens, A. (1976), *New Rules of Sociological Method* (London: Hutchinson & Co.).

Giddens, A. (1984), *The Constitution of Society* (Cambridge: Polity Press).

Gidron, B. (1978), "Volunteer Work and its rewards", *Volunteer Administration,* Vol. 11, pp. 18-25.

Glaser, B. and A. Strauss (1967), *The Discovery of Grounded Theory: Strategies for Qualitative Research* (Chicago: Aldine).

Goldner, F. (1979), "Internal Belief Systems and Ideologies about the Organizational Structure of Church and Industry", in Lammers, C. and D. Hickson (Eds), *Organizations Alike and Unlike: International and Inter-Institutional Studies in the Sociology of Organizations* (London: Routledge and Kegan Paul), pp. 124-136.

Gollin, J. (1971), *Worldly Goods: The Wealth and Power of the American Catholic Church, the Vatican and the men who control the money* (New York: Random House).

Gordon, D., Edwards, R. and M. Reich (1982), *Segmented Work: Divided Workers, the Historical Transformation of Labor in the United States* (Cambridge University Press).

Gouldner, A. (1954), *Patterns of Industrial Bureaucracy* (Glencoe, Illinois: Free Press).

Gowler, D. and K. Legge (1983), "The Meaning of Management and the Management of Meaning: a View from Social Anthropology", in Earl, M. (Ed), *Perspectives on Management: A Multidisciplinary Analysis* (Oxford University Press).

Griffiths, Sir R. (1988), *Community Care: Agenda for Action. A Report to the Secretary of State for Social Services* (London: Her Majesty's Stationery Office).

Hagg, I. and G. Hedlund (1979), "'Case Studies' in Accounting Research", *Accounting, Organizations and Society,* Vol. 4, No. 1/2, pp. 135-143.

Halfpenny, P. (1979), "The Analysis of Qualitative Data", *Sociological Review,* Vol. 27, No. 4, pp. 799-825.

Hamburger, P. (1989), "Efficiency Auditing by the Australian Audit Office: Reform and Reaction under Three Auditors-General", *Accounting, Auditing and Accountability Journal,* Vol. 2, No. 3, pp. 3-21.

Hammersley, M. and P. Atkinson (1983), *Ethnography: Principles in Practice* (London: Tavistock).

262   *Managment Control in a Voluntary Organization*

Handy, C. (1988), *Understanding Voluntary Organizations* (London: Penguin Books).

Harper, B. and P. Harper (1988), "Religious Reporting: Is It the Gospel Truth?", *Management Accounting* (U.S.), February, pp. 34-39.

Harris, C. (1969), "Reform in a Normative Organization", *Sociological Review* (new series), Vol. 17, No. 2, July, pp. 167-185.

Harris, Marlys (1982), "The Squeeze on Churches and Synagogues", *Money*, April, pp. 97-106.

Harris, Margaret (1990), "Review Article: Working in the UK Voluntary Sector", *Work, Employment and Society*, Vol. 4, No. 1, pp. 125-140.

Harris, Margaret and D. Billis (1986), *Organizing Voluntary Agencies: A Guide through the Literature* (London: Bedford Square Press / National Council for Voluntary Organizations).

Hastings, A. and C. Hinings (1970), "Role Relations and Value Adaption: A Study of the Profession Accountant in Industry", *Sociology*, Vol. 4, No. 4, pp. 353-366.

Hay, L. (1980), *Accounting for Governmental and Nonprofit Entities* (Homewood, Illinois: Richard D. Irwin).

Hayes, D. (1977), "The Contingency Theory of Management Accounting", *The Accounting Review*, Vol. LII, No. 1, pp. 23-39.

Hayes, D. (1983), "Accounting for Accounting: A Story about Managerial Accounting", *Accounting, Organizations and Society*, Vol. 8, No. 2/3, pp. 241-249.

Henke, E. (1986), *Accounting for Nonprofit Organizations*, (Boston: Kent Publishing Company, fourth edition).

Hertenstein, J. (1985), *Inflation Adjusted Accounting in Management Control Systems: Case Studies of Two Adopting Firms* (working paper, Harvard Business School).

Hines, R. (1988), "Financial Accounting: in Communicating Reality, We Construct Reality", *Accounting, Organizations and Society*, Vol. 13, No. 3, pp. 251-261.

Hinings, C. (1979), "Continuities in the Study of Organizations: Churches and Local Government", in Lammers, C. and D. Hickson (Eds), *Organizations Alike and Unlike: International and Inter-Institutional Studies in the Sociology of Organizations* (London: Routledge and Kegan Paul), pp. 137-148.

Hinings, C. and A. Bryman (1974), "Size and the Administrative Component in Churches", *Human Relations*, Vol. 27, No. 5, pp. 457-475.

Hinings, C. and B. Foster (1973), "The Organizational Structure of Churches: A Preliminary Model", *Sociology*, Vol. 7, January, pp. 93-106.

Hinings, C. Clegg, S., Child, J., Aldrich, H., Karpik, L. and L. Donaldson (1988), "Offence and Defence in Organization Studies: A Symposium", *Organization Studies*, Vol. 9, No. 1, pp. 1-32.

HMSO (1989), *Charities: A Framework for the Future* (London: Her Majesty's Stationary Service).

Hofstede, G. (1967), *The Game of Budget Control* (Assen: Van Gorcum).

Hofstede, G. (1981), "Management Control of Public and Not-For-Profit Activities", *Accounting, Organizations and Society*, Vol. 6, No. 3, pp. 193-211.

Hopper, T., Cooper, D., Lowe, T., Capps, T. and J. Mouritsen (1986), "Management Control and Worker Resistance in the National Coal Board: Financial Control in the Labour Process", in Knights, D. and H. Willmott (Eds), *Managing the Labour Process* (Aldershot: Gower), pp. 109-141.

Hopper, T. and A. Powell (1985), "Making Sense of Research into the Organizational and Social Aspects of Management Accounting: A Review of its Underlying Assumptions", *Journal of Management Studies*, Vol. 22, No. 5, pp. 429-465.

Bibliography 263

Hopper, T., Storey, J. and H. Willmott (1987), "Accounting for Accounting: Towards the Development of a Dialectical View", *Accounting, Organizations and Society*, Vol. 12, No. 5, pp. 437-456.

Hopwood, A. (1972), "An Empirical Study of the Role of Accounting Data in Performance Evaluation", *Empirical Research in Accounting: Selected Studies*, Supplement to *Journal of Accounting Research*, Vol, 10, pp. 156-182.

Hopwood, A. (1977), "Editorial", *Accounting, Organizations and Society*, Vol. 2, No. 2, pp. 99-100.

Hopwood, A. (1978a), "Editorial: Accounting Research and the World of Action", *Accounting, Organizations and Society*, Vol. 3, No. 2, pp. 93-95.

Hopwood, A. (1978b), "Towards an Organizational Perspective for the Study of Accounting and Information Systems", *Accounting, Organizations and Society*, Vol. 3, No. 1, pp. 3-13.

Hopwood, A. (1983), "On Trying to Study Accounting in the Contexts in which it Operates", *Accounting, Organizations and Society*, Vol. 8, No. 2/3, pp. 287-305.

Hopwood, A. (1984), "Accounting and the Pursuit of Efficiency", in Hopwood, A. and C. Tomkins (Eds), *Issues in Public Sector Accounting* (Oxford: Phillip Allen).

Hopwood, A. (1987), "The Archaeology of Accounting Systems", *Accounting, Organizations and Society*, Vol. 12, No. 3, pp. 207-234.

Hopwood, A. (1989), "Behavioral Accounting in Retrospect and Prospect", *Behavioral Research in Accounting*, Vol. 1, pp. 1-22.

Hopwood, A. and C. Tomkins (Eds) (1984), *Issues in Public Sector Accounting* (Oxford: Philip Allan).

Horngren, C. and G. Foster (1987), *Cost Accounting: A Managerial Emphasis*, (Englewood Cliffs, NJ: Prentice-Hall, sixth edition).

Isaac, S. and W. Michael (1980), *Handbook in Research and Evaluation*, (San Diego: EDITS Publishers, thirteenth edition).

Jablonsky, S. and M. Dirsmith (1978), "The Pattern of PPB Rejection: Something about Organizations, Something about PPB", *Accounting, Organizations and Society*, Vol. 3, No. 3/4, pp. 215-225.

Jick, T. (1979), "Mixing Qualitative and Quantitative Methods: Triangulation in Action", *Administrative Science Quarterly*, Vol. 24, December, pp. 602-611.

Johnson, H. (1978), "Management Accounting in an Early Multidivisional Organization: General Motors in the 1920s", *Business History Review*, Winter, pp. 490-517.

Johnson, H. (1983), "The Search for Gain in Markets and Firms: a Review of the Historical Emergence of Management Accounting Systems", *Accounting, Organizations and Society*, Vol. 8, No. 2/3, pp. 139-146.

Johnson, T. and R. Kaplan (1987), *Relevance Lost: The Rise and Fall of Management Accounting* (Boston: Harvard Business School Press).

Jones, C. (1986), "Organizational Change and the Function of Accounting", *Journal of Business Finance and Accounting*, Vol. 13, No. 3, pp. 283-310.

Junker, B. (1960), *Field Work: An Introduction to the Social Sciences* (Chicago: University of Chicago Press).

Kaldor, P. (1987), *Who Goes Where? Who Doesn't Care?* (Sydney: Lancer).

Kaplan, R. (1984), "The Evolution of Management Accounting", *The Accounting Review*, Vol. LIX, No. 3, July, pp. 390-418.

Kaplan, R. (1986), "The Role of Empirical Research in Management Accounting", *Accounting, Organizations and Society*, Vol. 11, No. 4/5, pp. 429-452.

Katz, A. (1970), "Self-help Organizations and Volunteer Participation in Social Welfare", *Social Work*, Vol. 15, No. 1, pp. 51-60.

264   *Managment Control in a Voluntary Organization*

Keister, O. (1974), "Internal Control for Churches", *Management Accounting* (U.S.); January, pp. 40-42.

Kerlinger, F. (1973), *Foundations of Behavioral Research*, (New York: Holt, Rinehart and Winston Inc., second edition).

King, A. (1988), "Automating Church Accounting", *Management Accounting* (U.S.), March, pp. 18-20.

Kramer, R. (1981), *Voluntary Agencies in the Welfare State* (Los Angeles: University of California Press).

Kramer, R. (1990), "Voluntary Organizations in the Welfare State: On the Threshold of the '90s", *Working Paper No. 8*, The Centre for Voluntary Organization, London School of Economics and Political Science.

Kreiser, L. and P. Dare (1986), "Shaker Accounting Records at Pleasant Hill: 1830-1850", *The Accounting Historians Journal*, Vol. 13, No. 2, pp. 19-36.

Laughlin, R. (1984), *The Design of Accounting Systems: A General Theory with an Empirical Study of the Church of England* (Unpublished Phd thesis, University of Sheffield).

Laughlin, R. (1987), "Accounting Systems in Organizational Contexts: A Case for Critical Theory", *Accounting, Organizations and Society*, Vol. 12, No. 5, pp. 479-502.

Laughlin, R. (1988), "Accounting in its Social Context: An Analysis of the Accounting Systems of the Church of England", *Accounting, Auditing and Accountability Journal*, Vol. 1, No. 2, pp. 19-42.

Laughlin, R. (1990a), "A Model of Financial Accountability and the Church of England", *Financial Accountability and Management*, Vol. 6, No. 2, Summer, pp. 93-114.

Laughlin, R. (1990b), *Field Study in Accounting: A Case for Middle Range Thinking* (Paper presented the Adelaide Accounting Research Meeting, Flinders University, July).

Laughlin, R. and E. Lowe (1990), "A Critical Analysis of Accounting Thought: Prognosis and Prospects for Understanding and Changing Accounting Systems Design", in Cooper, D. and T. Hopper (Eds), *Critical Accounts* (London: Macmillan), pp. 15-43.

Lavoie, D. (1987), "The Accounting of Interpretations and the Interpretation of Accounts: the Communicative Function of the 'Language of Business'", *Accounting, Organizations and Society*, Vol. 12, No. 6, pp. 579-604.

Layton, E. (1969), "Science, Business and the American Engineer", in Perrucci, R. and J. Gerstl (Eds), *The Engineers and the Social System* (New York: John Wiley & Sons), pp. 51-72.

Leahy, J. (1974), "Pastoral Planning", *Management Controls (PMM&Co.)*, January, pp. 14-17.

Leat, D. (1988), *Voluntary Organizations and Accountability* (London: Policy Analysis Unit, National Council for Voluntary Organizations).

Leathers, P. and H. Sanders (1972), "Internal Control in Churches", *The Internal Auditor*, May/June, pp. 21-25.

Libby, R. (1981), *Accounting and Human Information Processing: Theory and Applications* (Englewood Cliffs, NJ: Prentice Hall).

Littler, C. (1982), *The Development of the Labour Process in Capitalist Societies* (London: Heinemann Educational).

Littler, C. and G. Salaman (1982), "Bravermania and Beyond: Recent Theories of the Labour Process", *Sociology*, Vol. 16, No. 2, pp. 251-269.

Loft, A. (1986), "Towards a Critical Understanding of Accounting: The Case of Cost Accounting in the U.K., 1914-1925", *Accounting, Organizations and Society*, Vol. 11, No. 2, pp. 137-169.

Bibliography

Lord, A. (1989), "The Development of Behavioral Thought in Accounting, 1952-1981", *Behavioral Research in Accounting*, Vol. 1, pp. 124-149.

Lowe, E. and R. Shaw (1968), "An Analysis of Managerial Biasing: Evidence from a Company's Budgeting Process", *Journal of Management Studies*, Vol. 5, pp. 304-315.

Macintosh, N. (1981), "A Contextual Model of Information Systems", *Accounting, Organizations and Society*, Vol. 6, No. 1, pp. 39-53.

March, J. and J. Olsen (1976), *Ambiguity and Choice in Organizations* (Bergen, Norway: Universitetsforlaget).

March, J. and H. Simon (1958), *Organizations* (New York: John Wiley & Sons).

Markus, L. and J. Pfeffer (1983), "Power and the Design and Implementation of Accounting and Control Systems", *Accounting, Organizations and Society*, Vol. 8, No. 2/3, pp. 205-218.

Martin, D. (1969), *The Religious and the Secular* (London: Routledge and Kegan Paul).

McGregor, M., James, S., Gerrand, J. and D. Carter (1982), *For Love Not Money: A Handbook for Volunteers* (Blackburn, Victoria: Dove Communications).

Mellor, H. (1985), *The Role of Voluntary Organizations in Social Welfare* (London: Croom Helm).

Merchant, K. and R. Simons (1986), "Research and Control in Complex Organizations: An Overview", *Journal of Accounting Literature*, Vol. 5, pp. 183-203.

Meyer, J. (1980), "The World Polity and the Authority of the Nation-State", in Bergesen, A. (Ed), *Studies of the Modern World System* (New York: Academic Press), pp. 109-137.

Meyer, J. (1986), "Social Environments and Organizational Accounting", *Accounting, Organizations and Society*, Vol. 11, No. 4/5, pp. 345-356.

Meyer, J. and B. Rowan (1977), "Institutionalized Organizations: Formal Structure as Myth and Ceremony", *American Journal of Sociology*, September, pp. 340-363.

Meyer, M. (1987), "The Growth of Public and Private Bureaucracies", *Theory and Society*, Vol. 16, pp. 215-235.

Meyer, M. and M. Brown (1977), "The Process of Bureaucratization", *American Journal of Sociology*, Vol. 83, No. 2, pp. 364-385.

Miles, M. and A. Huberman (1984), *Analyzing Qualitative Data: A Sourcebook for New Methods* (Beverly Hills, CA: Sage).

Miller, M. (1983), "From Ancient to Modern Organization: The Church as Conduit and Creator", *Administration and Society*, Vol. 15, No. 3, November, pp. 275-293.

Miller, P. (1990), "On the Interrelations between Accounting and the State", *Accounting, Organizations and Society*, Vol. 15, No. 4, pp. 315-338.

Miller, P. and T. O'Leary (1987), "Accounting and the Construction of the Governable Person", *Accounting, Organizations and Society*, Vol. 12, No. 3, pp. 235-265.

Milofsky, C. (Ed) (1988a), *Community Organizations: Studies in Resource Mobilization and Exchange* (New York: Oxford University Press).

Milofsky, C. (1988b), "Networks, Markets, Culture, and Contracts: Understanding Community Organizations", in Milofsky, C. (Ed), *Community Organizations: Studies in Resource Mobilization and Exchange* (New York: Oxford University Press), pp. 3-15.

Milofsky, C. (1988c), "Structure and Process in Community Self-Help Organizations", in Milofsky, C. (Ed), *Community Organizations: Studies in Resource Mobilization and Exchange* (New York: Oxford University Press), pp. 183-216.

Mintzberg, H (1975), *Impediments to the Use of Management Information* (National Association of Accountants).

266   *Managment Control in a Voluntary Organization*

Mitchell, J. (1983), "Case and Situation Analysis", *The Sociological Review*, Vol. 31, No. 2, May, pp. 187-211.

Mol, J. (1971), *Religion in Australia* (Australia: Thomas Nelson).

Moores, K. (1988), *Organization Theory and Management Accounting Research: the contingent design of management accounting systems* (paper presented at the First Management Accounting Research Conference, University of New South Wales).

Morgan, G. (1983), "Social Science and Accounting Research: A Commentary on Tomkins and Groves", *Accounting, Organizations and Society*, Vol. 8, No. 4, pp. 385-388.

Morgan, G. (1988), "Accounting as Reality Construction: Towards a New Epistemology of Accounting Practice", *Accounting, Organizations and Society*, Vol. 13, No. 5, pp. 477-485.

Morgan, G. (1990), *Organizations in Society* (London: Macmillan).

Nahapiet, J. (1988), "The Rhetoric and Reality of an Accounting Change: A Study of Resource Allocation", *Accounting, Organizations and Society*, Vol. 13, No. 4, pp. 333-358.

O'Connell, B. (1988), "Values Underlying Nonprofit Endeavour", in O'Neill, M. and D. Young (Eds), *Educating Managers of Nonprofit Organizations* (New York: Praeger), pp. 155-162.

O'Leary, T. (1985), "Observations on Corporate Financial Reporting in the Name of Politics", *Accounting, Organizations and Society*, Vol. 10, No. 1, pp. 87-102.

O'Neill, M. and D. Young (Eds) (1988a), *Educating Managers of Nonprofit Organizations* (New York: Praeger).

O'Neill, M. and D. Young (1988b), "Education Managers of Nonprofit Organizations", in O'Neill, M. and D. Young (Eds) *Educating Managers of Nonprofit Organizations* (New York: Praeger), pp. 1-21.

Odom, R. and W. Boxx (1988), "Environment, Planning Processes, and Organizational Performance of Churches", *Strategic Management Journal*, Vol. 9, pp. 197-205.

Olofsson, C. and P. Svalander (1975), *The Medical Services Change Over to a Poor Environment - "New Poor" Behaviour* (working paper, University of Linkoping).

Otley, D. (1980), "The Contingency Theory of Management Accounting: Achievement and Prognosis", *Accounting, Organizations and Society*, Vol. 5, No. 4, pp. 413-428.

Otley, D. (1984), "Management Accounting and Organization Theory: A Review of their Interrelationship", in Scapens, R., Otley, D. and R. Lister (Eds), *Management Accounting, Organizational Theory and Capital Budgeting* (London: Macmillan), pp. 96-163.

Otley, D. and C. Wilkinson (1988), "Organizational Behavior: Strategy, Structure, Environment, and Technology", in Ferris, K. (Ed), *Behavioral Accounting Research: A Critical Analysis* (Columbus, Ohio: Century VII Publishing), pp. 147-170.

Pallenberg, C. (1971), *Vatican Finances* (London: Peter Owen).

Paton, W. and A. Littleton (1940), *An Introduction to Corporate Accounting Standards* (American Accounting Association Monograph No. 3).

Perrow, C. (1986), "Economic Theories of Organization", *Theory and Society*, Vol. 15, Nos 1/2, pp. 11-46.

Potts, J. (1977), "The Evolution of Budgetary Accounting Theory and Practice in Municipal Accounting from 1870", *The Accounting Historians Journal*, Vol. 4, No. 1, Spring, pp. 89-100.

Prentice, K. (1981), "Church Accounting: Good Intentions and Good Accounting", *The Woman CPA*, April, pp. 8-14.

Preston, A. (1986), "Interactions and Arrangements in the Process of Informing", *Accounting, Organizations and Society*, Vol. 11, No. 6, pp. 521-540.

Bibliography

Preston, A. (1990), *Diagnosis Related Groups Prospective Payment and the Politics of Welfare in the U.S.* (paper presented at the second biennial Management Accounting Research Conference, University of New South Wales).

Pugh, D., Hickson, D., Hinings, C. and C. Turner (1968), "Dimensions of Organization Structure", *Administrative Science Quarterly*, Vol. 13, June, pp. 65-105.

Pugh, D., Hickson, D., Hinings, C. and C. Turner (1969a), "The Context of Organization Structure", *Administrative Science Quarterly*, Vol. 14, March, pp. 91-114.

Pugh, D., Hickson, D., Hinings, C. and C. Turner (1969b), "An Empirical Taxonomy of Structures of Work Organizations", *Administrative Science Quarterly*, Vol. 14, March, pp. 115-126.

Ramanathan, K. (1985), "A Proposed Framework for Designing Management Control Systems in Not-for-Profit Organizations", *Financial Accountability and Management*, Vol. 1, No. 1, Summer, pp. 75-92.

Ranson, S., Hinings, C. and R. Greenwood (1980), "The Structuring of Organizational Structures", *Administrative Science Quarterly*, Vol. 25, No. 1, March, pp. 1-17.

Roberts, J. and R. Scapens (1985), "Accounting Systems and Systems of Accountability - Understanding Accounting Practices in their Organizational Contexts", *Accounting, Organizations and Society*, Vol. 10, No. 4, pp. 443-456.

Robins, J. (1987), "Organizational Economics: Notes on the Use of Transaction-Cost Theory in the Study of Organizations", *Administrative Science Quarterly*, Vol. 32, March, pp. 68-86.

Robins, S. and N. Barnwell (1989), *Organization Theory in Australia* (Sydney: Prentice Hall).

Rosenberg, D., Tomkins, C. and P. Day (1982), "A Work Role Perspective of Accountants in Local Government Service Departments", *Accounting, Organizations and Society*, Vol. 7, No. 2, pp. 123-137.

Rothschild-Whitt, J. (1979), "The Collectivist Organization: An Alternative to Rational-Bureaucratic Models", *American Sociological Review*, Vol. 44, August, pp. 509-527.

Rowe, T. and G. Giroux (1986), "Diocesan Financial Disclosure: A Quality Assessment", *Journal of Accounting and Public Policy*, Spring, pp. 57-74.

Rudge, P. (1968), *Ministry and Management* (London: Tavistock).

Salaman, G. (1979), *Work Organizations* (London: Longman).

Scapens, R. (1984), "Management Accounting: A Survey Paper", in Scapens, R., Otley, D. and R. Lister (Eds), *Management Accounting, Organizational Theory and Capital Budgeting* (London: Macmillan).

Scapens, R. (1990), "Researching Management Accounting Practice: The Role of Case Study Methods", *British Accounting Review*, Vol. 22, No. 3, September, pp. 259-281.

Scapens, R., Otley, D. and R. Lister (1984), *Management Accounting, Organizational Theory and Capital Budgeting* (London: Macmillan).

Schiff, M. and A. Lewin (1970), "The Impact of People on Budgets", *The Accounting Review*, Vol. VL, No. 2, pp. 259-268.

Schutz, A. (1967), *The Phenomenology of the Social World* (Evanston: Northwestern University Press).

Schwartz, H. and J. Jacobs (1979), *Qualitative Sociology: A Method to the Madness* (New York: The Free Press).

Scofield, B. and D. Milano (1984), "Managerial Accounting for Churches and Related Enterprises", *The National Public Accountant*, Vol. 29, September, pp. 40-49.

Scott, D. (1981), *Don't Mourn for Me - Organize...: The Social and Political Uses of Voluntary Organizations* (Sydney: George Allen & Unwin).

Seville, M. (1987), "The Evolution of Voluntary Health and Welfare Organization Accounting: 1910 - 1985", *The Accounting Historians Journal*, Vol. 14, No. 1, Spring, pp. 57-82.

Sills, D. (1957), *The Volunteers: Means and Ends in a National Organization* (Glencoe: The Free Press).

Silverman, D. (1985a), *Qualitative Methodology and Sociology: Describing the Social World* (Aldershot: Gower).

Silverman, D. (1985b), *Telling Convincing Stories: A Plea for Cautious Positivism in Case Studies* (plenary address to the British Sociology Association, Sociology of Medicine Conference, University of York).

Silverman, D. (1989), "Six Rules of Qualitative Research: A Post-Romantic Argument", *Symbolic Interaction*, Vol. 12, No. 2, pp. 25-40.

Simon, H., Guetzkow, H., Kozmetsky, G. and G. Tyndall (1954), *Centralization Versus Decentralization in Organizing the Controller's Department* (New York: Controllership Foundation).

Simon, H. (1990), "Information Technologies and Organizations", *The Accounting Review*, Vol. 65, No. 3, July, pp. 658-667.

Smith, H (1975), *Strategies of Social Research: The Methodological Imagination* (Englewood Cliffs, NJ: Prentice Hall).

Snodgrass, R. (1986), "Religious Organizations Need Sound Business Arrangements, Too", *CA Magazine*, January, pp. 81-85.

Solomons, D. (Ed) (1968), *Studies in Cost Analysis*, (New York: Sweet and Maxwell, second edition).

Spicer, B. (1990), *The Resurgence of Interest in Cost and Management Accounting: Practice, Theories and Case Research Methods* (paper presented at the Annual Conference of the Accounting Association of Australia and New Zealand, July).

Sproull, L. (1981), "Beliefs in Organizations", in Nystrom. P. and W. Starbuck (Eds), *Handbook of Organizational Design*, Vol. 2 (New York: Oxford University Press), pp. 203-224.

Stanton, A. (1989), *Invitation to Self Management* (Middlesex: Dab Hand Press).

Starbuck, W. (1981), "A Trip to View the Elephants and Rattlesnakes in the Garden of Aston", in Van de Ven, A. and W. Joyce (Eds), *Perspectives on Organization Design and Behaviour* (New York: John Wiley and Sons), pp. 167-198.

Sterling, R. (1970), "On Theory Construction and Verification", *The Accounting Review*, Vol. XLV, No. 3, pp. 444-457.

Stinchcombe, A. (1974), *Creating Efficient Industrial Administrations* (New York: Academic Press).

Storey, J. (1985), "The Means of Management Control", *Sociology*, Vol. 19, No. 2, May, pp. 193-211.

Sundem, G. (1981), *Future Perspectives in Management Accounting Research* (paper presented to the Seventh Accounting Research Convocation, University of Alabama).

Swanson, B. (1978), "The Two Faces of Organizational Information", *Accounting, Organizations and Society*, Vol. 3, No. 3/4, pp. 237-246.

Swanson, G. and J. Gardner (1986), "The Inception and Evolution of Financial Reporting in the Protestant Episcopal Church in the United States of America", *The Accounting Historians Journal*, Vol. 13, No. 2, pp. 55-63.

Swanson, G. and J. Gardner (1988), "Not-For-Profit Accounting and Auditing in the Early Eighteenth Century: Some Archival Evidence", *The Accounting Review*, Vol. LXIII, No. 3, July, pp. 436-447.

Tarling, L. (1980), *Thank God for the Salvos: The Salvation Army in Australia - 1880 to 1980* (Sydney: Harper & Row).

Bibliography 269

Taylor, S. and R. Bogdan (1984), *Introduction to Qualitative Research Methods: The Search for Meanings*, (New York: John Wiley & Sons, second edition).

Theobald, W. (1985), *The Evaluation of Human Service Programs* (Champaign, Illinois: Management Learning Laboratories).

Thompson, J. (1967), *Organizations in Action* (New York: McGraw-Hill).

Thompson, K. (1970), *Bureaucracy and Church Reform* (Oxford: The Claredon Press).

Thompson, K. (1975), "Religious Organizations", in McKinlay, J. (Ed), *Processing People: cases in organizational behaviour* (London: Holt, Rinehart and Winston), pp. 1-40.

Thompson, P. (1989), *The Nature of Work*, (London: Macmillan, second edition).

Tinker, A. (1980), "Towards a Political Economy of Accounting: An Empirical Illustration of the Cambridge Controversies", *Accounting, Organizations and Society*, Vol. 5, No. 1, pp. 147-160.

Tinker, A. (1985), *Paper Prophets* (London: Rinehart and Winston).

Tinker, A., Merino, B. and M. Neimark (1982), "The Normative Origins of Positive Theories: Ideology and Accounting Thought", *Accounting, Organizations and Society*, Vol. 7, No. 2, pp. 167-200.

Tomkins, C. and R. Groves (1983a), "The Everyday Accountant and Researching His Reality", *Accounting, Organizations and Society*, Vol. 8, No. 4, pp. 361-374.

Tomkins, C. and R. Groves (1983b), "The Everyday Accountant and Researching His Reality: Further Thoughts", *Accounting, Organizations and Society*, Vol. 8, No. 4, pp. 407-415.

Tremblay, M. (1982), "The Key Informant Technique: A Non-Ethnographic Application", in Burgess, R. (Ed.), *Field Research: A Sourcebook and Field Manual* (London: George Allen and Unwin), pp. 98-104.

Tricker, R. (1979), "Research in Accounting", *The Chartered Accountant in Australia*, May, pp. 15-26.

van Gunsteren, H. (1976), *The Quest for Control: A Critique of the Rational-Central-Rule Approach in Public Affairs* (London: John Wiley & Sons).

Van Til, J. (1988), *Mapping the Third Sector: Voluntarism in a Changing Social Economy* (New York: The Foundation Centre).

Vladeck, B. (1988), "The Practical Differences in Managing Nonprofits: A Practitioner's Perspective", in O'Neill, M. and D. Young (Eds), *Educating Managers of Nonprofit Organizations* (New York: Praeger), pp. 71-81.

Wallis, R. (1984), *The Elementary Forms of the New Religious Life* (London: Routledge and Kegan Paul).

Ware, A. (1989), *Between Profit and State: Intermediate Organizations in Britain and the United States* (Cambridge: Polity Press).

Webb, E., Campbell, D., Schwartz, R. and L. Sechrest (1966), *Unobtrusive Measures: Non-reactive Research in the Social Sciences* (Chicago: Rand McNally).

Weber, M. (1927), *General Economic History* (translated by F. Knight) (Glencoe, Illinois: The Free Press).

Weber, M. (1930), *The Protestant Ethic and the Spirit of Capitalism* (translated by T. Parsons) (New York: Scribner's).

Weber, M. (1947), *The Theory of Social and Economic Organization* (translated by Parsons, T. and A. Henderson) (New York: Free Press).

Weber, M. (1978), *Economy and Society* (Berkeley, Calif.: University of California Press).

Weick, K. (1979), *The Social Psychology of Organising*, (Reading: Addision-Wesley, second edition).

Weiss, J. (1988), "Substance versus Symbol in Administrative Reform: The Case of Human Services Coordination", in Milofsky, C. (Ed), *Community Organizations: Studies in*

270   *Managment Control in a Voluntary Organization*

Resource Mobilization and Exchange (New York: Oxford University Press), pp. 100-118.

Whitley, R. (1988), "The Possibility and Utility of Positive Accounting Theory", *Accounting, Organizations and Society*, Vol. 13, No. 6, pp. 631-645.

Wildavsky, A. (1975), *Budgeting: a Comparative Theory of Budgeting Processes* (Boston: Little, Brown and Company).

Williams, K., Mitsui, I. and C. Haslam (1990), *How Far Japan? A Case Study of Management Calculation and Practice in Car Press Shops* (paper presented to the Organization and Control of the Labour Process Conference, Aston University).

Williamson, O. (1975), *Markets and Hierarchy: Analysis and Antitrust Implications* (New York: Free Press).

Williamson, O. (1983), "Organization Form, Residual Claimants and Corporate Control", *Journal of Law and Economics*, Vol. 36, pp. 351-366.

Willmott, H. (1983), "Paradigms for Accounting Research: Critical Reflection on Tomkins and Groves' 'Everyday Accountant and Researching His Reality'", *Accounting, Organizations and Society*, Vol. 8, No. 4, pp. 389-405.

Willmott, H. (1986), "Organising the Profession: A Theoretical and Historical Examination of the Development of the Major Accountancy Bodies in the U.K.", *Accounting, Organizations and Society*, Vol. 11, No. 6, pp. 555-580.

Wilson, B. (1961), *Sects and Society* (London: Heinemann).

Wilson, B. (1967), *Patterns of Sectarianism* (London: Heinemann).

Wilson, B. (1969), *Religion in Secular Society* (Harmondsworth: Pelican).

Wilson, D. (1989), "New Trends in the Funding of Charities: The Tripartite System of Funding", in Ware, A. (Ed), *Charities and Government* (Manchester: Manchester University Press), pp. 55-81.

Wolfenden Committee (1978), *The Future of Voluntary Organizations: Report of the Wolfenden Committee* (London: Croom Helm).

Wood, S. (1979), "A Reappraisal of the Contingency Approach to Organisation", *Journal of Management Studies*, Vol. 16, No. 3, pp. 334-54.

Woodfield, Sir P., Binns, G., Hirst, R. and D. Neal (1987), *Efficiency Scrutiny of the Supervision of Charities, Report to the Home Secretary and the Economic Secretary to the Treasury* (London: Her Majesty's Stationary Office).

Yin, R. (1989), *Case Study Research: Design and Methods*, (Beverly Hills: Sage, revised edition).

Zietlow, J. (1989), "Capital and Operating Budgeting Practices in Pure Nonprofit Organizations", *Financial Accountability and Management*, Vol. 5, No. 4, Winter, pp. 219-232.

Zucker, L. (1983), "Organizations as Institutions", *Research in the Sociology of Organizations: A Research Annual*, Vol. 2, pp. 1-47.

Zucker, L. (1987), "Institutional Theories of Organization", *Annual Review of Sociology*, Vol. 13, pp. 443-464.

MAINSTEAM CHURCH REFERENCES

Note: Actual details of references have been disguised in a manner consistent with the disguising of the identity of the organization used in the book.

Communication Services Unit (1984), *A Guide to the Mainstream Church (Northern Division)* (Northern Division of the Mainstream Church).

Limerick, D. and J. Kable (1983), *Report on the 'Mission and Management' Survey of the Members of the Mainstream Church, Northern Division* (Northern Division of the Mainstream Church).

Bibliography

271

Northern Division (1977), *Minutes of the First Annual General Meeting* (Northern Division of the Mainstream Church, October 9th-14th).

Northern Division (1978), *Minutes of the Second Annual General Meeting* (Northern Division of the Mainstream Church, October 8th-13th).

Northern Division (1979a), *Reports of the Third Annual General Meeting*, Volume 1 (Northern Division of the Mainstream Church, October 5th-12th).

Northern Division (1979b), *Minutes and Supplementary Reports of the Third Annual General Meeting*, Volume 2 (Northern Division of the Mainstream Church, October 5th-12th).

Northern Division (1980a), *Reports of the Fourth Annual General Meeting*, Volume 1 (Northern Division of the Mainstream Church, October 3rd-10th).

Northern Division (1980b), *Minutes and Supplementary Reports of the Fourth Annual General Meeting*, Volume 2 (Northern Division of the Mainstream Church, October 3rd-10th).

Northern Division (1981a), *Reports of the Fifth Annual General Meeting*, Volume 1 (Northern Division of the Mainstream Church, October 9th-16th).

Northern Division (1981b), *Minutes and Supplementary Reports of the Fifth Annual General Meeting*, Volume 2 (Northern Division of the Mainstream Church, October 9th-16th).

Northern Division (1982a), *Reports of the Sixth Annual General Meeting*, Volume 1 (Northern Division of the Mainstream Church, October 8th-15th).

Northern Division (1982b), *Minutes and Supplementary Reports of the Sixth Annual General Meeting*, Volume 2 (Northern Division of the Mainstream Church, October 8th-15th).

Northern Division (1983a), *Reports of the Seventh Annual General Meeting*, Volume 1 (Northern Division of the Mainstream Church, October 7th-14th).

Northern Division (1983b), *Minutes and Supplementary Reports of the Seventh Annual General Meeting*, Volume 2 (Northern Division of the Mainstream Church, October 7th-14th).

Northern Division (1984a), *Reports of the Eight Annual General Meeting*, Volume 1 (Northern Division of the Mainstream Church, October 5th-12th).

Northern Division (1984b), *Minutes of the Eight Annual General Meeting*, Volume 2 (Northern Division of the Mainstream Church, October 5th-12th).

Northern Division (1985a), *Reports, Recommendations and Financial Statements of the Ninth Annual General Meeting*, Volume 1 (Northern Division of the Mainstream Church, October 4th-11th).

Northern Division (1985b), *Minutes of the Ninth Annual General Meeting*, Volume 2 (Northern Division of the Mainstream Church, October 4th-11th).

Northern Division (1986a), *Reports and Recommendations of the Tenth Annual General Meeting*, Volume 1 (Northern Division of the Mainstream Church, October 3rd-9th).

Northern Division (1986b), *Minutes of the Tenth Annual General Meeting*, Volume 2 (Northern Division of the Mainstream Church, October 3rd-9th).

Northern Division (1987a), *Reports and Recommendations of the Eleventh Annual General Meeting*, Volume 1 (Northern Division of the Mainstream Church, October 9th-15th).

Northern Division (1987b), *Minutes and Supplementary Reports of the Eleventh Annual General Meeting*, Volume 2 (Northern Division of the Mainstream Church, October 9th-15th).

Northern Division (1987c), "Called to Worship, Witness and Service: The Budget", *'Before the Next Step' Programme Brochure* (Communication Services unit, Northern Division of the Mainstream Church).

Mainstream Church (1977), *Minutes of the First National Council Meeting* (Mainstream Church).

Mainstream Church (1979), *Minutes of the Second National Council Meeting* (Mainstream Church).

Mainstream Church (1982), *Minutes of the Third National Council Meeting* (Mainstream Church Press).

Mainstream Church (1984a), *Constitution of the Mainstream Church* (Mainstream Church Press).

Mainstream Church (1984b), *Regulations of the Mainstream Church* (Mainstream Church Press).

Mainstream Church (1984c), *Basis of Union* (Mainstream Church Press).

Mainstream Church (1985), *Minutes of the Fourth National Council Meeting* (Mainstream Church Press).

Index

Abdel-Khalik and Ajinkya, 75
Accountants
    capitalist firms, 41
    churches, 69
    crises, 38
    critical structuralist
        framework, 36
    management group, 9
    uses of accounting, 167
    voluntary organizations, 57
Accounting
    as implementation
        constraint, 160
    capitalist firms, 37
    changes over time, 6
    comparative research, 248
    crises, 38
    distrust, 35
    dominant interests, 42
    financial control, 169
    functional imperatives, 3 - 5
    functionality of, 7
    Japanese practices, 222
    made purposeful, 5
    managers, 9
    objective effects, 10
    occupational groups, 9, 34
    purposefulness - boundary
        conditions, 7

    purposefulness - limits to,
        12
    quantitative measures, 143,
        168, 174, 180
    rationalization, 11, 52
    rules - indexical nature, 8
    situated practice, 3, 61, 221
    skeletal model, 11
    socially constructed, 4 - 6,
        74, 163, 221
    subjective effects, 10
    tool for mission, 165, 172,
        211
    trust, 13
    type of use codes, 144
    variable significance of, 21,
        143, 226
Accounting profession, 10, 11,
    33, 38 - 40, 45, 70 - 72,
    222
    British developments, 37
    interests, 43
    within global function of
        capital, 37

274 *Managment Control in a Voluntary Organization*

Accounting system
  comparative analysis, 112
  defined, 5, 102
  distinctive features of, 102
  management reports, 106
  measurement and
    communication
    system, 6
  occupational groups, 134
  origins in Northern
    Division, 107
  rationalization, 108
  sophistication of, 121, 225
Albrow, 8
Amigoni, 102, 103, 104
Anthony, 4, 18, 19, 52, 225
Anthony and Young, 4, 19, 52,
  225
Argyris, 35, 99
Armstrong, 4, 9, 13, 22, 25, 27,
  28, 30, 31, 32, 33, 34,
  35, 36, 37, 38, 40, 41,
  45, 71, 178
Arndt and McCabe, 72
Ashbrook, 63

Baiman, 12, 34
Bariff and Galbraith, 10
Barnes, 25
Bartunek, 63, 64
Batstone, 9, 10
Berger, 60, 67, 68
Berry et al, 3, 6, 15, 35
Beyer, 72
Billis, 17, 45, 46, 54
Birnberg and Shields, 100
Birnberg et al, 75, 96, 99
Boland and Pondy, 26
Bolton, 243, 244

Booth, 10, 20, 42, 61, 69, 85, 86,
  205, 217, 240, 245
Bourn and Ezzamel, 20
Boyce, 72
Braverman, 29, 30
Bray and Littler, 22, 29, 30
Brownell and Trotman, 75
Bruns, 75
Brunsson, 6
Budgeting
  balancing process, 208
  budget formulation, 197
  committed (fixed) costs, 111
  contested terrain, 215
  coverage of, 111
  financial crises, 192
  formulation issues, 124
  formulation timetable, 110
  history of (Northern
    Division), 188
  major features (Northern
    Division), 188
  official goal, 110, 126, 194
  participatory nature, 109
  political approach, 150
  rational approach, 170, 203
  structures of negotiations,
    190
Burawoy, 30
Burchell et al, 3, 5, 10, 43, 74,
  221
Burckel and Swindle, 72
Burgess, 82

Callus et al, 15
Capitalist firm, 8, 9, 11 - 13
Caplan, 13, 35
Carchedi, 32
Carmichael, 13, 35

Index

Case study, 73
  ability to generalize from, 96 - 98
  major attributes, 74
  observer role, 92
Chandler, 4, 22, 25, 29, 122, 225
Chandler and Deams, 4, 25, 122, 225
Chua, 3, 13, 15, 26, 75, 221, 248
Churches
  accounting, 61
  control problems, 60, 67
  crises, 65
  finances, 240
  goals, 60, 63
  importance of, 20
  membership, 76
  non-calculable ideals, 60, 63
  occupational groups, 64
  resistance, 19
  sacred and secular divide, 20 - 22
  selection of, 19
Clawson, 30
Clegg, 9, 22, 25, 29
Clegg and Dunkerley, 29
Colignon and Covaleski, 9
Comparative research
  accounting, 248
Control processes explanation, 22 - 25, 239
Cook, 53
Cooper, 25, 42, 73
Cooper and Hopper, 25
Cooper and Sherer, 42
Cooper et al, 25
Covaleski, 9, 75, 150
Covaleski and Dirsmith, 75
Crises

financial, 123
Critical structuralist framework, 4, 22 - 28, 36, 221, 225, 232 - 234, 239
  accounting, 34, 36
  accounting - summary of, 43
  accounting and interests, 42
  adaptation to voluntary organizations, 57
  advantages, 42
  capitalist organizations, 28
  churches, 60
  control problems in churches, 67
  control problems in voluntary organizations, 53
  crises, 31
  limitations, 41
  occupational groups, 31
  rationalization, 44
  sacred and secular divide, 67
  summary of, 69
  trust, 35
  voluntary organizations, 45, 58
Cultural diffusion, 22, 233
Cultural rationalization, 51, 59, 67, 68, 108
  accounting, 69
  resistance, 53
  voluntary organizations, 57
Cunningham and Reemsnyder, 72

Daniel, 72
Day and Klein, 56
Denzin, 93, 96, 97
Dermer and Lucas, 6

DiMaggio, 11, 22, 49, 50, 53, 54, 55, 57, 67, 108, 242, 246
DiMaggio and Powell, 11, 22, 49, 50, 67, 108
Donaldson, 22, 29

Economic goals, 8
Economic means-ends relationships, 7 - 9, 23, 222
Edwards, 30, 31
Ellis, 72
Ezzamel and Bourn, 84

Faircloth, 61
Fichter, 63
Financial crises, 123, 237
    causes of, 129
    use of accounting, 127
Financial stress, 63, 65, 198, 247
    Northern Division, 84
Flesher and Flesher, 61
Floyd, 72
Forms of rationality, 6, 23, 244
Foucault, 12, 53
Fox, 13, 34, 178, 249
Friedman, 30, 31
Futcher and Phillips, 72

Gardner, 61, 62
Gerard, 46, 48, 54, 55, 57, 190, 246
Giddens, 218
Gidron, 45
Glaser and Strauss, 14, 97
Goldner, 63
Gollin, 240, 241, 243, 245, 247, 249

Gordon, Edwards and Reich, 30
Gowler and Legge, 9, 10
Griffiths, 52, 108

Hagg and Hedlund, 75
Halfpenny, 98
Hamburger, 52
Hammersley and Atkinson, 98, 99
Handy, 14, 16, 17, 48, 60
Harper and Harper, 72
Harris, 15, 45, 46, 47, 48, 55, 56, 58, 63, 64, 65, 68, 205, 217, 245
Hay, 26
Henke, 26
Hertenstein, 84
Hines, 25
Hinings, 29, 63, 65, 69, 72, 84
Hofstede, 99
Hopper and Powell, 26
Hopper et al, 12, 15, 30, 43, 71
Hopwood, 3, 4, 6, 10, 11, 12, 15, 42, 52, 73, 100, 103, 221
Horngren and Foster, 4, 122
Human rationality, 6

Institutional isomorphism, 50, 52
Institutional theory, 50

Jablonsky and Dirsmith, 50
Jick, 97
Johnson, 4, 25, 122, 222
Jones, 102, 103, 104
Junker, 92

Kaldor, 20, 89

Index 277

Kaplan, 73, 75, 122, 222, 225
Katz, 45
Keister, 72
King, 72
Kramer, 15, 47, 48, 50, 52, 55,
    56, 58, 241, 245
Kreiser and Dare, 61

Labour process, 11, 29, 30, 31,
    32, 34, 38, 70, 71
  critical structuralist
      approach, 32
  managerial control
      strategies, 30
  managerial strategy and
      control, 28
Laughlin, 5, 11, 15, 20, 61, 62,
    63, 65, 66, 72, 73, 75,
    86, 88, 98, 102, 111,
    119, 122, 217, 225, 240,
    241, 243, 245, 246, 247,
    249
Lavoie, 5
Layton, 31, 32
Leahy, 72
Leat, 54, 55, 56, 190
Leathers and Sanders, 72
Littler, 22, 28, 29, 30, 31
Loft, 6, 10, 25, 38, 225
Lord, 100
Luckman, 60, 67

Meyer, J., 49, 50, 51, 67
Meyer, M., 49
Mainstream Church
  importance of, 83
  membership, 76
  religious beliefs, 84

Management control strategies,
    24, 27, 32, 36, 41, 42,
    58, 69, 234, 239, 242,
    244, 246
  churches, 60
  historical development of,
      29
  occupational groups, 33
  rationalization, 30, 44, 52
  trust, 35
Management control systems
  distrust, 13, 34
Managerial control strategies
  resistance in voluntary
      organizations, 55
Managers
  control function, 12
  trust, 13
Market failures, 29
Markus and Pfeffer, 10
Martin, 60
McGregor, 48
Mellor, 49, 55, 56
Meyer and Rowan, 11, 12, 22,
    49, 50, 67
Miles and Huberman, 97
Miller, 6, 10, 12, 25, 52, 63
Miller and O'Leary, 6, 10, 12,
    25
Milofsky, 45, 48, 49, 54, 55, 57,
    241
Mitchell, 14, 74, 86, 89, 98, 240
Modes of rationality, 244
  conflict between, 175
Moral orders, 10, 23, 183, 222
Morgan, 8, 9, 10, 11, 12, 17, 18,
    20, 26, 28, 49, 52, 53,
    55, 60, 75

278   *Managment Control in a Voluntary Organization*

Nahapiet, 3, 15, 74
Northern Division
    new organizational
        structure, 79
    size, 77
    size of, 83

O'Connell, 48, 54, 55, 60, 190,
    242
O'Neill and Young, 45, 48, 52,
    241
Occupational groups
    accountants, 69, 167
    accounting, 63
    churches, 63, 68
    competition between, 22, 32,
        44, 56, 64, 68, 174,
        236, 246
    in Northern Division, 113
    managers, 9
    sacred, 143
    solutions to control
        problems, 32
Odom and Boxx, 63
Olofsson and Svalander, 84
Otley, 122

Pallenberg, 240
Perrow, 29
Prentice, 72
Preston, 3, 52, 116

Ramanathan, 45
Rationality
    formal and substantive, 244
Rationalization, 234
    capitalist organizations, 30
    churches, 60
    cultural, 51

    general tendency, 8, 11
    Mainstream Church, 83
    religious organizations. *See*
        churches
    resistance, 12
    role of accounting, 8
    voluntary organizations, 57
Rational-legal bureaucracies, 8
Religious organizations. *See*
    churches
Resistance, 8, 12, 14 - 19, 23,
    72, 121, 223, 231
    accounting, 234
    accounting systems, 117
    budget strategies, 206
    budgeting, 196, 156, 205
    churches, 60 - 61
    crises, 65, 237
    critical structuralist
        framework, 43
    financial crises, 65, 135, 137
    non-calculable ideals, 235
    occupational groups, 55,
        163, 229, 235
    outcomes of, 211
    reduction of, 172
    religious belief systems, 63
    sacred and secular divide,
        62, 67, 156
    sacred ends, 202
    setting of action, 157
    trust, 236
    voluntary organizations, 53,
        54, 246
Robbins and Barnwell, 190
Roberts and Scapens, 9, 10, 248
Rosenberg, 52
Rothschild-Whitt, 14, 16, 17, 48,
    50, 54, 60, 190, 242

Index

Rowe and Giroux, 61
Rudge, 63

Sacred and secular divide, 61,
    63, 70, 183, 243
   accountants, 170, 236
   accounting, 234
   accounting systems, 117
   budgeting, 193
   crises, 68
   functions of departments,
    113
   major features of, 66
   modes of rationality, 244
   occupational groups, 178,
    216
   rationalization, 223
   resistance, 156
   success of, 214
Salaman, 8, 28
Scapens, 9, 10, 12, 14, 73, 74,
    75, 98, 99, 248
Scheme of Arrangement
   Mission Outreach, 159
Schutz, 6
Schwartz and Jacobs, 25
Scofield and Milano, 72
Scott, 54
Secularisation, 60
Sills, 45
Silverman, 92, 97, 99, 104, 144,
    146
Simon, 13, 34, 99, 190
Situated practice, 3, 22, 221, 249
Skeletal model, 11, 12, 14
Smith, 97
Spicer, 73
Sproull, 72
Stanton, 54, 55

Starbuck, 29
Stinchcombe, 7, 8, 10, 26
Storey, 9
Strategic contingencies, 29
Swanson, 5, 61, 62

Tarling, 240
Taylorism, 30, 31, 33
Theobald, 52
Thompson, 4, 11, 19, 26, 28, 60,
    63, 64, 190
Tinker, 13, 42
Tomkins, 4, 11, 15, 52, 75
Tremblay, 93
Triangulation, 76, 89, 93 - 100
Tricker, 25, 69
Trust, 13, 14, 23, 34 - 36, 57, 58,
    71, 106, 137, 142, 178,
    185, 228, 235, 249
   churches, 60
   critical structuralist
    framework, 34
   rationalization, 35
   resistance, 236
   voluntary organizations, 56

Van Til, 46
Vladeck, 46, 48, 55, 57

280   *Managment Control in a Voluntary Organization*

Voluntary organizations
  as extreme cases, 14
  churches, 18, 19, 60
  control problems, 17, 53, 57,
      136
  defined, 16, 47
  importance of, 15
  major characteristics of, 16,
      49
  management control in, 45
  model of dynamics of
      management
      control, 248
  nature of goals, 48, 54, 190
  non-calculable ideals, 14,
      47, 54
  occupational groups, 55
  rationalization, 12, 49
  religious organizations. *See*
      churches
  resistance, 14, 205
  skeletal model, 14
  trends in management
      control, 240
  trust, 13
  typology of, 16

Voluntary sector
  defined, 46
Volunteers, 45, 46, 47, 54
  interactions with paid staff,
      48
  occupational groups, 57

Wallis, 60
Ware, 45
Webb, 97
Weber, 8, 9, 11, 49, 63, 244
Weiss, 55, 56, 245
Wildavsky, 205
Williams, 222
Williamson, 22, 29
Willmott, 41, 43, 75
Wilson, 52, 57, 60, 63, 69, 246
Wolfenden Committee, 57, 247
Wood, 29
Woodfield, 52, 108
Written communication, 7, 25

Yin, 14, 74, 82, 85, 86, 98

Zietlow, 61
Zucker, 50, 67